Shifting Ground

Studies in Feminist Philosophy is designed to showcase cutting-edge monographs and collections that display the full range of feminist approaches to philosophy, that push feminist thought in important new directions, and that display the outstanding quality of feminist philosophical thought.

STUDIES IN FEMINIST PHILOSOPHY
Cheshire Calhoun, *Series Editor*

Published in the series:

Shifting Ground

Knowledge and Reality,
Transgression and Trustworthiness

Naomi Scheman

OXFORD
UNIVERSITY PRESS

OXFORD
UNIVERSITY PRESS

Oxford University Press, Inc., publishes works that further
Oxford University's objective of excellence
in research, scholarship, and education.

Oxford   New York
Auckland   Cape Town   Dar es Salaam   Hong Kong   Karachi
Kuala Lumpur   Madrid   Melbourne   Mexico City   Nairobi
New Delhi   Shanghai   Taipei   Toronto

With offices in
Argentina   Austria   Brazil   Chile   Czech Republic   France   Greece
Guatemala   Hungary   Italy   Japan   Poland   Portugal   Singapore
South Korea   Switzerland   Thailand   Turkey   Ukraine   Vietnam

Copyright © 2011 by Oxford University Press, Inc.

Published by Oxford University Press, Inc.
198 Madison Avenue, New York, New York 10016

www.oup.com

Oxford is a registered trademark of Oxford University Press

Scheman, Naomi.
Shifting ground : knowledge and reality, transgression and trustworthiness.
p. cm.   (Studies in feminist philosophy)
ISBN 978-0-19-539511-2 (hardcover : acid-free paper)
ISBN 978-0-19-539510-5 (pbk. : acid-free paper)   1. Philosophy.   I. Title.
B29.S355 2011   191—dc22

9 8 7 6 5 4 3 2 1

Printed in the United States of America
on acid-free paper

One might say: the axis of our examination must be rotated, but about the fixed point of our real need.

Ludwig Wittgenstein, *Philosophical Investigations* §108

The alternative to relativism is partial, locatable, critical knowledges sustaining the possibility of webs of connections called solidarity in politics and shared conversations in epistemology.

Donna Haraway, "Situated Knowledges: The Science Question in Feminism and the Privilege of Partial Perspective"

Acknowledgments

All of the essays collected here were elicited by people who believed, even when I did not, that I had something to say about the topic of a volume or a conference they were planning. I owe them my career, and I thank them collectively. Individual thanks accompany each essay, as do thanks to the many friends and colleagues who listened and responded as I figured out just what it was I had to say and who helped me to say it. Beyond those specific acknowledgments, two friends especially accompanied me as I pulled this collection together—Ruth-Ellen Joeres and Amy Kaminsky— and it is a pleasure to thank them for their companionship, their thoughtful encouragement, and the inspiration of their own work. To Michael Root I owe an apology for my grumpiness at his exhortations, and my thanks for his detailed criticisms and suggestions (some of which I actually heeded) and for his sticking with me through it all, from the earliest of these essays to the final stages of the book, including the Sunday afternoon he brought sandwiches to his office and insisted we were staying until we pulled everything together, made all the copies, and finally sent the manuscript to Cheshire Calhoun and Peter Ohlin.

Thanks to Cheshire for asking me to submit these essays for her Studies in Feminist Philosophy series and for the excellent company my book gets to keep. The idea of my publishing a second volume of collected essays was actually originally Hilde Lindemann's, and I appreciate the good grace with which she took my choosing Oxford. One way or another I usually do what Hilde tells me to, and I am better for it.

Over the time span of the work collected here I have come to have a life in Sweden. Like the topics on which I have written, this life came as a surprise to me. I have enjoyed it from the start—a year in what was then the Women's Studies Department at Gothenburg University—and I am finally taking its continuing place in my life seriously. From 2009 to 2013 I am a part-time visiting researcher at the Umeå Centre for Gender Studies, a vibrant and exciting place to work; and to prepare for my time there I have been studying Swedish and have resumed lindy hop classes. I have by now a large number of Swedish friends and colleagues, who are helping me think about—among other things—the language in which we theorize and its relationships to the languages in which we live our everyday lives. For their friendship and intellectual companionship

I want to thank especially Eva Borgström, Mats Forsberg, Ulla Holm, Berit Larsson, and Agneta Wiren in Gothenburg, and Hildur Kalman, Erika Alm, and Marianne Winther Jørgensen in Umeå.

Many thanks to the editors and production staff at Oxford for their excellent work as well as for their helpfulness, patience, and good cheer. Thanks to Martha Peach for the index and to Stuart Klipper for the beautiful cover photograph. When I thought of an image for the cover, Stuart's photographs came immediately to mind: they are what loving attention looks like.

These essays are published with permission of their original publishers.

"Non-Negotiable Demands: Metaphysics, Politics, and the Discourse of Needs," in *Future Pasts: Reflections on the History and Nature of Analytic Philosophy*, edited by Juliet Floyd and Sanford Shieh. Copyright © 2001 Oxford University Press.

"Feminist Epistemology," *Metaphilosophy* 26:3 (July 1995).

"On Waking Up One Morning and Discovering We Are Them," in *Pedagogy: The Question of Impersonation*, edited by Jane Gallop. Copyright © 1995 Indiana University Press.

"Terminal Moraine," in *Jewish Locations: Traversing Racialized Landscapes*, edited by Bat-Ami Bar On and Lisa Tessman. Copyright © 2002 Rowman and Littlefield.

"Against Physicalism," in *Cambridge Companion to Feminism in Philosophy*, edited by Miranda Fricker and Jennifer Hornsby. Copyright © 2000 Cambridge University Press.

"Feeling Our Way toward Moral Objectivity," in *Mind and Morals*, edited by Andy Clark, Marilyn Friedman, and Larry May. Copyright © 1995 MIT Press.

"Queering the Center by Centering the Queer: Reflections on Transsexuals and Secular Jews," in *Feminists Rethink the Self*, edited by Diana Tietjens Meyers. Copyright © 1997 Westview Press.

"Forms of Life: Mapping the Rough Ground," in *Cambridge Companion to Wittgenstein*, edited by Hans Sluga and David Stern. Copyright © 1996 Cambridge University Press.

"The Trustworthiness of Research: The Paradigm of Community-Based Research," coauthored with Catherine Jordan and Susan Gust, *Metropolitan University's Journal* 16(1) (March 2005).

"Narrative, Complexity, and Context: Autonomy as an Epistemic Value," in *Naturalized Bioethics: Toward Responsible Knowing and Practice*, edited by Hilde Lindemann, Marian Verkerk, and Margaret Urban Walker. Copyright © 2008 Cambridge University Press.

"Epistemology Resuscitated: Objectivity as Trustworthiness," in *(En)Gendering Rationalities*, edited by Sandra Morgen and Nancy Tuana. Copyright © 2001 SUNY Press.

Contents

Shifting Ground

Introduction

Or, rather, multiple introductions. In addition to needing to be introduced to several diverse groups of readers, the essays in this collection need to be introduced to each other. They were each written in response to a specific request, framed around a specific set of questions, and for a more or less specific audience. They appear here essentially unrevised, in part to reflect the fact that my most productive philosophical thinking is provoked by conversations about topics as diverse as controversies between Native Minnesotans and University plant genomics researchers about wild rice, and the experiences of variously transsexual and transgendered people in navigating through social spaces that render them unintelligible. I suspect that this sort of attachment to questions and problems that are not, as initially encountered, distinctively philosophical is more than an idiosyncrasy. Rather, it suggests one sort of answer to the question of what a philosopher moved by Wittgenstein's *Philosophical Investigations* might go on to do.

In addition to attending to problems that are not specifically—and, in Wittgenstein's view, problematically—philosophical, the essays reflect several other features of my Wittgensteinian approach: I do not aim at a *theory* of anything, but rather at ways of seeing sets of practices as connected to each other and my accounts of them as connected to the work of others. Thus, I suggest that we need, not concepts or even conceptualizations, so much as ways of attentively and critically looking and listening—of theorizing, recognizing that theorizing is itself a set of shared practices, materially situated and subject to critique. Similarly, I do not attempt to provide foundational justifications, aimed at convincing any rational reader. Rather, I take my readers to be "fellow travelers": not adherents to some party line or other, but *literally*, on a journey away from some things and toward others, sharing—depending on the particular contexts and conversations each essay seeks to intervene in—enough of what we take those things to be. And while I intend to be persuasive, I think less of logical coercion than of an invitation—to dinner, for example, including the likelihood of finding yourself seated next to someone you thought you couldn't or wouldn't talk with, who perhaps seems initially utterly unintelligible.

3

More substantively, the essays focus on theorizing from explicitly transgressive social locations, both as a contribution to various politics of resistance and social transformation, and as a way of replacing the philosophical problems that are the object of Wittgensteinian therapy with the practical, moral and political problems we *ought* to have—problems with our language and the other practices that shape what does and does not make sense, problems that we (or those whose allies we would be) encounter as obstacles to our making a sense we can live with. A question that runs through the essays is: What happens when we take Wittgenstein's urging us "back to the rough ground" not as calling us to attend to "what we do" as though that were clear, unequivocal, and unproblematic, but rather as directing our attention to how "our" discursive practices appear from the perspectives of those whom those practices render unintelligible or grotesquely hyper-intelligible—"known" in ways that distort or silence their own voices—those for whom the roughness of the ground provides not, as Wittgenstein suggests, traction, but obstacles and potholes.

The volume can be seen as spanning, in the sense of joining, typically unrelated (if not actively hostile) theoretical terrains: analytic epistemology and metaphysics on the one side and, on the other, feminist, anti-racist, post-colonial, and queer theory. The essays collectively argue for the value of the spanning—for the practical contributions of specifically philosophical theorizing to feminist, queer, and other liberatory politics, and for the transformation of epistemology and metaphysics—of philosophy as a discipline—by such theorizing. The hostility of the two camps leads to a conception of normativity (how we ought to form beliefs, what constitutes real knowledge) as essentially foundationalist, ahistorical, and non-self-reflexive, and to a conception of post-modern theorizing (involving a rejection of the traditional canons of rationality) as dismissive of such things as truth, reality, and objectivity. While feminist and other liberatory theorizing does, I argue, mark a decisive break with philosophical modernity, it can, at (what I take to be) its best, challenge the idea that such dismissiveness follows from that break. Rather, I want to suggest, such projects can help us move beyond these impasses: the normativity they have at their heart is non-foundationalist and historically specific and requires reflexive critique.

One of the paths traced in this collection is a return, with liberatory theorizing in mind, to some of the traditional concerns of philosophers, including of contemporary analytic philosophers. In one sense the philosophical problems actually dissolve: we no longer demand what our language seems to require but our practice doesn't provide. In this sense the task is a negative one; in Wittgenstein's words, "Philosophy is a battle against the bewitchment of our intelligence by language." But, having become unbewitched, what, if anything, can we, as philosophers, go on to do? My suggestion, throughout these essays, is that we can shift attention from wheel-spinningly frustrating philosophical problems—

"gears that move though nothing moves with them," to use Wittgenstein's image—to appropriately difficult problems, requiring, as Wittgenstein puts it a "change in our form of life," as we "rotate our investigation around the axis of our real need."

That exhortation is explicitly addressed in the essays that open and close the volume, "Non-Negotiable Demands: Metaphysics, Politics, and the Discourse of Needs" and "Epistemology Resuscitated: Objectivity as Trustworthiness." The short answer to the obvious question—What *are* our real (in this case epistemic) needs?—is that we need usable and defensible answers to questions that arise in ordinary life: questions about things and events in the world (water, food, drugs, bridges, airplanes, wars, climate change, elections, and religious strife), about what we ought—prudentially or morally—to do, and about whom to trust about all these things. The essays in the first section, "Knowledge," start with the idea that the challenges posed by these questions now and the resources for addressing them call for radically different responses from those that were articulated by early modern philosophers and that still shape epistemology and (to a much lesser extent) philosophy of science.

Building on the essays in my earlier collection, *Engenderings: Constructions of Knowledge, Authority, and Privilege,* as well as the work of other feminist epistemologists, I argue that the core tenets of epistemology—the spoken and unspoken, taken-for-granted and rigorously disciplined, rules for good knowing—served a specific historical project and the creation of a revolutionary historical subject: the universal Man of liberal democratic theory and practice, the bourgeois individual, the citizen of the nation-state, the autonomous actor, the objective observer and theorizer. Those at the margins (women, people of color, homosexuals, the poor, the disabled, children) have lacked political and epistemic enfranchisement not despite the tenets of liberal democracy, but specifically because of them. They have existed, that is, outside the bounds of epistemic and political theory, which applied, as Hobbes stated with characteristic bluntness, to men presumed to have, like mushrooms, sprung up fully grown overnight. Privileged men were presumed to speak for all the rest of us, either generically and universally (paradigmatically as the scientist), or individually, each on behalf of everyone within his (private) sphere, all of whom (women and children, of course, but at various times and places, also servants and wage-earners in his employ) were under a sort of *couverture.* Liberal democratic struggles for epistemic as well as political enfranchisement have thus consisted in the staking of claims to being, in all relevant ways, indistinguishable from the already enfranchised.

Along with many others, I argue that, for better and worse, we have entered post-modernity, which is marked by a politics of difference (however shifting, fragmented, or multiple those differences might be). While the growing dangers of unchecked assertions of inassimilable difference, along with the still outstanding promissory notes of liberal democracy, may make it seem exceedingly ill-advised to pull away from the ideals of modernity, I don't think we have a choice. Epistemologically—no less than politically—we need to grapple with the proliferating refusals of liberal modernity's difference-denying offers of inclusion. Precisely because we urgently need to call on notions like objectivity, reality, truth, evidence, justification, authority, and expertise, we need ways of thinking of them that don't rest on what is increasingly seen as an unpersuasive, if not positively oppressive, difference-denying logic.

In response to these challenges, I suggest that such notions (objectivity, truth, and their ilk) can be given robust, usable articulations that take diversity not as a problem, but as the ground for a solution. I use the term 'ground' advisedly: Its appearance in the title of this volume reflects my (Wittgensteinian) conviction that we need to replace problematically foundationalist demands for (not only metaphorical but mythical) grounds with critical attentiveness to the ground that lies literally beneath our literal feet, as well as to the practices that (metaphorically but actually) ground the claims we make, accept, dispute, and contest. I find resources for such theorizing in the work of those who are acutely aware of the practical perils of a playful pluralism (such as one finds in the work of many explicitly post-modern theorists) that takes "post-modern epistemology" to be oxymoronic, eschews all talk of grounding, and tosses away any means of adjudicating conflicting claims. Epistemology re-emerges as a normative (albeit historicized and self-relexive) enterprise when we confront the bearers of institutionalized authority and demand that they earn the credibility we are expected to accord them. I find resources for theorizing such a demand—in the name of diverse and shifting publics, multiple "we"s—in feminist philosophy of science, as well as in the transgressive theory and politics of those marked as "different" by virtue of race, gender, sexuality, disability, class, ethnicity, or religion.

From the perspective of present-day analytic epistemology I seem not to be talking about the same thing, and I'm not. For some time the field has been seeking a definition of knowledge, a set of necessary and sufficient conditions for saying of some person s that s/he knows some proposition p. The demand that there must or should be such conditions is, on a Wittgensteinian account, misplaced: as he says of the concept of a game, "We do not know the boundaries because none have been drawn. To repeat, we can draw a boundary—for a special purpose. Does it take that to make the concept usable? Not at all!" (Wittgenstein 1958 §69) Knowledge is not something—like, say, gold—about which we can wonder if we have, in defining it, "carved nature at the joints."

Rather, all the discussions about defining conditions have usefully drawn our attention to the wide variety of things we care about when we care about whether or not people really know certain things. Thus, as internalists argue, we care about how responsibly they have formed their beliefs; but we also care, as externalists argue, about how reliable they tend to be: are we well-advised in seeking their counsel? The counter-examples serve to sharpen our intuitions about questions such as these, meaning that they help us articulate the concerns that lie behind our ascriptions of knowledge; they help clarify our practices. But there is no reason to believe that all these concerns and practices cohere, that there is one way of specifying them so as to draw a sharp boundary around cases of knowledge. If for some particular purpose we need a clear definition, we can provide one, either adapting a concept already in use or inventing a new one. So if, for example, we wanted to speak precisely about when we would take a computer to know something, we could define precise conditions for using that concept, which would differ from our ordinary concept of knowledge in various ways, including in having necessary and sufficient conditions.

The demand for clear boundaries is not a uniquely philosophical one, though it has specifically philosophical manifestations. But it is a feature of much of our ordinary discourse that we insist on placing people, in particular, in clearly marked categories, notably those of sex, gender, and sexuality. That, and how, we make these demands varies from time to time and place to place, and one concern in some of these essays (most clearly in "Queering the Center by Centering the Queer" in Section 2) is to destabilize our classificatory habits. It is an explicit aim of that essay to produce, rather than attempt to alleviate, conceptual confusion, by exposing some of the practices that hold our concepts in place and showing them to be neither coherent nor, upon reflection, ones we can in good conscience endorse. Conceptual clarity may not only—as with knowledge—prove elusive; it may, when we think we have it, be achieved—that is, produced—at a deeply problematic cost. This attention—to the productive, not merely descriptive—feature of our apparently descriptive practices is taken up more explicitly in the following section.

The second section, "Reality," takes on an explicitly metaphysical, ontological set of questions, concerning the nature of ordinary objects and states of objects—what it means to say that they exist and that they cause things to happen (over and above the existence and causal powers of whatever fundamental stuff they are made of). That I had something to say about something so apparently abstruse emerged as I was working on "Narrative, Complexity, and Context: Autonomy as an Epistemic Value," the most recent essay in this collection, an essay that brought me back to issues I took up in my dissertation thirty years ago and returned to years later in one of my most mainstream or analytical essays, "On Physicalism."

There I argued that complex mental phenomena are socially constructed, meaning that their "holding together" as particular states, events, or processes is dependent on their being embedded in a context of social practices in relation to which they form a coherent whole: they are, that is, like constellations rather than galaxies. Galaxies are real astronomical objects—the stars that make them up share a common history, spatial contiguity, and likely fate—while constellations are, astro-nomically speaking, merely a random collection of stars: they make up a constellation only from the perspective of earth-dwelling creatures given to finding patterns in the "night sky" and associating them with characters in Greek mythology. The answer to the question of whether such socially constructed things as constellations or (I argue) mental phenomena really exist is not a simple yes or no. Some constructions are sturdier than others, more tightly woven into our lives. While most of us could imagine giving up on constellations—our commitment to them is relatively shal-low—that is not the case with such things as emotions, beliefs, attitudes, and desires. We are, I argue—even those of us who, as a matter of philosophical theorizing, claim otherwise—committed to the practices in terms of which psychological phenomena are real and really cause and are caused by other, psychological and physical, phenomena.

When I laid out the account in "Against Physicalism" to John Dupré (who was my commentator at a session at Birkbeck College organized by Jennifer Hornsby and Miranda Fricker in connection with their editing of the book in which that essay appeared), I claimed to be agnostic about the metaphysics of causation. John persuaded me that actually I wasn't, that I had crossed over the line into being committed to what is called "emer-gence," the view that not all causality belongs to the objects (whatever they might be, probably not at all object-like) of fundamental physics, but rather that, as complex objects come into existence, they carry with them new causal capabilities and susceptibilities. I crossed the line when I argued that the causes and effects of psychological phenomena inhered in them as the socially salient patterns that they are: if my anger causes your resentment, or my own sense of empowerment, that causal connec-tion is both real and irreducible to anything that might be caused or affected by any physical states of me (or of you), where being a physical state means being a coherent entity in abstraction from social context—anger is causally efficacious because of what it means.

What I came to think as I worked on "Narrative, Complexity, and Context" is that this way of thinking about complex psychological entities could be carried over to thinking about complex entities in general, including ordinary physical objects. The central notion is narrative, which I defined—in its core or minimalist sense—as space and time made salient (the move from space-time coordinates to here or there, now or then). To be a thing, I suggest, is to have a sufficiently robust narrative, a story of how you came into existence as the sort of thing you are and of what in your environment was and is salient to you, and some tendency to continue into the future as the thing that you are (what Spinoza called "conatus"). Thingness is a matter of mattering, of being a certain sort of locus of salience in the context of a network of relation-ships—as psychological states are patterns of salience in a context of human sociality. It follows that thingness is essentially vague and admits of degrees—another core metaphysical position I find myself committed to: vagueness is a feature of reality. We can mark sharp boundaries when we have some reason to (Wittgenstein 1958 §69), but in Alice Dreger's words, "Humans like categories neat, but nature is a slob." (quoted in the *New York Times*, "Gender Test After a Gold-Medal Finish," Christopher Clarey, 20 August 2009, p. B15) Since to be a thing is to be at least one sort of thing, particular objects and phenomena inherit this vagueness.[1]

As abstruse as all this sounds, the idea is actually a rather common-sensical one. (The abstruseness comes, I would suggest, from the need to counter a metaphysical picture that resolutely defies both common sense and science.) Common sense, as well as science, marks a difference between a heap of sand and a stone, even if the two contain exactly the same amounts of the same minerals. The stone has a rich story to tell about how it came to be. (Is it igneous, sedimentary, metamorphic? Was it once part of a larger mass of rock? Did it once lie somewhere far from here? How has it been affected by erosion? And how many insects has it squashed, or other smaller stones dislodged? Has it broken any windows?) The heap of sand, as a heap, has no such trove of stories; its integrity (to the extent that it has any) is minimal, and scattering it requires minimal effort (certainly compared to the force needed to disaggregate the stone); and although each individual grain of sand has a rich history, the heap itself has hardly any (I just scooped it up from the beach), nor does it lay claim to anything much in the way of causal powers (if I throw it a window, the window has nothing to fear, largely because *it*—the heap—will cease to exist before reaching the window).

The anthromorphic language of the last paragraph (having a story to tell) is, I suggest, eliminable. All that is needed is the notion of salience, meaning that things respond to and affect the environment around them selectively, as the sorts of things that they are: stones respond to steady streams of water, not to streaming sunlight, trees to sunlight, not to the color of the birds nesting in them, birds' predators to birds' colors, not (perhaps) to birdsong, and birds to other birds' singing. Pollination, erosion, photosynthesis, digestion, the flight of airplanes: all depend on selective capacities and susceptibilities—and it is that selectivity, I want to suggest, that makes a thing a thing. For more complex things (us, for example) selectivity will be not only generic (what matters to humans, or mammals or animals or physical objects, and what such things can do) but also idiosyncratic (who and what in particular affect me and how I in particular affect the people and things around me). Difference is at the heart of thingness: one could say that things just are the forms of non-indifference that characterize the relationships between them and their worlds, the differences they and their surroundings make to each other.

---

1. I belatedly encountered Lynne Rudder Baker's work in this area. I find her position on the metaphysics of ordinary things congenial, and I appreciate the analytic rigor of her arguments, including for the vagueness of reality. (See Baker 2007)

The impetus for and implications of my thinking in this way about thing-ness have two aspects. The first, which applies to things that are socially constructed and underlay my thinking about psychological states, was to conceptualize such states as real, their realness resting on our commitment to the practices that construct them. Similarly to many who have been arguing that such categories as race and gender are socially constructed, the point is to draw our attention to our practices, to our responsibility for them, and to questions about whether or not we ought to modify them. And all these questions need to include reflection on just who "we" are, since we are diversely placed in relation to the practices that construct us and the meanings of our lives. "Feeling Our Way toward Moral Objectivity" specifically takes on moral questions that arise when we think of ourselves and our inner lives as, in this sense, in each other's hands.

The second aspect is epistemological: if we think about things in general—even those that are not socially constructed—as being what they are because of their complex interconnectedness with other things, then knowledge about them needs to include knowledge about those interconnections, including how the things in question are "perceived" (what is salient about them) from the point of view of the things to which they are related. And coming to know is also to enter materially into that web of relationships, not to stand outside observing it. "Queering the Center," in addition to drawing attention to the apparatus of sex and gender, problematizes the various perspectives that claim to have the truth about our bodies and identities.

The third, concluding section, "Transgression and Trustworthiness," articulates what I have come to think of as "practical epistemology," which takes as its subject matter the problems posed by the need to form rationally grounded beliefs about things that require expertise we do not possess, especially when some of the relevant expertise is authoritatively wielded by the inequitably privileged, and some of it is hidden in the "subjugated knowledges" of the inequitably marginalized. One thing that emerges in these investigations is a connection between such an epistemology (a version of standpoint epistemology) and an ontology like the one I just sketched, according to which things are what they are because of the specificities of their relationships to other things, including to those who know about them. I choose the label 'practical' for this epistemology, rather than 'applied' to make the point that—as with the best of practical ethics—such investigations are substantive contributions to (rather than applications of) the theoretical field. More radically—and this point is one I take to be Wittgensteinian—we ought to cultivate the ground we stand on, rather than dig for the hidden, unifying depths presumed to lie beneath its complex topography.

The essays in this final section pull together the themes of the first two to address explicitly normative epistemological questions: What makes for genuine knowledge? In particular, how ought we decide which knowledge claims to accept? What constitutes epistemic responsibility in a post-modern world? As the section title suggests, the answers to these questions will be explicitly value-laden, embracing a politics of social justice, of disloyalty to practices that unjustly marginalize some people and privilege others. Against the charge that it is dangerous and wrong to politicize epistemology, I refer back to the arguments in the first section of this volume and in *Engenderings* that point out the politics that implicitly inform present-day analytic, "liberal" epistemology and that were explicit in the work of the philosophers who originally modern epistemology's questions. Those politics aimed at epistemically empowering generic, representative individuals and underwriting our trust in what they came to know, trust that is no longer either psychosocially likely or rationally justifiable.

The epistemological aspect of the account of thingness in the second section underwrites an epistemology of engagement, of creating the conditions under which one's object of knowledge (human or otherwise) can return one's gaze, and one is able to learn from those (human and otherwise) that are connected to that object and that help to constitute it as the thing it is. Thus, in "The Trustworthiness of Research: The Paradigm of Community-Based Research," I argue, along with my co-authors (a pediatric neuropsychologist and a community organizer who collaborated in a project addressing the problems of childhood lead poisoning in an inner-city neighborhood), for the epistemic value of community-based participatory research. Other essays in this final section look at other epistemic practices—film, autobiographical narrative, and clinical treatment and research—to explore the ways in which relationships shape both our objects of knowledge and our ways of knowing them. The concluding essay, "Epistemology Resuscitated: Objectivity as Trustworthiness," is both programmatic and polemical. It lays out the argument for shifting the defining projects of epistemology—away from problems framed in terms of an individual knowing subject and toward explicitly politicized social problems—and sketches what epistemology would look like if we were in this way to "rotate our investigation around the axis of our real need."

This concluding theme points toward work in practical epistemology (begun when I was an associate dean in the University of Minnesota Graduate School, from 2000 to 2003, and continuing with the various projects and conversations that occasion some of these essays) on the value and responsibilities of public research universities, as sites for institutionally authorized knowledge claims. To frame the themes of this collection in practical terms, I am interested in contributing both to ongoing policy discussions about the future of public research universities and to epistemology, by arguing that diversity, as it is increasingly being framed *by*—rather than *about*—various of modernity's marginalized or excluded others, undermines currently hegemonic, difference-denying practices and rationales for reconciling democracy and expertise. Such undermining will be seen as an epistemic threat so long as the relevance of diversity of perspective to accounts of the world is assessed against a conception of objectivity as disinterested and purged of all traces of either idiosyncratic or group-based identity.

The argument of these essays, taken collectively, is that so long as such a distinctively modern conception is taken—equally by its adherents and its critics—to be a necessary support for knowledge claims, we will be unable to say anything useful about the core "real" problem of epistemology: how to respond to pervasive and ineradicable epistemic dependency. When so much of what we need to know—from the safety of the water we drink to the facts behind rationales for going to war—is impossible for us to independently verify, we need ways of thinking about the trustworthiness of the authorities on whom we depend and of the institutions that discipline and certify their expertise. It is my hope that through a combination of theoretical reflection and concrete case studies, the current collection lays the ground for the articulation of a "postmodern" epistemology, which puts diversity and a politics of social justice in place of the universalistic abstract individualism that have framed the epistemology and politics of modernity.

PART I

KNOWLEDGE

The essays in this section move from diagnosing forms of philosophical, specifically epistemological, malaise to an overview of feminist epistemology as a response to that malaise, to exercises in one aspect of that response—the politically reflective placement of one's own voice.

"Non-Negotiable Demands: Metaphysics, Politics, and the Discourse of Needs" was written for a *Festschrift* for Burton Dreben, one of my graduate school teachers and a strong influence on many years of Harvard philosophy graduate students, especially on our reading of Wittgenstein and on our sensitivity to history in understanding philosophers and their views. The essay explores the demands placed on philosophical, especially epistemological, theory and explanation, demands that can't be met, but—more importantly—that would not, if met in the terms in which they are posed, actually satisfy the need that underlies the demand. This sort of situation—a genuine human need that takes on the form of a demand that the world (or the mind, or language, . . .) *must* be a certain way—is one that Stanley Cavell, in particular, has explored as fundamental to Wittgenstein's therapeutic method. I differ from Cavell and most other readers of Wittgenstein in locating the demand (the distortion of the need) in the historically specific construction of privileged modern subjectivity—the man of liberal political and philosophical life and thought.

"Feminist Epistemology," which was written for a symposium in *Metaphilosophy*, where it was followed by a critique by Louise Antony and my response, is influenced by W.V. Quine, another of my graduate school teachers, although the way I think about his work probably owes more to Dreben than to Quine himself. The closing sentence of "Feminist Epistemology," which refers to the "mutual containment of philosophy and politics" is a reference to Quine's naturalized epistemology, which rests on the mutual containment of epistemology and psychology (or, more generally, of philosophy and science): epistemology is that part of psychology that discusses our acquisition of beliefs, and psychology is among the empirical sciences that epistemology critically examines. The essay as a whole is framed by Quinean naturalism, which repudiates any epistemology that purports to be grounded in anything beyond what people actually do in acquiring and evaluating beliefs. I also agree with Quine that such a naturalized project can be normative: in his terms "normative epistemology is a branch of engineering." It is, he explains, a technology for making better predictions. (Hylton, p.84)[1]

Quine takes the scientific explanations of belief acquisition to be specifically psychological because he frames the questions of epistemology in individualistic terms. But as I suggest above and in this essay, and explore at greater length in "Resuscitating Epistemology" in Part 3, we can challenge that framing and shift the questions that epistemology—and the empirical science(s) connected to it—are called upon to address. In particular, there is no reason to limit questions about belief acquisition to individuals and individual cognitive processes. Lynne Hankinson Nelson proposes, starting from an explicitly Quinean perspective, that we treat the subject of knowledge as, in the first instance, an epistemic community: "we know" is analytically prior to "I know." (Nelson 1990) Heidi Grasswick wants to hold onto individual knowers and individual epistemic responsibility, while theorizing individuals as always in community (Grasswick 2004); and Miranda Fricker examines "epistemic injustice," practices that wrongly undermine some people's credibility. (Fricker 1998) If issues such as these are epistemology's concern, then the site of empirical investigation shifts from individual psychology to various social sciences, and the site of normative critique shifts from individual to collective practice: normative epistemology becomes, at least in part, a branch of politics.

"Terminal Moraine" and "On Waking Up One Morning and Discovering We Are Them" were both requested for volumes dealing with issues of identity, the first about Jewish identity in the context of racialization and racism, and the latter for a conference and later volume on identity and pedagogy. They have in common the conviction that it is often far from simple to describe the world as it appears from where one is located in it, that it can actually be easier—feel more natural—to ventriloquize, throwing one's voice so that it seems to emerge from a different social location. One may, for example, learn to describe the world as one thinks it would appear from the vantage point of someone more privileged (meaning more likely to be taken as epistemically reliable) than oneself. Alternatively, for those who feel guiltily privileged, it can be difficult to acknowledge the specificity of one's location and the ways in which it shapes one's view of the world.

The sort of location I claim in both essays exemplifies what I have termed (in "Mapping the Rough Ground" in Part 3) "privileged marginality." By that I do not mean the combination of privilege with marginality (the situation of, for example, economically privileged African-Americans); rather I'm pointing to particular forms of privilege constructed specifically on the margins, taking as a starting point the

---

1. I address the possibility of naturalized normativity—norms, even radically critical norms, that are not grounded in anything beyond practice—most directly in "Forms of Life: Mapping the Rough Ground," in Part 3.

position of wealthy Jews in early modern Europe, whose wealth came from their engaging in the money-lending forbidden to Christians: their wealth and social advantage stemmed from and was the indelible mark of their marginality, easily mobilized as a rationale for anti-Semitism. "Terminal Moraine" explores the location of middle-class post-WWII (i.e., post-Holocaust) white suburban politically progressive Jews, especially in relation to the civil rights movement, while "Waking Up" looks at the aging cohort of what, in the book of the same name, Roger Kimball has called "tenured radicals."

Although both essays are explicitly autobiographical (and, as autobiography, "Waking Up" is also decidedly dated), I am attempting in them to explore subject locations that will resonate with some readers with some significant degree of familiarity, and help facilitate difficult conversations with others in markedly different locations. I'm concerned, that is, with the problem of how to say "we" after the relatively privileged among us have been chastened for arrogant over-generalizing. One response to that chastening has been to claim to speak only for oneself, a response that does nothing to address the problem of whose voice gets a hearing and who often gets taken as speaking for a larger group, no matter how idiosyncratic one intends one's words to be. It's also impossible to form a political movement or theorize forms of subordination in the first person singular. What is needed is neither the eschewing of "we" nor its easy deployment. It ought always to be a question whom one is speaking for, or in solidarity with, and we (and here I mean those who engage in or have a stake in liberatory theorizing) need to hold each other responsible for how we address that question. We owe each other our best efforts at figuring out how our views of the social world are shaped by where we are standing in it, how that world itself is shaped by our practices, and how our participation in those practices sustains the ground on which some of us cannot move freely or find our feet.

Chapter 1

Non-Negotiable Demands

Metaphysics, Politics, and the Discourse of Needs

> One might say: the axis of our examination must be rotated, but about the fixed point of our real need.
>
> Wittgenstein, *Philosophical Investigations*, §108

> I do not explicitly learn the propositions that stand fast for me. I can *discover* them subsequently like the axis around which a body rotates. This axis is not fixed in the sense that anything holds it fast, but the movement around it determines its immobility.
>
> Wittgenstein, *On Certainty*, §152

> I am by no means sure that I should prefer a continuation of my work by others to a change in the way people live which would make all these words superfluous.
>
> Wittgenstein, *Culture and Value*, p. 61

Perhaps, one might say, we discover our real need by the movement around it: as we attempt to rotate the axis of our examination—learn to ask different questions, problematize the taken-for-granted, stir up trouble where there seemed to be consensus—we discover something about who "we" are, what our stake is in the forms of life within which we are made intelligible. If we succeed in changing the ways people live, will the philosophical problems that have engaged us become superfluous, no longer articulating anxieties that arise from our attempts to make sense of who and how we are? Might what we now take to be the problems of philosophy cease to be *our* problems?

I want to address these questions by bringing together two lines of thought: Cora Diamond's articulation (1991e, pp. 13–38) of a Wittgensteinian critique of philosophical demands (her term is "requirements") and Nancy Fraser's work (1989) (drawing critically on Habermas and Foucault) on the politics of needs discourse. What I want to suggest is this: what our "real need" might be in any particular case will frequently be deeply contested; discovering it will mean discovering who we are and whom we might best become. Such discovery (merging with invention) is what serious politics, in an Aristotelian sense, is about; such discovery also creates, in an unavoidable circle, the possibility of serious politics. Serious politics is the struggle to create the possibility of engaging in the social activity of self-discovery and self-creation by means of socially discovering and creating ourselves as persons capable of engaging in that struggle. Serious politics must be, then, disorienting, as it involves excavating the ground under your own feet, chipping away at the bedrock that ordinarily turns your spade (Wittgenstein 1958, §217)[1]; and it calls for the deepest of trust in one's fellow citizens—trust that issues only from long political struggle.

The circularity is Aristotelian: it takes the well-ordered polis to create the citizens who can create the well-ordered polis, much as an individual becomes virtuous by cultivating the habit of acting virtuously. In either case, however, the circle needn't be vicious: it can be, and ideally is, precisely virtuous. But if the polis or the person is initially vicious, it can be hard to see how the circle could fail to be so; and actual politics is frequently marked by the various suspicions that variously located political actors have that the conditions for the circle's being virtuous are not—perhaps cannot be—met. In the face of this despairing of serious politics, the two most common twentieth-century replacements for it are aiming for the satisfaction of what are taken to be scientifically determined "real needs" and fighting for the granting of painstakingly detailed rights or "demands." These strategies, though, are especially fraught with tension for the relatively disenfranchised, who are rightly suspicious both of the supposedly objective specification of their real *needs* by those who control the production of knowledge and by the embodiment of *rights* in institutions that have historically explicitly or implicitly excluded them.

The tensions between the two strategies—rights versus needs—have fueled much of recent political philosophy,[2] and it is not my intent to recapitulate those controversies. Rather, I want to develop a way in which we can better understand both the problematic nature of the "demands" that (as Diamond argues Wittgenstein (1967, §314)[3] shows) philosophy typically and problematically makes and the sources of those demands: why it is that we (and Wittgenstein, in the recurring voice of his interlocutor) find it so hard to stop, to find peace (*PI* §133), to accept that, in refusing to meet those demands, Wittgenstein is not "denying something" (*PI* §305).

1. References hereafter will be to *PI* and will be made parenthetically in the text.
2. For particularly insightful discussions of these tensions, see the disputes between critical legal theorists and critical race theorists. The former argue against the discourse of rights as enshrining a problematically bourgeois conception of the individual; the latter historicize that discourse rather in terms of black antislavery and enfranchisement struggles and argue for its continuing relevance. See Williams (1991) and Delgado (1995). Nancy Fraser (1989) also addresses these tensions in an especially illuminating way.
3. References hereafter will be to *Z* and will be made parenthetically in the text.

THE EVASION OF HISTORY

> When Americans say something is history, that means it's irrelevant.
>
> Polish journalist
>
> More dangerous than Hitler?
>
> Caption on a photograph of John Dewey,
> cover of *Time* magazine, March 17, 1952

In *The American Evasion of Philosophy*, Cornel West (1989, p. 4) examines the role of pragmatism in American philosophical and cultural life and emphasizes its resolute evasion of ("epistemology-centered") philosophy, in favor of an "unashamedly moral emphasis and...unequivocally ameliorative impulse." What I want to suggest in the present essay (in line with West's own arguments) is that analytic philosophy, especially as practiced in the United States after World War II, focusing on ahistorically articulated abstract "problems," has identified with and deepened the obverse evasion—of a moral and (politically ameliorative) conception of philosophy in favor of epistemological projects that rest on and reinforce the idea that knowledge, though it will in various ways be in the service of power, is not fundamentally constituted by it. The protection of philosophy from politics similarly rests on and reinforces the idea that philosophy's demands—for example, for theoretically tidy accounts of our moral and epistemic relationships to each other and to the rest of the natural world—can be met by purely intellectual investigation, that there are answers to philosophy's questions that lie in something other than what we do, something out of our hands and not of our making, something that has no significant (extraphilosophical) history.

The abstraction of the problems of philosophy from historical context is something that has, itself, a history, one that can be understood in the context of the specifically American evasion of serious politics, especially after World War II. Serious history (meaning history that makes a difference to how we experience the present)—along with serious politics—was regarded as suspiciously European: to the extent that it was not already dead, it was dangerous. For the generation born after the war, a too-vivid sense of history stood in the way of our all becoming self-made "men," even those of us whose cousins had, shortly before our birth, been murdered on a continent that took (and still takes) history very seriously indeed.[4] For the generation of our teachers, however, history must have been an ever-present ghost, something I dare say they had in mind even as they wove for our delight and empowerment a "problem-oriented" introduction to this marvelous twenty-five-hundred-year conversation. My

---

4. Konstanty Gebert, the Polish journalist quoted in the epigraph to this section, goes on to say, "When we say [that something is history], it means just the opposite." I take this quote from an editorial in the *New York Times*, August 28, 1997.

own philosophical mentors were overwhelmingly women and Jewish men. Their own places in the profession and the academy, and subsequently mine, had needed within their lifetimes to be fought for, a fact that cannot have escaped their notice; and it was, I now recognize, an extraordinary gift that they so arranged things that for a shockingly long time it utterly escaped my notice. I managed to regard myself as an entirely unexceptional heir to the history of philosophy, an enabling ignorance made possible only by the abstraction of philosophy's history from history more generally.

"History," however, was what brought analytic philosophy to North America, via refugees from Hitler's Europe. But the flight from Nazism became in effect a flight from politics, as the post-war mood in the United States was hardly receptive to the often left-wing political convictions of many of the refugees, convictions that in many cases had actually passionately motivated what came to be characterized as the excessively dry and formal abstractions of logical positivism.[5] Cold war attitudes stigmatized ideas associated, rightly or wrongly, with Communism; and a revulsion against the Nazi labeling of "Jewish" science and philosophy reinforced the view of both those fields as ideally independent of any ideological considerations. The attempt to stamp out suspiciously "un-American" political thinking led to the McCarthy era's terrorizing of the politically serious professoriate, both immigrant and native-born. Ironically, distinctively American philosophy was among the casualties, surviving only as a marginalized and neglected specialty, whose recent resurgence owes much to the raising of explicitly historical and political questions in relation to metaphysics and epistemology. Pragmatism was tainted both by its association with progressive politics and by its being insufficiently pragmatic (in the popular sense of that term) because of its attention to why we ask the questions we do and why we care about the answers.

Formalisms of various sorts—the best known example being New Criticism in literature—can be seen in part as responses to the chilling effect of McCarthyism on American universities. "Problems" are formal puzzles whose raison d'être is simply that they are there—and that we have tools that seem suited to answering them. For my peers and those who have followed us, this ahistorical inheritance of the field has made it more readily ours, since we did not, in theory, have to confront what it meant that the likes of us should be among its heirs—including, as we do, not only Jews but many white women and, though far too few, men and women of color. In practice, many of us have come to believe that we do have to confront the terms of this inheritance and to ask, not only if the answers philosophers have given will work in the varying contexts of our

5. The role of progressive politics in the discussions in the Vienna Circle is discussed in Carnap (1963, especially pp. 22–4). Whether or not political commitments ought explicitly to inform philosophizing was, according to Carnap's reminiscences, a frequent topic of conversation. His own view was that they should not; his main adversary in this regard was Otto Neurath.

lives, but more deeply if—and in what ways—the questions philosophers have asked are ours.[6] The dehistoricizing of the field, seen in connection with the depoliticizing of the academy, has facilitated the inclusion in philosophy of many who are coming to question the terms of that inclusion—much as the liberal inclusion of previously excluded groups in political discourse has led to the questioning of liberalism. In both cases, those who facilitated our inclusion, in part by shielding us from the depth of the historical resistance to it, understandably tend to see such questioning as counterproductive, dangerous, and ungrateful: it troubles our relationship to a field that only too recently allowed us in at all.[7]

THE PROBLEMS OF PHILOSOPHY

I have argued in a series of essays (see Scheman 1993b) that central philosophical problems (among those that West sees pragmatism as evading, arising from worries about whether or not the world is my world, whether I can know it or be known in it, whether my words can refer and my sentences be true or false, whether I inhabit it with intelligible others and whether I am intelligible to them, whether we matter to each other or to anything beyond ourselves) are not best understood as timeless and acontextual, nor is that how they were understood by the earlier philosophers who first articulated them in something like their present form. Rather, they are attempts to meet the specific needs that arose as the irresolvable residue of projects of crafting and enacting privileged subjectivity, projects in which canonical philosophers were explicitly engaged in ways that clearly connect with their epistemological and metaphysical questioning and theorizing. Philosophy could not actually meet those needs (nothing could), but expressing them in the form of philosophical demands helped to allay the symptoms (for everyone but philosophers) of the "dis-ease" they represented—the disconnection, for example, of the knowing subject from the objects of his knowledge, starting with his own body.

---

6. My use of "we" (and, alternatively, "they") in this essay will be intentionally unstable and shifting, reflecting the unstable and shifting nature of my own identifications. In particular, I will sometimes say "we" and sometimes "they" when speaking either of those who are privileged or of those who are marginalized or subordinated. Not only do I and other radical academics occupy a variety of different subject positions, some privileged, some marginalized or subordinated, but we share a particular complex position I have elsewhere called "privileged marginality." See chapter 8, p. 154–156. Such complexity needs to be seen both as an epistemic tool and as a reminder of the importance of concrete forms of moral, political, and epistemic responsibility. For the first point, see Collins (1986, pp. 14–32).

7. Taking the problems of philosophy in this way seriously, as requiring us to ask why it is that they matter to us and matter in a way that brain-teasers or (mere) puzzles do not, in fact characterized much of my own philosophical education—explicitly from Stanley Cavell and, as importantly, implicitly from Burton Dreben, of blessed memory. Whatever reservations either of them has or had about my work attach, I am certain, not to my raising such questions but to my too quickly answering them.

Thus, philosophy did, indirectly, meet (some of) the needs of those who benefited from the construction of privilege: the placebo effect does work. The situation is more complicated with respect to those who are variously marginalized or subordinated. The same philosophical problems will be ours to the extent that we come to have, or to believe we have, a stake in the structures of privileges we lack (and that we will frequently have such a stake and even more frequently be justified in believing we do is one of the reasons political organizing against these structures is so difficult). It may even seem, for reasons I will discuss, that those who are marginalized or subordinated have a specific, perhaps even greater, interest in the posing of philosophical demands.

I want to argue, however, with respect to three deeply entrenched metaphysical pictures, that—though each seems to meet the real needs of those who are marginalized or subordinated—that offer is an illusion. In each case, I will argue, the metaphysical picture promises what it cannot deliver and diverts attention away from the commitment to political struggle that might, to paraphrase Wittgenstein's words, change the way we live and dissolve the philosophical problem to which the metaphysics was meant to be a solution.[8] I want to suggest that the failure in each case stems from a similar move—the initial one in the conjuring trick, the one that escapes notice (PI §308): for understandable reasons, the circularity of genuine needs discourse is rejected in favor of the posing of demands that are taken, in a way that precludes examination, to represent the satisfaction of real needs—to be what must be the case if our needs are to be met.

MIND-INDEPENDENT REALITY

Arguments about the nature of reality—in particular, about what it means to say, and whether it is true, that the physical world exists independently of our attempts to know it—are in some form or other as old as philosophy. One recent turn on these disputes starts with the argument, often from the academic left, that realism is politically suspect, that the requirement of mind-independent reality as the ground for truth claims about the world is an ideological fiction that serves to occlude the human activities of world-structuring. A reply to that argument, from political allies, is that it is those who contest the status quo who most need independence—as the ground for the truth of such claims as that gender is a system of subordination, whether or not anyone thinks so. Furthermore,

---

8. I need to guard against the tendency to oversimplify the political and to believe I know more than I possibly can about what such changes can and should be like. What I want to argue here—as will, I hope, become clear below—is that what is at issue is not the actual achievement of specific political changes, but rather the commitment to what I am calling serious politics, which I see as connected to Wittgenstein's attempt to get us to acknowledge both the absence of anything underneath our practices and the depth of those practices.

it is argued, surely we want to be able to say that those who promulgate sexist, racist, homophobic theories about the nature of women, people of color, gays and lesbians, are just wrong and that the theories we and our allies come up with are not just more to our liking, but are actually true (or, at least, truer).[9]

One standard way of explaining what is meant by mind-independent reality is to say that it entails that no matter how far we may progress in our understanding of the world, no matter how confident we may be in the truth of our theories, we could turn out to be wrong, even if we might never actually or perhaps even possibly discover that fact. No amount of justification entails truth: metaphysics (what is true) is independent of epistemology (what we are justified in believing).[10]

It does seem right to me that liberatory theorists have good reasons to be realists. Those reasons include a recognition of the problems of arrogance: surely it is salutary to cultivate an attitude of openness to being surprised by reality, a discipline of attentiveness, a readiness to discover that the world eludes one's classificatory and explanatory grasp, rather than conforming to it as a matter of definition (see Code 1991; Haraway 1988; Harding 1986; Heldke and Kellert 1995). What is seriously at issue is how to characterize realism—in particular, what characterization best captures the insights into the necessarily perspectival nature of knowledge that have been developed by feminist theorists and others?

Such insights (including arguments against an Archimedean point, or God's-eye, objectivity, and for the relevance of social location to how one comes to conceive of the world) have often been interpreted as arguments against realism—replacing reality with views of reality. Such arguments are, I think, fundamentally misguided: perspectivalism (which I take to be basically correct, in some form or other, and there are many) makes sense only as a form of realism. To say that perspectives differ is to say that those who are relevantly differently located will perceive things differently—and this simply makes no sense unless what is being perceived, the perceivers, and their locations are all real. One can, in fact, often differentiate between real and imagined things precisely by asking if those who are differently placed have different perspectives on them—if from where you stand, you can see the pink elephant I see, and if the way it looks to you is different in the ways it ought to be from the way it looks to me. It's not only that, if you fail to see it, we may conclude that it's my

9. The arguments have been around for quite some time but took in the 1990s a heated turn. See, for example, the fracas surrounding Alan Sokal's spoof of post-modern science studies: Alan Sokal (1996a, pp. 62–4; Sokal's exposure of the spoof), Alan Sokal (1996b, pp. 217–52; the spoof itself), and Sokal et al. (1996, pp. 54–64; discussion by the editors of *Social Text*, Sokal, and others of the significance of the spoof). For a left-feminist attack on feminist and other approaches to science studies, see Ehrenreich and McIntosh (1997, pp. 11–16).

10. Scientific realists, such as Richard Boyd, want to emphasize that the independence emphatically does not go the other way around: we have good reason to conclude that those among our beliefs that are justified are so precisely because they are (approximately) true. See Boyd (1991, pp. 195–222).

hallucination, but, if, standing on the other side of the room, you see just what I see, we may conclude that we're *both* hallucinating: perspectives are supposed to differ, and to do so predictably, or at least in ways we can come to understand.

Metaphysical realism may well be compatible with perspectivalism. But, as Wittgenstein put it, "a wheel that can be turned though nothing else moves with it, is not part of the mechanism" (*PI* §271). Whether or not something is part of the mechanism has to do with what we are doing: what is the "real need" to which mind-independent reality is the answer?[11] While all persons have an interest in their theories' being true, independently of anyone's thinking that they are, the need for realism specifically on the part of those who are marginalized or subordinated is acute, since the alternative—truth's consisting in some sort of agreement in practice—would leave them not only epistemically but metaphysically in the cold, their beliefs condemned to being not only unjustified but false.

But does metaphysical realism answer this real need? What it does is to put the truth beyond a necessarily receding horizon: anything that could be known to turn with the parts we have our hands on could, on this view, not be reality—the possibility of not being part of the mechanism is its whole point. It is, in this way, suspiciously like a Kingdom of Heaven promised especially to those who are on the losing end of all the kingdoms on earth. The keys to this heavenly kingdom do not unlock any earthly doors; the message of transcendence is necessarily one of deferral. One suspects that the function of the two transcendent gestures is the same— the deflection of attention from what might change the situation of the wretched of the earth here on the earth, by shifting the structures of power that keep them wretched.

What might this point come to in the case of metaphysical realism? What other account of realism might meet those real needs in reality, not just in fantasy? Rather than being able to say, without being able to show, that there is a fact of the matter that makes one's views the truth, or at least nearer the truth than one's opponents, what would actually do some work would be making a space for critical engagement. An account of realism that starts with the perspectival nature of knowledge provides such a space by its insistence on the problematic partiality of any account that has failed to engage relevant critiques. What makes a critique relevant, and what counts as engagement, are matters for argument: but for a perspectival realist, it remains always an open possibility that, however stable a current consensus might be, there are potential critics who ought to be heard and who, if heard, would properly upset that

11. To frame the issue this way may seem, on a meta-level, to beg the question against the metaphysical realist, who might either reject the question or answer it by saying that our real need is for the truth of the matter. The point supports my argument: metaphysical realism is attractive insofar as one does not historicize the question to which it is an answer.

consensus. A perspectival account of realism places on those who would maintain a particular view the burden of seeking out critics or, at the very least, of scrutinizing the practices that might be keeping critics silent or distorting what they might say. It requires that a commitment to objectivity and truth be backed up by vigorous projects of discursive affirmative action (see Longino 1990). Rather than resting with the metaphysical possibility that we might be wrong—a possibility that, since it is necessarily transcendent, remains with equal force no matter what we do—it draws our attention to what we need to *do* if we care about truth. To say that reality might turn out to be different from what we take it to be doesn't direct our attention; to say that our accounts of reality are incomplete because relevant perspectives have not contributed to them directs us to those who have been marginalized or subordinated by social structures.

Another way of putting the point is that metaphysical realism is a thesis about the ontological status of the objects of knowledge; it is mute about the subjects of that knowledge. By contrast, the recognition that specific forms of bias inhere in privileged perspectives on the world underwrites the call for what Sandra Harding (1991, p. 161) calls "strong objectivity," which "puts the subject or agent of knowledge in the same critical, causal plane as the object of her or his inquiry."[12] What responds to the real needs of the marginalized or subordinated is realism about knowing subjects as rigorous as the realism about the objects of their knowledge. Such a need is especially crucial when the objects of knowledge are the marginalized or subordinated themselves—scrutinized, pathologized, exoticized, and anatomized by those whose epistemic privilege consists precisely in their being exempt from such scrutiny, in their occupying subject positions encoded as generic, and in their being allowed (often, in fact, required) to present what they claim to know in anonymous, impersonal, "objective" form, a requirement that idealizes the conditions of their knowledge-construction, effectively masks their social location, renders them "unreal," and removes them from reciprocal critical examination.[13]

In seeming to offer a ground for truth claims, metaphysical realism may be a source of comfort for liberatory theorists, but it has—can have—no teeth. At best, one can hope that reality will eventually bite back against one's opponents. Perspectival realism, by contrast, is programmatic: it

12. The point is strikingly similar to Quine's call for a naturalized epistemology. However differently Harding and Quine might characterize the relevant explanatory sciences, they share the insistence that subjects of knowledge need equally to be objects and in the same terms as other objects. See Quine (1969a).

13. Such antirealist, Archimedean-point conceptions of objectivity do not, it should be noted, follow from metaphysical realism: One can hold such a conception of realism alongside an equally robust realism about knowing subjects. But the placement of mind-independent conceptions of reality at the definitional heart of realism does in practice serve to deflect attention from subjects to objects of knowledge—so that, for example, the contamination of test tubes poses an obvious epistemic threat, while the sexual harassment of lab assistants does not.

allows one to distinguish between those who have a genuine commitment to objectivity and truth and those who do not. Such a view of realism can be argued for independently of any particular perspective, but those whose voices are already heard are less likely to see, from their own perspective, the need for it: it doesn't, in the same direct way, respond to their "real needs." But rotating the axis of our examination around the real needs of the "others"—needs for legitimated entry into the processes of knowledge-creation—shifts the constraints on an adequate account of the nature of realism and moves us away from the metaphysical demand for—and problem of—inaccessible reality and toward the politics of democratic critical engagement.

As with any serious politics, however, such a project is unavoidably circular. In particular, what are the terms of democratic critical engagement, starting with the question of how "we" are to decide who is to participate in it? There is no way prior to such a project to lay down the rules for engaging in it. In the absence of the trust that could ground such boot-strapping, there may be no way effectively to answer the interlocutor who persists in the demand for absolute, metaphysically guaranteed bedrock. What would allow us to give peace to such a demand would be the confidence that the real needs that give it force stood some real chance of being, at least, attended to. For this reason, breaking the hold of the metaphysical picture requires a change in the way we live.

TRANSCENDENT MORAL STANDARDS

Similar arguments have occupied moral philosophers. A standard question has been: Are there grounds for moral judgment that transcend particular, historically and culturally variable forms of practice? Further, are such grounds required if moral judgments are to be objectively (or even universally intersubjectively) true or false? What might the source of such moral authority be, and how might we be connected to it epistemically and motivationally? How do we know what it commands, and why do its commands speak to us? Arguments for one or another form of moral realism have mirrored those for metaphysical realism, including the point that it is especially those whose interests are not reflected in dominant practices who have the greatest stake in not reducing claims about what we ought to do to claims about what we in fact do or even what we think we ought to do.[14] It would seem that some sort of moral realism is required to make sense of the claim of the radical critic that the form of life she inhabits is an immoral one.

As with metaphysical realism, the apparent need is to have it both ways—to ensure the objectivity of moral judgments by locating their

---

14. For an explicit connection between scientific and moral realism, see Boyd (1988).

source outside of our practices, but also to connect those judgments to our practices in ways that make them both knowable to us and binding on us. Plausible accounts of moral epistemology or of moral motivation risk losing moral objectivity, while accounts of moral objectivity risk making moral truths inaccessible or alien. Attempts at reconciling these conflicting demands have frequently rested on substantive claims about allegedly universal human needs or interests: the problem comes in specifying those needs or interests in ways that avoid being either too thin to do any real work or too thick to be nontendentious.

Wittgenstein is frequently read as urging us to forego these attempts altogether—to recognize that justification is itself a practice, which, like all practices, rests not on some transcendent ground but on what we do, on our agreement "in form of life" (*PI* §241). "The end is not an ungrounded presupposition: it is an ungrounded way of acting." (Wittgenstein 1969, §110)[15] This "pluralist conservative" reading of Wittgenstein (see Nyiri 1982 and 1986) has been contested, notably by Sabina Lovibond (1983), who has argued that Wittgenstein is best read as a moral realist and, as such, provides a way of making the radical critic intelligible by construing objectivity in terms of a project rather than an already existing ground. Properly understood, moral practices are intrinsically critical. Rather than a transcendent ground, we have a rolling horizon, and keeping it rolling is the work of the moral critic: this is what we—at least some of us—do.[16]

Putting the matter this way makes moral objectivity not a given, but a commitment. If "we" *don't* contest the status quo, then justification may well come to an end, not because it *couldn't* be carried further, but because no one has taken on the task of disturbing its grounds. Wittgenstein writes, "If I have exhausted the justifications I have reached bedrock, and my spade is turned. Then I am inclined to say: 'this is simply what I do'" (*PI* §217). "Bedrock" is no more absolute, however, than is the riverbed in *On Certainty*. It may be that the "hard rock" of the bank is "subject to no alteration or only to an imperceptible one" (OC §99), but that doesn't mean that it can't be disturbed: it's simply a matter of fact that it isn't. So if we find its obduracy problematic, we have our work cut out for us. If our demands for justification are met with the reply "this is simply what I do," we need to ask ourselves: "Is this what *I* do? And, if so, do I do it less than wholeheartedly," as Lovibond puts it (1983 pp. 159–63)? Do I know others who are similarly (or perhaps differently) estranged from this "we"? Why, precisely, does what is being justified seem to me or to others to be unjustified?

It is a peculiar feature of commitments to both moral and metaphysical realism that they typically take as definitive a resistance to being thus "cashed out." In the terms of such resistance, "where your mouth is" is

---

15. References hereafter will be to OC and will be made parenthetically in the text.
16. For approaches to extending this account, see chapter 8 and O'Connor (2002).

precisely where your money is not supposed to be. This can seem especially responsive to the needs of those without money: indefinite deferral means that the line of credit will never come due. But, as in the financial realm, getting credit requires more assurance of solvency than simply pointing out that there's a lot of time before one will have to make good. The "real needs" of the moral critic are not met by an inner assurance of ultimate vindication. If one's criticisms are ignored (the privileged insist that their spades are turned), such inner assurance will be cold comfort, assuming one is even able to maintain it. To take moral realism seriously would mean to be committed to the belief that, if others did or could live a form of life deeply different from ours, there would still be the possibility of critical engagement with them, that their different ways are possibilities for us and pose a critical challenge to us, that they might be right to do what they do and we might be wrong.

In this sense, those who are subordinated or marginalized have, one might say, moral realism thrust upon them: that others might live differently is not just a matter for theoretical speculation. The mores of the dominant are everywhere around them, constantly being touted as the right way to live. In the light of those mores, the subordinated or marginalized see themselves stigmatized as culpably defective, their forms of life as inferior, either lacking in values or informed by the wrong ones. Whether we internalize these judgments of ourselves or reject them, we can hardly ignore them or see them as emanating from forms of life that are just different, neither better nor worse. Questions about right or wrong are not idle, nor can one say "this is what we do," as though that settles the matter, when the "we" one appeals to is stigmatized as perverse. Critical engagement, for some, is not a theoretical possibility; it is a necessity for survival.

From nonprivileged vantage points, moral realism is practical and concrete rather than metaphysical. It does some work because there is work that needs to be done. Moral questions are real questions, with real answers—moral judgments are true or false—because that is how they are treated, as matters literally of life and death, whether one is confronting gay-bashers or those who would deny food, shelter, and health care to children without two, married parents. Ultimate vindication in the light of principles that transcend any form of practice is beside the point: what makes moral judgments objective is the intelligibility of continuing dispute.[17]

The privileged, by contrast, might well come to a point where such intelligibility runs out, where it seems either that no-one really

17. The issues here are similar to those raised by critical race theorists about, for example, talk of rights. Critical legal theorists argue against the appeal to rights, on the grounds that the concept lacks the sort of practice-transcendent ground that would give it standing independent of its use by those in power. Critical race theorists agree that the meaning of the concept is its use, but point to its use by, for example, blacks in the civil rights struggle. They argue that such use makes rights real in any meaningful sense of that term: real enough, that is, to use; too real to ignore.

could, seriously, think or act differently, or that their doing so is of merely aesthetic interest: quaint or exotic or titillating. In either case, there's nothing to argue about, no real possibility that others might show me to be mistaken. One might subscribe nonetheless to metaphysical moral realism—holding on, as a matter of principle, to the intelligibility of dispute, without any idea of how in practice to carry it on, but the principle is an empty one. What it would take for one's spade *not* to be turned would be the actual chipping of the bedrock, a cracking open of the earth beneath one's feet, a real instability calling for a real effort to regain one's footing, to find a better ground for one's convictions, or, perhaps, a change in one's form of life.[18] Moral realism is a demand, from the less to the more privileged, that the latter take such a challenge seriously. To reply that the challenge can only truly be set, or met, by practice-transcendent values is to evade the demand: Let them eat pie-in-the-sky.

Here, however, once more the turn toward serious politics presumes a discursive space that in general does not exist: "Just say 'No'" works no better against metaphysics than it does against drugs. In both cases what is likely to be lacking is the justified belief in something to which to say "yes." One can admit that a serious moral conversation (or a well-paying, rewarding job) is what one really needs, but, if one thinks there is no chance of getting one, it can be hard to let go of one's surrogate satisfactions.

PRIVILEGED ACCESS

Metaphysical and moral realism seem to offer protection from the abuses of power and privilege by positing a realm of truth that is beyond the grasp equally of prince and of pauper. The thesis of privileged access to our mental states offers such protection by putting those states equally within the grasp of each of us—and us alone. Each of us gets to be the ultimate insider, possessed of the insider's edge, when it comes to the crucial questions about what we believe or feel, desire or despise. Since it is those without sanctioned social power—for example, women, children, gays and lesbians, transsexuals, those declared insane—who are

---

18. One can evade the demand that one change one's life and attempt to regain one's footing on new, more democratic ground, by embracing the conditions of instability and mocking any call for grounding as theoretically suspect. Though my quarrel in this essay is with analytic philosophers, it is important to point out that many (not all) postmodern, anti-Enlightenment theorists are equally guilty of an evasion of politics. Rather than arguing, or assuming, that the structures of liberalism are adequate to liberatory politics, they argue against the notion that anything could be adequate, or even meaningfully responsive. Such theorists may be effective seismographs, in recognizing the instability of the ground that most analytic philosophers take to be quite stable, but their evasion of agency and responsibility is a refuge for privilege, as Spelman (1988, pp. 183–5) characterizes epistemic nihilism or relativism on the part of the privileged. For a discussion of the relationships between poststructuralist theory and (specifically feminist) politics, see Benhabib et al. (1995).

typically subjected to allegedly authoritative pronouncements by others as to what we really feel or mean or intend or want, it would seem that we would have particular reason to embrace a philosophical position that made us the only true ultimate authorities on such matters. It would seem helpful to be able to say, "You—whoever you are—are merely in the position of putting together pieces of evidence, trying to acquire reasons to believe what I, and I alone, already directly and infallibly know."

Certainly the problem of being subjected to others' socially sanctioned expertise over one's inner states is a real one. Children are told their anger is merely overtiredness (the word "cranky" exists largely for this purpose); women are told by men that our no's really mean yes; the meaning of homoerotic desire is claimed by those whose authority stems largely from their supposed immunity to it (see Halperin 1995); transsexuals have had to struggle with a range of expert discourses that claim to know better than they do what genders they are or can possibly be; and a declaration of insanity is tantamount to a loss of all epistemic authority over oneself. In these ways, it can be evident that what appears to be a metaphysical thesis, applying equally to everyone, functions instead like a property right: privileged access is just what it sounds like—a right to (epistemic) access that tracks privilege.[19] But why shouldn't we argue for granting in practice what the thesis offers in theory—privileged access for each of us to our own inner lives?

There are two reasons why such an offer is, like the offers of metaphysical and moral realism, more apparent than real, a distraction from the changes in our form of life that would address the real needs that privileged access appeals to. The first concerns what we don't get with privileged access; the second concerns what we too often do.

What we don't get is an acknowledgment of the roles that we play in each other's intelligibility, of the ways in which we "listen each other into speech," create the grounds of each other's possibility (see Lugones 1987; see also chap. 6). It is an illusion of privilege to believe that our inner lives have meaning and structure independently of the social worlds in which we are embedded. The illusion comes about from the closeness of fit the privileged are likely to experience, the ease with which they can make sense of themselves using the available language and explanatory frameworks—even when they are articulating their own supposed divergence from what they take to be the norm (there is, at least in the late twentieth-century United States, a ready vocabulary for disaffection, alienation, and eccentricity). It can seem that one just does directly encounter one's inner self, and that its meaning is clear.

As post-Freudian sophisticates, we do not really believe in such simple self-transparency.[20] But, depending on our social locations, we have

19. For a fuller discussion of this point, see Scheman (1980). This essay is reprinted in Scheman (1993b).
20. Thanks to Mary Mothersill for reminding me of this.

wildly diverse encounters with the various expert discourses that purport to have or to be able to uncover the truth about us, a truth of which we might be unaware or which we might actively resist. For the privileged, such encounters tend to be voluntary and to be aimed at providing explanations over which we exercise ultimate authority; and the terms of those explanations are likely to be familiar, even if their application in one's own case is initially disconcerting. The "designated others," by contrast, encounter experts implacable in their claims to ultimate authority, an authority that is quite independent of whether or not we ever come to accept their stories about us as the correct ones. Nor are the terms of those expert discourses likely to be useful to us in fashioning livable narratives of our own lives: it is certainly not a condition on their explanatory adequacy that they do so—as it is in practice for the explanatory stories about the privileged. In the face of such pervasive arrogance, it can be a matter of survival to be convinced that one has privileged access to one's own inner being.[21]

There is a burgeoning literature about and from the perspectives of those whose identities are, according to dominant constructions, "impossible." Marilyn Frye (1983d), for example, starts her essay "To Be and Be Seen" with a comment by Sarah Hoagland that lesbians are impossible beings, and that being so offers distinctive epistemic advantages. María Lugones (1990a) writes in "Hispaneando y Lesbiando" about the impossibility of being what she is: an Hispanic lesbian. Jacob Hale (1995), Kate Bornstein (1994), Susan Stryker (1994), and Sandy Stone (1991) write variously about the ways in which transsexual subjectivity is a struggle against a dichotomous sex/gender system that offers intelligibility only at the cost of a continuous, truthful life story and the agreement to conform to stereotypical notions of gender. In all these cases, the need is acute to be able to say: I exist as what I know myself to be, in the face of a normalizing discourse that says no one can possibly be such a thing— a lesbian (someone whose attention is drawn to women) or a Hispanic lesbian (rather than a pervert or an exotic caricature) or a person whose gender identity has shifted in varying relation to one's also shifting sexed body.

Though privileged access can seem especially appealing to those subject to routine epistemic predation, one striking feature of the writing of these theorists is that, though they may acknowledge temptations in that direction, they argue, explicitly or implicitly, against such access. For one, they are acutely aware that those who do not find usable representations of themselves, narratives in which to insert their own singularity, need more than mere permission to say how it is with them and a readiness on the part of others to accept what they say. They first need a language, and a set of stories, that make them intelligible, that let them string

---

21. And thanks to Peg O'Connor for reminding me of this.

together descriptors that add up to something other than an "impossible being." Something needs to be there to make one's articulations of identity more than meaningless babble, even in one's own ears—a "something" that the privileged tend to take for granted.

Part of that "something" is provided by the discursive resources of our cultural surroundings. But we also need more focused uptake from those with whom we interact—we need acknowledgment and, beyond that, critical engagement with our ongoing projects of self-creation. Simply being left alone, as the ultimate authorities on ourselves, will too often leave us without the resources to figure out just what it is that we are supposed to know. We are neither as opaque to (all) others nor as transparent to ourselves as the thesis of privileged access would have it. To a great extent, we are what others take us to be, and, if we think that is not so, that is likely to be because the "others" are sufficiently culturally ubiquitous and sufficiently on our side for us to be oblivious to their contributions. When that is not the case, what we need is not to be left to our own devices, infallibly introspecting, supposedly protected by metaphysically guaranteed, universally privileged access. Locking others out serves equally to lock us in, deprived of sense-making resources.

We may, however, know that the culturally available discursive resources fail to make sense of our lives without ourselves knowing how better to tell the story. And an initial step toward constructing a usable narrative may well be the exposure of the contingency of those resources, an exposure that comes when the gaze of those who are rendered impossible is directed back at the structures of intelligibility. It is the invisibility of those structures to those for whom they work that fosters the illusion of direct self-knowledge, even as it allows for the idea that such self-knowledge may frequently fail and need to be supplemented by experts who can see the truth when we are ourselves unaware of it. Exposing structures of intelligibility as the contingent effects of normalizing practices is a first step in the concrete, political work of taking responsibility for our complicity in setting or refusing the conditions of each other's possibility.

If the notion of privileged access promises the discursively marginalized what it cannot deliver—unmediated access to an already existing coherent truth about themselves—it equally problematically imposes on them a form of self-knowledge from which they can have no distance and which is unusable in their hands. All they can do—what they are expected to do as "native informants"—is to hand over the infallible knowledge of themselves on which they will in all likelihood be impaled. Those designated "primitives" or "natives" are ironically taken to be in possession of (or to be possessed by) straightforward truths about their own lives, truths ready for consumption by those who take an interest in them.

These points have been made with greatest clarity by postcolonial theorists like Chandra Talpede Mohanty (1991) and Uma Narayan (1997). In a culture that privileges scientific knowledge—that is, knowledge gained by disciplined adherence to a prescribed method—the self-knowledge of the marginalized and subordinated is taken to inhere effortlessly in them and to exude naturally from them: a natural resource for more privileged knowers to gather up and refine in the production of "real" knowledge. Presumed incapable of real, disciplined understanding of their own situation, "natives" are no more empowered by their "privileged" relationship to the truths of their lives than indigenous peoples have been by their relation to the land on which they lived. (For further discussion see chap. 10.)

Elaine Scarry (1985, especially chap. 1) makes a similar point about pain, especially the pain of torture, on which the sufferer is impaled, disempowered by what she or he cannot but know but cannot say, the suffered pain made available for appropriation by the torturer. This pain comes to signify the torturer's power and control precisely because the torturer is the one who stands at the authoritative distance from it. In arguing that the experience of pain is private, in the sense of being incommunicable, Scarry might seem to be at odds with Wittgenstein. But there is, I think, an insight they share. Both see knowledge as an achievement—a matter, as Wittgenstein would stress, of justification, reasoning, overcoming of challenges, establishment of grounds and of authority. That is why Wittgenstein says that we do not know our own pain. We do not stand in the right relation to it. We are not separate from it; it is not an object for us, hence not an object of knowledge.

Wittgenstein clearly does not mean to single out in particular the sort of pain Scarry writes about: he would include pain we can straightforwardly communicate, as when we tell the doctor where and how it hurts—or, for that matter, when we cry out or moan. Somewhat less clear is the question: Why pain? Isn't what Wittgenstein says true of all sensations, perceptions, and so on? My sense about that is that there is something special about pain, and that Scarry's discussion of the pain of torture strikingly brings it out. In general, my "inner states," including my pain, can be the objects of the knowledge of others; but, especially in the case of pain, what I may primarily need from others is not that they know how it is with me, but that they acknowledge it—and me (Cavell 1969b). When my pain is acknowledged, I am connected as a subject with others; and their knowledge, if grounded in that acknowledgment, is available to me: I am part of the community that comes to know how it is with me—even though my own relation to what I feel is not the same as that of the others. We are, reciprocally, subjects and objects for each other; and what I come to know about you inflects how I experience myself. In the absence of that reciprocity and trust—commonly, when my experiences put me beyond the range of what others are able to acknowledge, as can happen with extreme pain, or, horrifically, when the others are not to be trusted with my experience, as when, most extremely, they are my torturers—those experiences (and pain is at least the paradigm example here) are not known within a community of which I am an equal member.

Instead, knowledge happens in the absence of acknowledgment. A chasm opens up between my having and others' knowing: each stands as a reproach to the other, contests the other's authority. My body becomes contested epistemic terrain—and the contest is one I cannot win, if the winner is the one who knows.

What is the "real need" of the marginalized and subordinated with respect to the truths of their/our own lives? The answer to that question starts from the recognition that, construed as a struggle for something that already exists, it is one we are doomed to lose. Insofar as such truths are seen as proper objects of knowledge, others are far better placed to possess them; and if such truths are seen as naturally inhering in us, they possess us rather than the other way around. If, however, the truths of our lives are to be created—not by making ourselves up, though we may need to do that, but by creating the explanatory and narrative frames within which we can make a sense we can live with—then what we need are contexts of trust and reciprocity, contexts in which, in Marilyn Frye's terms (1983a), we are "lovingly perceived." It is the strength of diverse separatisms to create such contexts. Moving beyond those confines has met with some, albeit limited, success, but to the extent that relationships with dominant discourses remain hostile, privileged access will retain its appeal to those who feel themselves wrongly stigmatized by those discourses.

WHAT PHILOSOPHY CANNOT DO, AND WHY

In suggesting that we rotate the axis of our examination, Wittgenstein presumably had in mind (not solely, but centrally) the examination he had undertaken in the *Tractatus* of language, the world, and the relationship between them. That examination had culminated—*philosophy*, he argued, therein culminated—in a proof by ostension (showing, not saying) that both language and the world were, necessarily, *mine*. The "real need" to which such a "proof" was meant to respond concerns one's belonging in, or to, the world—knowing and being known, understanding and being understood, mattering and having things matter. It makes no sense, in *Tractatus* terms, to think oneself marginal to or excluded from sense-making: wherever I am is the center of my world, the place from which sense is made.

Some interpreters of Wittgenstein (see, e.g., Lear 1984) have read especially the private language "argument" in the *Investigations* as continuing this line of thought, with the crucial shift from "I" to "we." On this reading, Wittgenstein's later work provides the same sort of minimal metaphysical guarantee of intelligibility and deflection of the threat of radical skepticism as did the earlier work: by our use of language, we place ourselves within a form of life the living of which provides the ground for shared judgments. There is, I think, something right about this picture. To the extent that our judgments are grounded, this is what it comes to. But the air of bourgeois complacency many commentators attribute to Wittgenstein—we all go on the same, doing what we do, our spades turned—could not be more alien to his sensibility. The interlocutor's unwillingness to stop demanding something more absolute by way of bedrock can, I have argued elsewhere (see chap. 8), best be understood as an expression of anxiety on the part of someone whose attachment to "what we do" is by no means simple or to be taken for granted. It may well be that only if I take what we do for granted (which includes not worrying about just who "we" are) can I be fully intelligible, even to myself—but there is no guarantee that I am intelligible.

Nor is intelligibility an all-or-nothing affair. As both subjects and objects of knowledge, each of us moves in the world as one medium-sized physical object among many, finding our way around with a degree of success—whoever we may be—sufficient to ground the objectivity of a plethora of judgments. We wouldn't (couldn't) argue as we do about, for example, preserving the environment, if we didn't agree about being mortal creatures inhabiting the same planet. But when it comes to more subtle and vexed ways of sense-making, our relationships to the practices that ground intelligibility differ widely. "What we do" is a matter of what Wittgenstein calls our natural history, including under that rubric "[c]ommanding, questioning, recounting, chatting" along with "walking, eating, drinking, playing" (*PI* §25). If one's commands are routinely ignored or mocked, one's questions consistently dismissed as silly, one's attempts to recount one's experiences rejected as fantasy, or one's chatting ignored as chattering; if one's ways of walking (or not) are unaccommodated, or one's experiences around food and drink are the source of shame, or if, as a boy, one prefers playing with dolls over what is referred to as "rough and tumble play," one is likely to be regarded by those around one as not quite making sense.

It is understandable that one might try to argue that one *does* make sense—that there is a truth about who and what one is, as well as about the moral rightness of one's being, and that, no matter what anyone else says, there are things about oneself that one just directly knows. One might, that is, call on metaphysics as a shield against others who seem to get one wrong, gesturing toward something that is not a matter of shared practices on which to ground the truth and rightness of one's claims to intelligibility.

Such arguments—or gestures in the directions of arguments—are understandable, but they are not, I have argued, effective. Like the soaring arches of Gothic cathedrals, they draw our attention away from the practices that ground intelligibility and from the need for concrete political struggle to change those practices, to shift the ground. Wittgenstein had little or nothing to say about such struggle, as deeply disaffected as he was with the Europe of his day, except to express profound suspicion of the idea that philosophy could figure out what should be done. He clearly rejected the possibility of sitting down and deducing from first principles how and where to relocate the riverbed.

But a suspicion of theory-driven radical utopianism doesn't preclude recognizing the radical potential in the perspectives of those whose connections to "what we do" are neither simple nor unconflicted. As María Lugones (1991) has argued, the tendency of privileged theorists to see all problems as matters to be dealt with by coming up with better theories expresses an unwillingness to engage with those who have been excluded or marginalized by dominant practices, including practices of theory-construction. What is avoided, Lugones points out, when we think what we need are better theories, is engagement, interaction, and submission by the privileged to the gaze of "others." By drawing our attention ("just look") to our practices, Wittgenstein can lead us to notice our complicity, our (diverse) investments and "real needs," and how what we do makes what others do—or try or want to do—difficult or impossible.

NEEDS AND DEMANDS

> To successfully negotiate an indefinite sequence of emergent resistances in the interplay of material, conceptual and social practices is a far more impressive and admirable achievement than simply to conform to a list of standards given in advance.
>
> Andrew Pickering, "Objectivity and the Mangle of Practice,"
> quoted in Heldke and Kellert (1995)

> Need is also a political instrument, meticulously prepared, calculated, and used.
> Michel Foucault, *Discipline and Punish*, quoted in Fraser (1989)

We can get clearer about the nature of philosophical "demands" by looking at the paradox of analysis.[22] One way of putting the paradox is this: we are looking for the analysis of some concept, say knowledge. Now, either we know what it is—in which case, why do we have to look for it?—or we do not—in which case, how will we recognize it when we find it? For analytic philosophers, the usual resolution to the paradox is via some form of what Rawls (1971, p. 20) calls "reflective equilibrium": we approach an analysis by tacking back and forth in response to the pressures on the one side from our considered judgments and on the other side from the demands of a theory meant to explain and justify those judgments: we have reached the analysis when we are, so to speak,

---

22. The paradox of analysis is stated in semantic, rather than epistemic, terms (either the analysans has the same meaning as the analysandum, in which case the analysis is trivial, or it does not, in which case the analysis is false) by Langford (1952). Thanks to Jagvar Johansson for pointing out to me that the epistemic version of the paradox first appears in Plato's *Meno*.

becalmed. "What we are inclined to say" is both a place to start and a pressure to which we need always to be responsive (otherwise we could not know that it was our concept we had analyzed), but it cannot be our only consideration, since there is no reason to believe that the concept itself will be perspicuously displayed in all our deployments of it. The concept "works" because of its underlying logic, which may or may not show up on the surface.

Philosophers' "demands" thus have at least two sources: on the one hand, an analysis must fit the form of whatever theoretical framework is being deployed; and, on the other, it must effectively account for our preanalytic judgments. There is, on the face of it, nothing to object to in this method: it seems laudably open to discovery and revision both from theoretical developments and from more careful examination of the data. Yet the problematic "a prioricity" to which Wittgenstein and Diamond draw our attention is smuggled in under cover of this apparent reasonableness, in what Wittgenstein refers to as "the initial move in the conjuring trick" (*PI* §308). We may be quite open as to the character of what fills the explanatory box; but the size, shape, and location of the box are set in advance: we are looking, for example, for a description of the state (event, process) that will play what we have determined is the necessary casual role in the explanatory scheme that seems to us to make sense of the phenomenon we are analyzing. Such a project may seem to leave everything open, while actually—starting with the identification of "*the* phenomenon"—setting unargued-for constraints on what we are in a position even to notice, let alone adequately to describe.

But surely we have to start somewhere, and, if we have no idea of what it is we are explaining or of what an acceptable explanation looks like, how are we even to get started? Don't we have to place demands on what we do in order to do anything at all? What might Wittgenstein have in mind in urging us to attend not to the demands of philosophers but to our "real needs"? How do we determine what those needs are and what might count as meeting them? Aren't philosophers' demands meant precisely to meet our needs for clarity, understanding, and confidence in what we take to be our best-founded judgments?

What I want to suggest is that a serious attempt to meet our real needs involves us in an open-ended search to articulate what those needs might be. It involves us, that is, in what in the introduction to this essay I called serious politics—that circular, Aristotelian crafting of virtuous citizens and a virtuous polis as the conditions for each other's possibility. If for whatever reason one disdains or despairs of such an attempt (and there are many reasons why one might; the understandable lack of trust on the part of the disenfranchised is the one that has most concerned me here, but equally worth noting is the cynicism of the overly comfortable), then one will be drawn to ways of thinking it unnecessary, impossible, or both. One way is to act as though real needs were discoverable without politics: thus, the arrogance of the welfare state as Nancy Fraser describes it. Another is to replace needs with demands: thus, the understandable attractiveness of fighting for something one has specifically delineated (ideally by identifying it as a right, a legitimated demand), the deeper meaning of which is nonnegotiable, when the circumstances preclude the trust required for negotiating (discovering, creating) our real needs.

In this light, philosophers' demands are another evasion of serious politics, though not because were we to turn from our books to the streets we would be able to change the world (or even have a clue about what to do in order to change the world) so as to "make all these words superfluous." It is not that philosophers are fiddling while Rome burns when we should be helping to put out the fires. That may be sometimes how to describe what we are and should be doing, but it is hardly what Wittgenstein has in mind. Rather, we need to turn toward serious politics precisely because it is more, rather than less, open-ended than philosophy. It is, for example, more intellectually serious, more genuinely difficult and challenging, more potentially revelatory of the deep structures of knowledge and of reality, to take on the task of answering the doubts of those who are alienated from the practices of rationality than it is to attempt to answer the skeptic of one's own imagination.[23]

Those of us who, for example, teach introductory logic classes may well be right about the universal validity of, say, modus ponens; I can't imagine that we're not. But my confidence that the impossibility stems from something deeper than the limitations of my own imagination needs to be tested against my attempts to find the grounds for mutual comprehension with those (who may be among my students) who claim not to recognize that validity. Modus ponens may seem to them not to be implicated in the practices in which they are seriously engaged: it seems to belong to an alien form of life confined to the classroom, to meet no needs deeper or more pervasive than passing a required course. To take those students and their skepticism seriously doesn't require that we think they might be right to deny the validity of modus ponens. Rather, just as we need to teach them that modus ponens is, in fact, woven into the fabric of their ordinary practices, they have to teach us that also woven into that fabric are some very problematic practices of domination. We may be convinced that, were we to reweave the fabric of our practices in more equitable ways (in ways that more fully met real needs), modus ponens would remain (as I said, I cannot imagine otherwise); but the proof that that is so will come through those transformations in practice. And taking our students, and the needs that would emerge from our engaging with

23. Descartes may have believed that in constructing the evil genius he was posing to himself a challenge more stringent than any real-world interlocutor could devise, but, on my view, what he ended up doing was providing himself (and, more importantly, his heirs) with an all-purpose excuse for not attending to the voices of others, especially not to those others for whom the very structures of authoritative reasoning appear as part of the problem.

them, seriously is one place to start.[24] Not only can we not know in advance what our shared, real needs are (hence, we cannot satisfy them in the form of political demands), but there is not and cannot be an answer to that question outside of our engaging with each other in creating one (hence, we cannot expect as philosophers meaningfully to articulate those demands).

Since most of us who are professional philosophers are among the relatively enfranchised, one thing we can do is work toward the conditions in which such engagement can occur, by doing what we can to make the trust required for serious politics neither an unnecessary expense for the privileged nor a fatally foolhardy gamble for the subordinated. One would "give philosophy peace" in part by shifting back onto all of us the perplexity that philosophers have taken on as peculiarly our own, by stopping being the scapegoats for cultural anxieties. It would require the acknowledgment of the fact that there is nothing beyond or below human practice that obviates the need to create trust, nothing that either practically or conceptually sets the terms of truth or of right or determines our real needs—however unlikely it may seem that human practice is adequate to the task of doing so. In this light, arguments that undermine the allegedly practice-transcendent guarantors of truth are hardly nihilistic. To argue that there is nothing beyond or below "what we do" that grounds truth is to argue not for the superficiality of truth but for the depth of practice. There is no "merely" about our lives; it's "not as if we *chose* this game!" (OC §317).

24. This discussion can be read as a reply to Martha Nussbaum's dismissive critique of Ruth Ginzberg's discussion of feminist logic pedagogy, which attempts just the sort of engagement I am urging here (and which I learned how to think about from Ginzberg). See Ruth Ginzberg (1989a and 1989b) and Martha Nussbaum (1994) a review of Antony and Witt (1992). In a reply to a letter to the editor I wrote in response to her review, Nussbaum argued that "feminism needs to be able to avail itself of robust notions of reason and objectivity": see Nussbaum (1995). I couldn't agree more. But the dispute concerns how to understand "robust." My argument has been that, seen as a real need, as I presume Nussbaum intends for us to see it, robustness requires precisely the sort of commitment to practical, politically aware engagement that feminist critics (and others: see the quote from Pickering that heads this section) urge. To be robust is to be willing and able to roll up one's sleeves, get to work, and get one's hands dirty. In this light, the philosopher's demand (for some practice-transcendent guarantor) is revealed as precisely not robust but effete, insisting that we disclaim as not the "real thing" anything we actually do by way of resolving the disputes between us. Henry James's novella *The Beast in the Jungle*, can be read as a parable of this sort of thinking. Henry Marcher spent his whole adult life waiting for and focused on the one big thing that was to happen to him, thereby failing to attend to his actual life, in particular to the love that (indeterminately) was or might have been between him and May Bartram, the woman friend who spent her life waiting with him. Focusing on what lies always just over the horizon assures that everything closer than optical infinity will be a blur and, consequently, that one will fail at just the sort of responsibility that, as Heldke and Kellert (1995) argue, constitutes objectivity.

Chapter 2

Feminist Epistemology*

My aims in this paper will be two: first, to argue that there is and should be such a field as feminist epistemology—that the term "feminist" is an appropriate modifier of "epistemology"; and, second, to convey some sense of the range of work that goes on in that field.[1]

The term "feminist epistemology" strikes many philosophers as oxymoronic. That was certainly how I would have thought of it had anyone mentioned it to me in the 1960s and early 1970s, when I was envious of my friends in moral, political, and social philosophy, who could find a congruence between their philosophical interests and the political commitments we shared. I, on the other hand, faced what I took to be an unbridgeable gulf between my philosophy and my politics, since my philosophical inclinations were toward epistemology and metaphysics, which seemed as apolitical as pure mathematics. No one, of course, did mention feminist epistemology to me then, since that view of epistemology and metaphysics as apolitical was, at least on this side of the English Channel, pretty universal. But sometime in the mid-1970s, that changed.

One important reason for the change was that the founding of the Society for Women in Philosophy meant that many women philosophers found ourselves in each other's presence more than our small numbers in graduate school and even smaller numbers in the faculty ranks would have predicted. Although one of the aims of SWIP was and still is to support women's pursuing whatever philosophical interests they may have in a world that is still deplorably sexist, many of us found that pursuing those interests in a woman-centered intellectual environment changed those interests, and changed us. One of those changes proved to be especially disconcerting. So long as we were relatively isolated from each other, in environments that were defined by a 2500-year long

---

* The following paper by Naomi Scheman and the comment by Louise Antony were given at the American Philosophical Association, Eastern Division Meeting on December 29, 1994, in Boston, MA. (Antony's comment and my reply to it, which follow this paper in *Metaphilosophy* 26.3, July 1995, are not included here.)

1. I will not give a comprehensive survey of that work; those who want to explore it further might start by consulting the excellent bibliography in Lennon and Whitford (1994).

conversation that, with few largely forgotten exceptions, had gone on as though we were either nonexistent or, at best, a problematic topic of conversation, certainly not a contributor to it, we had a stake in ignoring, and trying to get others around us to ignore, the fact that we were women, or that our being women might make a difference to our being philosophers. We had, that is, a stake in making an honest generic man of the subject of philosophy.

In the context of SWIP some of us came to believe that, although we were clearly as capable as our male colleagues at doing philosophy as we had been taught it, the experience was one of passing. The generic man, many of us came to believe, was, in philosophy as elsewhere in the culture, really a man, and our inclusion in the conversation, however welcome it might sometimes be, was as honorary men. And there seemed to be something wrong with that. Figuring out just what was wrong with it was not, however, easy. Few of us were tempted by ideas about innate differences between the sexes: such ideas seemed politically retrograde, and besides, empirically, we were ourselves counterexamples. Much of what was culturally associated with femininity was decidedly unappealing, consisting, as most of it seemed to, in training for subordination. As Louise Antony has argued, there's a reason why it's called "privilege": it would hardly make sense for those in power to reserve for themselves the appropriate exercise of ineffective epistemic strategies.

Despite such concerns, many of us came to believe that gender, along with other socially salient characteristics, such as race, class, and sexual identity, inflects the ways in which people come to have a sense of self, as well as of mind and body, develop conceptions of themselves as variously epistemically competent, enter into and sustain relationships of trust, learn to exercise and to recognize others' exercise of authority, and so on. That is, how we form beliefs and how we judge some beliefs—our own or others'—to be justified or not, how we take epistemic authority to be constituted and exercised are all matters that are shaped in part by gender, as by other features of our lives. To position the knowing subject somehow outside of these differences, somehow able to take them into account—as though they simply constitute differences in situations in which one finds oneself (the recognition that one needs to employ different epistemic strategies if one is surrounded by spies, after all, does not point to the need for "espionage epistemology")—is to under-appreciate the depth at which such structures operate in our lives. It is not that as a generic self I need to figure out how to deal with a world in which I am in the position of a woman; rather, my sense of myself as female is as deep as my sense of myself as a person, which is not to say that it is at all clear what either of them comes to.

I do not believe that we can write off the possibility of there being substantive things to be said about human knowledge *per se*. That there are such things is, in principle, no more unlikely than that there are things to be said about human biology: it is even likely that the two are connected. Rather, we need to ask whether we (meaning philosophers and those with whom we might engage in some sort of cognitive science) are here and now in a position meaningfully to ask and answer the relevant questions. As Elizabeth Spelman (1988) argues regarding generalizations about women, one needn't be a disbeliever in important, substantive human commonalities to be deeply skeptical about the prospects of learning about them by starting with the notion of a generic human being, when that notion is drawn from perspectives given to massively over-generalizing their own peculiarities. And if there is anything we know about masculism, racism, heterosexism, and various other expressions of privilege, it is precisely that: privilege in European modernity is distinctively marked by the tendency to take its own particularities as generic, to cast those who differ from its norms not just as inferior, but as deviant.

Such skepticism about (available models of) generic subjectivity—however little it may be expressed in essentialist appeals to such dubious constructions as distinctively female modes of cognition—is deeply at odds with analytic epistemology. Central to analytic epistemology is the conception of the knowing subject—the bearer of the knowledge that we seek to define and to explore the scope and limits of—as generic. It has, that is, no history; no gender, race, class, sexual identity, or other particularizing attributes; it is, perhaps, human, but if so, its cognitive apparatus is shared by all normal members of the species. Or so we are to believe. Much of the work of feminist epistemologists has been to argue that, unsurprisingly, the allegedly generic philosophical subject has for most modern philosophers been normatively male, white, Christian, able-bodied, nonworking class, and heterosexual—that is, negatively characterized as lacking in the stigmatizing qualities attributed to various "others."

Epistemologists differ on the relative roles of the descriptive and the normative in the explication of knowledge, and I don't intend to enter into these disputes. Rather, I will argue that neither the descriptive nor the normative task can be adequately accomplished by abstracting knowers and knowledge from their concrete, historically specific incarnations. Nor can either the descriptive or the normative tasks be undertaken in ways that transcend substantive political commitments, a claim that draws on arguments against the possibility of value-neutral social science and of practice-transcendent normativity.

There is no agreed-upon sense of exactly what it comes to for an epistemology to be feminist, but I will suggest that a useful umbrella under which to shelter diverse projects would be that of "anti-masculism," by analogy with anti-racism. Such a label, by focusing on the claim that there is deep and pervasive bias both in epistemology and in the epistemic practices that are the objects of the descriptive task, provides, if justified, both an answer to the question of why one should accept a feminist epistemology and a counter to charges that such an epistemology presupposes such questionable constructs as distinctively female or feminine modes of cognition. The link with anti-racism also points to the necessity for any feminist epistemology to be simultaneously committed to challenging the various other sorts of bias that may be found within dominant practices of acquiring, justifying, and accounting for knowledge, as well as in the practices of relatively privileged feminists.

Much of feminist epistemology has been, more precisely, feminist philosophy of science, reflecting, in part, a similar blurring of boundaries in the nonfeminist fields. Science, that is, has been taken, by many feminists as by many nonfeminists, to be paradigmatic of knowledge. But another reason why so much of the feminist work in epistemology has been in philosophy of science is that it has become far less common among philosophers of science to see scientists, scientific practice, or scientific knowledge in generic terms, as lacking a history that is relevant to any story—descriptive or normative—that we might tell about it. And once one conceptualizes science as a set of social practices, historically variable and in complex interaction with other parts of the culture, it becomes much harder not to recognize the legitimacy of questions about the relevance of gender (and of other socially salient variables) to how scientific programs are framed and supported, how metaphors shape scientific explanation, how competing hypotheses and theories do or do not get to be part of the background against which confirmation is judged, and so on.

It is, however, far from clear what one might mean by referring to *knowledge* as a set of social practices, and even if one could make some sense of this idea, it is clear that there is nothing that plays the role of the institutionalized structures that embody the historical and political specificities that are seen either as factors unavoidably shaping scientific knowledge or as that against which scientific knowledge needs to be guarded. Scientists, that is, are particular ones of us—selected, trained, socialized, authorized, funded, rewarded, and recognized in ways that cannot but reflect the values of the culture in complex ways. But "knowers R us", or so it would seem—all of us, or any one of us, standing in for all of us. Hence, the centrality to epistemology of the sort of example Lorraine Code points to, of "S knows that p," where S is anyone at all, and p is something like "the cat is on the mat," where any differences among us in how likely we are to know such a thing—or to take ourselves or be taken by others to know such a thing—are wholly uninteresting (Code 1991).

But once we take a broader view of the knowledge of which epistemology is to give an account, we have, I will argue, to recognize that, however uninstitutionalized, the practices through which knowledge is acquired and justified are diverse and contestable. We will have to recognize, in particular, that much of what any of us knows is beyond our ability independently to verify (consequently that the descriptive task will have to appeal as much to sociology and social psychology as to more individualist forms of psychology), and that relationships of epistemic dependency are no more immune from political considerations of power, authority, and privilege than are any other social relationships. Whether our focus is descriptive or normative, we will need both to uncover masculist bias and to construct accounts of epistemic practices that are free of such bias (as of other, interconnected biases) and adequate to the task of challenging it both in epistemology and, more importantly, in knowledge practices more generally—that is, adequate to a feminist (anti-masculist) politics.

What is it that leads feminist epistemologists, whatever the differences between them, to reject the possibility of a value-neutral account of knowledge, along with the idea of a generic knowing subject?[2] I want to discuss four themes in feminist epistemology that support these conclusions: (1) a nonindividualist conception of knowledge; (2) attention to diversity, especially to differences of power or privilege; (3) critiques of objectivity as a goal of, especially, scientific knowledge; and (4) a concern with how in practice knowledge is normatively defined, in contrast with opinion or belief.

1. NONINDIVIDUALIST CONCEPTIONS OF KNOWLEDGE AND KNOWING SUBJECTS

Feminist philosophers have frequently been critical of individualism in ethics, political theory, philosophy of mind, and elsewhere, including in epistemology. Different critics have had different things in mind, both as illustrative of individualism and by way of an alternative to it. In epistemology, Lynne Hankinson Nelson argues explicitly that "in the primary sense it is communities, rather than individuals, that know" (Nelson xi). Others have held onto the idea of knowledge as being in the first instance something an individual person has, while arguing that she or he can "have" it only in relation to some particular social context that shapes both the knower and the known (See, for example, Grasswick 2004). The arguments here are various and complex and are connected to critiques of individualism in other areas of philosophy, as well as in the culture more generally.

There are, however, some common themes: One is the ineliminability of epistemic dependency and the requirement of trust, which make any discussion of epistemic norms turn at least in part on the nature of our

---

2. This is as good a place as any to note that there are many epistemologists who are feminists, who may even take it as a requirement on any acceptable epistemology that it be useful (or at least not detrimental) to feminist politics, who would nonetheless not reject one or both of a value-neutral epistemology or a generic knowing subject. My sense is that they would—for something like this reason—not consider themselves feminist epistemologists, nor do I think they are generally so considered by others. It is, in other words, a matter of dispute *among feminists* whether or not there ought to be a specifically feminist epistemology.

varied relationships with those on whom we depend and who depend on us. (An early example of such work is Lorraine Code's *Epistemic Responsibility* (1987), which preceded her more explicitly feminist *What Can She Know?* (1991), and that drew on Annette Baier's notion (1985a) of second personhood to argue for the centrality of responsibility to what it means to be a knower.) Feminist epistemologists, along with social epistemologists, argue that it is misleading to think of epistemic agency as ideally exercised in solitude, perhaps weighing, along with the other evidence, the testimony of others. Rather, they argue, at every step of the way knowing and coming to know are social and interactive; they are things we *do*, and things we are appropriately held responsible for doing, in social and cultural settings that variously help and hinder our doing them well.

Another common theme is a critique of individualism as tending to abstract from the concrete specificities of persons-in-relation. Especially in epistemology, individualism is often appropriately referred to as "abstract individualism": the individuals in question are distinct but not distinctive. Attention to the essentially social nature of human identity—to the ways in which we are, as deeply as we are persons, other persons' child, sibling, friend, lover, coworker, parent, and so on, as well as, equally deeply, sexed, raced, and classed, with particular sexual desires and other distinctive ways of experiencing ourselves in relation to others, real or imagined—means attending to the ways in which we differ from one another, both along lines of institutionalized privilege and idiosyncratically. Theorizing the nature, scope, and limits of the knowledge possessed by idealized generic persons would be useful only insofar as such an idealization captured either something essential or something desirable about real, diverse persons.

2. ATTENTION TO DIVERSITY

Feminist epistemologists, along with feminist theorists more generally, have been increasingly attentive to the diversity among women, especially to differences that represent differential access to privilege and power. One reason for this attention has been the recognition that unless those of us who are relatively privileged keep such matters in the foreground of our thinking, we will, whether we mean to or not, take ourselves as paradigmatic, either ignoring the perspectives of others or treating them as in some way "different"—as special cases, exceptions, or deviations from a norm. María Lugones writes of what happens when women of color encounter feminist theory created by white women inattentive to the implications and the effects on others of their own privileged specificity: "When I do not see plurality in the very structure of a theory I know that I will have to do lots of acrobatics—like a contortionist or tight-rope walker—to have this theory speak to me without allowing the theory to distort me *in my complexity*" (Lugones 1991, p. 43, emphasis in the original).

One of the consequences of such attention to diversity is the explicit politicization of epistemology. Not only do people have differing sorts and degrees of access to the sources of knowledge, but, at least in many areas of knowledge, justificatory standards tend to reflect the norms of privilege. Thus, for example, norms of disinterestedness and emotional restraint characterize both the sorts of epistemic strategies that are taken to be most reliable and the modes of cognitive engagement normatively demanded of heterosexual, professional, or managerial, white men. There is, of course, a chicken and egg problem here, and few if any feminist epistemologists would argue that the valorization of such norms is nothing but arbitrary bias in favor of the styles of those who are in charge. What we have are sets of complex interactions among (at least) social, economic, cultural, pedagogical, and familial structures that, in thoroughly circular fashion, shape the world, shape people to occupy different positions in that world, and shape the norms in terms of which some of the beliefs those people have about that world will count as justified.

Certainly, if one is at all drawn either to evolutionary epistemology or to scientific realism, both of which make much of the success of certain epistemic norms, then one ought at least to suspect that what those norms succeed at is maintaining the illusions that sustain the status quo, *not* exposing its inequities and irrationalities. That is, one ought to have reason to suspect, as feminist and other liberatory epistemologists do, that epistemic norms drawn from the experiences and perspectives of the relatively disenfranchised might prove better at revealing the contradictions, the cracks and fissures, in the consensus of recognized experts or in what passes for common sense. Consider, for example, what Alison Jaggar (1989) refers to as "outlaw emotions." These are emotions that, according to the hegemonic view of a situation, one is not supposed to feel; they are somehow inappropriate—misguided, misdirected, excessive, or otherwise "wrong." Outlaw emotions are perceived as especially epistemically unreliable, a perception that underlies the process described by Adrienne Rich (1979c) as "gaslighting," whereby we convince each other or ourselves that something that feels to us to be so is not so, as Ingrid Bergman was persuaded by Charles Boyer in the film of that name to dismiss as timorous foolishness both her fear and her certainty, based on the dimming of the gas lights in the room where she was, that someone else was in the house when he went out for his evening walk.

Jaggar argues, and the film illustrates, that there are good reasons, from the perspectives of privilege, for dismissing as unreliable the perspectives of those in subordinated positions: from such perspectives are frequently revealed truths damaging to the maintenance of their subordination. Perspectives can differ not only in where they are (as some people are believed to be less well placed to arrive at a balanced overview of the situation) but in how they are inhabited. Thus, people who characteristically tend to trust their emotional responses, especially if they and their responses are out of step with dominant groups, are regarded as epistemically untrustworthy, and will gain a hearing, if at all, only in translation, relegating their perceptions, as it were, to the realm of discovery, and couching everything in the hegemonic language of the realm of justification. They need, that is, to impersonate the allegedly generic (read: privileged) subject, treating their own less-mediated perceptions as rather suspect data that have managed to pass muster, as one might, after careful scrutiny, decide that what an inveterate liar has reported is, on this occasion, true.

3. RETHINKING OBJECTIVITY

Feminists have been among those raising questions about the appropriateness of norms of objectivity as applied both to science and to other areas of knowledge acquisition. Such norms have been a central reason for the distrust of emotions: if, as has usually been believed, emotions are both idiosyncratic and involuntary, then they would seem to be epistemically unreliable, in leading to beliefs that would be sharable only by others who just so happened to share one's emotional responses. The one form of voluntarism thought by most philosophers to be possible in the emotional realm is that of bracketing off one's emotions, and one common ground for differential epistemic enfranchisement has been how well one is taken to be able to do this. (The double-bind for many women has been that such bracketing—the achievement of disinterestedness—has been taken to be at odds with the virtues of femininity, many of which have to do with emotional susceptibility and unshakable favoritism toward one's nearest and dearest. Thus a virtuous woman is, by definition, epistemically unreliable, while a woman who has earned the right to be considered epistemically reliable is suspect as a woman.)

   Feminist epistemological critiques of objectivity (which mirror the feminist critiques of objectivism in ethics) have drawn attention to the particularities of the objectifying stance. Rather than being a way of regarding the world as it is in itself, uncolored by our attitudes toward it, it is a quite distinct and distinctive attitude that, like any other, shapes what is perceived through it. We lose, in particular, the epistemic resources of outlaw emotions, in part because, given the near impossibility of actually bracketing all emotional responses, those that agree with the dominant perceptions, however emotionally colored, are likely to be regarded as objective. So, for example, forms of sexual behavior that are regarded by those with cultural power with distaste are described as disgusting or despicable, as though those properties resided in them (within some communities, such statements would qualify, on Quine's terms in "Epistemology Naturalized" (1969a), as observation sentences, with dissenters dismissed as "deviants"), while analogous perceptions on the part of nondominant groups—that, for example, traditional marriage is degrading—are dismissed as "emotional" and "subjective." Such double standards reflect what (at least many) feminists would argue is, in fact, the case: there are no disinterested, emotionally neutral judgments; we always, unavoidably, bring values, interests, and affect to our perceptions; nor can these be filtered out at some later stage.

It has, however, long been noted by feminists that relativisms of various sorts are deeply problematic for political reasons, in addition to whatever epistemological or logical qualms we may share about them with our nonfeminist colleagues. It cannot simply be a matter of an emotional response we happen to share with some others—as we notably fail to share it with many *other* others—to regard a belief in male intellectual superiority as a mistake. As problematic as objectivity may be—in particular, as linked as its norms may be with masculist and individualist norms of distantiation and disinterest—it has seemed to most feminist epistemologists that something needs to take its place, something that would make knowledge, in Lorraine Code's term, "commonable." Subjectivity—attentiveness to how it appears from here, the place where I am located in all my specificity—has, it is argued, an important contribution to make to knowledge, but the knowledge to which it contributes has, somehow, not to be mine alone.

One thing to note is that the problem of producing shared knowledge from diversely located subjects is not a new one, nor is it in any way peculiar to feminists. It is the central legacy of the epistemic democratization that marks European modernity, and every modern epistemologist has had something to say about it. The feminist critique of that tradition is an argument to the effect that the set of answers that have been given are inadequate, in large measure because they simply do not work on their own terms. It ought, on those terms, to be possible for all of sound and mature mind to occupy the privileged position from which objective knowledge is revealed, and to regard that occupation as in some deep sense natural. The estrangements required to get there—the bracketing of emotional responses and affective ties, for example—ought to seem, however difficult, not a fundamental violation of whom one takes oneself to be. One needs to be able to say, from that position, perhaps reluctantly or with pain: so that is how things really are; not: so that's how things appear to someone I can impersonate but whose perspective has no claim on me, however well it may serve me to know that that's how things look from there, if "there" is the place from which people who have power over my life regard the world.

The problem is the epistemic analog of the problem of moral motivation: what reason do I have to replace the judgments I am now inclined to make with others that are supposed to be more reliable, more nearly true? So long as I can intelligibly ask "supposed by *whom*, and why, and why should their so supposing carry any weight with me?" and so long as those questions don't have answers that I find persuasive—that is, so long as the norms that give rise to the allegedly preferable judgments are not ones I find it reasonable to accept—the claim to objectivity, which rests on its producing universally acceptable beliefs, will be undercut—unless, that is, I am dismissed as epistemically incompetent, as, of course, many erstwhile critics have routinely been, in more or less formal versions of the sentencing of political dissidents to insane asylums.

The point is not that all epistemic norms are repressive, nor that all potential contributions to the project of constructing knowledge are equally valuable, still less that we each have our own reality about which we are authoritative. Rather, as Susan Babbitt (1992) has argued, feminist epistemology is best regarded as an especially robust form of realism. Reality, whatever else we know about it, is tremendously complex; and we as knowers, whatever else we know about ourselves, are notoriously susceptible to mistakes, distortions, deception, oversights, over-simplifications, hasty generalizations, prejudices, and fallacious reasoning. Especially when some or all of these are motivated by their role in maintaining one or another useful bit of ideology, we are notoriously good at protecting ourselves from seeing the truth by dismissing critical voices as methodologically unsound. We do not, that is, have good empirical reason to trust our ability to come up with genuinely disinterested epistemic norms and very good reason to suspect that the epistemic norms that we do have ("we" being those with the cultural clout to set norms that get generally recognized) are not well suited to serve genuinely democratic ends.

Only explicitly political attention to the concrete workings of epistemology—how, in practice some beliefs are regarded as justified and others not—and the cultivation of what we might call discursive affirmative action will be likely to overcome the biases inherent in dominant epistemic norms. Like other forms of affirmative action, this form is grounded in a studied skepticism about our ability to recognize merit when we see it (not just individual meritorious examples, but types of merit), whether in a job or school applicant or in an argument, along with views about which forms are especially likely to escape our notice and which are especially lacking and especially needed. Feminists and others in diverse liberatory movements have been arguing, for example, that it is inadequate to regard our contributions to common knowledge as simply providing missing data: we are returning the gaze. And there is no telling in advance how disorienting that will be, nor how, ultimately, knowledge will be reoriented.

4. CRITICAL EXAMINATION OF EPISTEMIC NORMS

The division of questions of epistemology into the descriptive and the normative has tended to focus attention on the relationships between how we actually acquire beliefs and how we ought to acquire them.

What tends to get lost is attention to the norms by which various groups make judgments about how we ought to acquire beliefs, especially when the group in question is "us." Sociologists of science (or of knowledge generally) have, of course, raised such questions, but most philosophers have regarded an empirical stance toward normativity as undermining of the philosophical project, which needs to take on the question of what we ought to do, not just to describe what various groups think we ought to do. As with the question of relativism, feminists have for the most part agreed in not wanting to rest with the flatly empirical: this is what we do, though various "theys" may well do things differently. But, as with relativism, there needs to be a third path between an embrace of normativity that lacks any historical or social specificity and an acceptance of uncritical descriptivism. As Sandra Harding argues, we need to place the subject of knowledge, including the norms that structure its subjectivity, in the same "critical plane" as the object of knowledge, not by way of abandoning objectivity in favor of a purely descriptive account of what various groups, including our own, happen to believe, but precisely to achieve what she calls "strong objectivity" (Harding 1991, esp. Ch. 6).

It is an illusion to think that we can, for example, define knowledge in a way that will be neither formally empty nor tendentiously value laden. The discussions that have followed Gettier-type counterexamples to the definition of knowledge as justified true belief illustrate the point. The examples rest on the possibility that one might be justified in believing p, p might in fact be true, but nonetheless one would not properly be said to know p, because the connection between p's being true and your believing p is merely fortuitous. The argument does not depend on how justification is characterized, nor on what sorts of connection are regarded as merely fortuitous: given any account of those, one can construct a suitable counterexample. (If your epistemic faith is in tea leaves, imagine that the cup that gave the right answer was not in fact yours but had been surreptitiously switched.) But what the counterexamples are generally taken to reveal is that no account of justification can wholly bridge the gap between the world and our beliefs about it—no methodology is foolproof; the Cartesian dream of an internal vetting procedure strong enough to ward off the possibility of mistake is unrealizable.

Attention has consequently shifted to the nature of that gap and to what goes on in it, to how we acquire the beliefs we have and what modes of acquisition are in fact reliable, what sorts of connection need to obtain between world and belief for a belief not only to be justified but to count as knowledge. The shift is from subjectively to semi-objectively defined justification: the point of the counterexamples is that my belief may have been a justified one in the sense that I was justified in holding it (I had what according to the relevant norms were good enough grounds for holding it), but semi-objectively—looking at my epistemic state from some omniscient position—that belief was not in fact justified, in that my grounds for holding it were, for reasons it was not my responsibility to be aware of, inadequate or irrelevant or undermined. "Semi-objectively," since, by hypothesis, the belief is actually true: "objectively unjustified" therefore cannot mean "unjustified by any grounds whatsoever." Rather, there had to have been something wrong with the reasons I *had* for the belief, though, since my belief was justified, it could not have been my fault that I was unaware of what that was.

At this point—the identification of something wrong that was not my fault—we are on doubly normative ground: what counts as wrong, and what's not my fault? As soon as we move away from the sorts of generic examples that characterize most of this literature, it becomes apparent that answers to these questions that will have sufficient content to actually *be* answers will frequently rely on tendentious, explicitly or implicitly political, assumptions. Consider, for example, what we take ourselves to know about atomic testing or about our government's intentions towards other countries. Many people would deny that other people's beliefs about such things, if based on official government statements and mainstream press accounts, are justified, on the grounds that these are issues of the sort that our government has a track record of lying to us about. If, however, one takes such skepticism to be misguided paranoia, one will regard at least some such beliefs as justified. If, then, it comes out that the relevant government officials were lying, but, fortuitously, the belief in question (say, that the government did not release radioactive dust in my community) was nonetheless true (the army did secretly release radioactive dust in a lot of places, and lied about it, but it happens to be true that they didn't do it *here*), then one will have a Gettier-type counterexample if and only if one takes the initial faith in the government to be reasonable—otherwise the original, as it turns out true, belief wouldn't count as justified.

As in the example of the tea leaves, one can give the formal structure of Gettier-type counterexamples while remaining agnostic about what actually constitutes justification. But one cannot remain agnostic if what one is aiming for is a substantive definition of knowledge, that is, a substantive account of which ways of bridging the gap between belief and the world are reliable and which are not. The point is that what fills that gap is in deep ways social and political, having to do with relationships of trust and dependency, with values and interests, with solidarity and the negotiating of power and privilege. Epistemic norms, including those we use in our epistemological theorizing, are undetachable from such issues—which means that they need to be the objects of scrutiny, however circular such scrutiny inevitably is. But this result ought not to be dismaying or even unfamiliar to any but foundationalists: what it amounts to is the reciprocal containment of philosophy and politics.

Chapter 3

On Waking Up One Morning and Discovering We Are Them

I.

I suppose it was inevitable. If you're talking about the personal these days, the erotic is on the scene—if not by its explicit presence, then by its conspicuous absence. And if the scene is the pedagogical, the site of instruction, of knowledge and self-knowledge, the language of psychoanalysis presents itself, bidden or not. And once you're on the terrain of transference and counter-transference, there it is: students in love with (or at least drawn to) teachers, and vice versa. A distaste for psychoanalysis, or even for modernity, won't help, either: for those more classically inclined, the Platonic route takes us to the same destination.

Not that teacher/student erotic encounters, fantasized or otherwise, don't happen. But something about their unquestioned centrality in our discussions throughout the conference[1] troubled me, and I couldn't quite tell why. Of course, there are all the reasons to be wary about potential and actual abuses of power and trust, but those seem taken care of (in theory, at least) by the psychoanalytic model, since sex between analyst and analysand is more strictly forbidden than sex between teacher and student (in theory, at least).

Then, speaking from the floor, Patsy Schweickart told a story. At the age of ten she asked herself one day, with no sense of anxiety, only puzzlement: "What are parents for?" In retrospect she takes her question to be both a tribute to her parents—a reflection of their having instilled in her a sense of security and agency that left their role invisible—and a model of what she hopes to be, as a teacher, in her students' lives. Now, at some point, an analysand might calmly and bemusedly wonder (it might, perhaps, even be a sign of successful termination), "What was my analyst for?," but certainly not in the midst of transference.

When Patsy told her story, with its moral, my unease suddenly made sense: all the talk of student-teacher eroticism had no connection at all

1. The conference was "Pedagogy: The Question of the Personal," organized by Jane Gallop through the Center for Twentieth Century Studies at the University of Wisconsin-Milwaukee in April 1993. The conference led to a book, in which this chapter was published (Gallop 1995). (Note added in 2010)

with my experience, as a student or as a teacher. Not that I didn't find classrooms sexy. At least since graduate school[2] I have found them very sexy indeed, but the eroticism I found there was among the students, a site totally occluded by the psycho-analytic model, where all one's "siblings" are, however vividly, only imagined.

My graduate school experience was as positive as that of any other woman I know, something for which I have Barnard and my teachers there, Sue Larson and Mary Mothersill, largely to thank. Had I come to Harvard needing to be assured that I had what it took, that I could plausibly aspire to becoming a philosopher, I would have been dependent on my teachers' good opinion in a way that I suspect might well have precluded my getting it. As it was, not only did I feel confident that I could aspire to being a philosopher, I took myself already to be one. Freed of an anxious dependency on my teachers, I reveled in the comradeship of my peers. We used to joke, in fact, that the best thing the faculty had done was to admit all of us, leaving us for the most part in each other's hands: that's what they were for. (Or so it seemed: as with Patsy's parents, there was a lot more to it than that.)

One of the best parts of my experience of those days was the permeability of the boundaries between the sorts of relationships we had with each other. It was, I think, essential to the permeability in particular between the sexual and the intellectual that we met each other on terms of equality. Between teacher and student, inequality is unavoidable, even if it is not a defining part of the erotic equation (and we might doubt that that could ever be the case; certainly the transference model would lead one to be skeptical, as would by now commonsense feminist reflections on the social construction of desire). It may have taken chutzpa for me to have known then that I was a philosopher, but it would have been madness to have thought myself the intellectual peer of my teachers. But it was not madness—it ought not even to have taken chutzpa, though perhaps, sadly, for a woman it did—to think myself the intellectual peer of my fellow students.

Equality between women and men was and is a rare thing, and usually sex messes it up. Part of why I remember those days as utopian is that I don't think that happened. (This is, of course, fertile ground for self-deception, but after twenty-five years, a feminist consciousness verging on the fanatical, and a reasonably successful career, I haven't had to reconsider. I do, however, need to be careful. I know that for all sorts of reasons my experience was far more positive than that of most women, there or elsewhere, then or at any other time. Even more problematically, there

2. I was an undergraduate at Barnard, and the experience made me an ardent advocate of women's colleges. But the feminism of Barnard when I was there (I graduated with my class in 1968, but I left the year before, when I married a Columbia student and followed him to MIT) was of an earlier era: there was nothing to hold me back, after class, from immersion in politics and romance on the other side of Broadway. And in those days of official homophobia and silent closets, the last thing I associated with women's spaces, be they dormitories or classrooms, was eroticism.

were ways in which my choices—both that I had them and how I made them—were the cause of pain to other women. So I can't generalize and I shouldn't romanticize what it was like. But, having said that, I do still believe that what I lived was a utopian possibility—that is, that its value did not depend on my carelessness about it, nor on its rareness.)

I see the same spirit among the students I work with today, though, so far as I can tell, they act it out with less abandon than we did—a not uncommon difference between the seventies and the nineties. The major difference, though, is the open and pervasive lesbian eroticism among them, characterized by a playful inclusiveness that embraces the heterosexual women students who are unthreatened by it.

It also embraces me. In the early days of the pioneering feminist graduate students in my department I was in a frequent panic about boundaries. It seemed that they needed me far too much, needed my support, my good opinion, my honest and tough criticism, my attention, and my care. All of the above, all of the time. If, for example, the criticism threatened to weaken the support, there was nowhere else for them to get it, no one I could take turns with. (I'm sure I'm exaggerating, and I probably did then, but I'm quite certain not only of my own anxieties, but also of corresponding ones on their part, even if mine outstripped theirs.) And playful friendship, let alone anything hinting of the erotic, scared the hell out of me.

I'm no more likely now than I would have been then to have a sexual relationship with a student I work with, but playful, even erotically tinged, friendship is one of the blessings to me of the flourishing of the graduate student community.[3] The particularities of my relationship to any one of them are mediated, buffered, by my relationship to them as a group and by their relationships with each other. I attend and host potlucks, get teased, go dancing at the country and western bar (taking turns leading when we two-step), join in celebrating their commitments and their children. Neither they nor I forget that I'm not one of them, that I have power they rely on and a position they aspire to, that they, just as did their predecessors, depend on me for tough criticism as well as support. But moving into and out of different roles, meeting different needs, is far less awkward when they and I know that they have each other and when the less formal, more friend-like interactions between us are for the most part communal.[4]

---

3. The description that follows is dated. Neither the feminist graduate student community nor my relationships to the students I work with are as vibrant as they were, for reasons I don't really understand. My aging might account for the latter, but not for the former. This chapter generally is not only more specifically autobiographical than the others in this volume; it is also more dated and more uncomfortable for me to reread. My including it, against the advice of one of the Press's reviewers, reflects my hope that the squirmy discomfort it occasions will speak to at least some readers, despite its idiosyncrasies and datedness. (Note added in 2010)

4. The other thing that helps is that over the years they have taught several of my colleagues how to be good teachers for them, so, for example, mine is not the only faculty criticism they can trust nor the only faculty support they can count on.

Part of what I'm negotiating in these relationships is my transformation from sixties student radical to full professor. It is a point of honor to belong to the group dubbed by Roger Kimball "tenured radicals." However uncomplimentarily he meant the term, it is for me, as for many others, a matter of intellectual as well as political integrity to retain a right to the "radical" in light of the safety from personal consequence implied by the "tenured." That is, of course, not an easy thing to do. Although I don't worry about inappropriately using the students I work with to satisfy my erotic needs, I do worry about inappropriately using them to satisfy my need to appear to myself and others as genuinely radical, as not having sold out, not having accepted the implicit bribes that went along with my academic success, able to be counted on if need be to bite the hands that feed me, even as I'm on friendly, first-name terms with many of the people whose hands they are.

In my own case, I was out of the country from the summer of 1968 to the fall of 1969, and when I returned, my political home, Students for a Democratic Society, had dissolved, many of its members going into the Weather Underground. I wouldn't have known how to follow them had I wanted to, and I couldn't quite bring myself to want to, though I have never been confident about why I didn't. I had, for what seemed to me irrelevant reasons, not been at Columbia when my comrades had gotten beaten in the police riot, and I could point to no differences between us prior to that year's events that gave me any confidence that I'd not have joined in their despairing exit from being the good children that most of us were: we really did think (for what it's worth, I still do think) that we were saving what was best in universities and in American society from evil people who were selling us all down the river for their sick dreams of unlimited power and monetary gain.

But, as I said, I didn't know where the others were; besides, graduate school beckoned, and I did love philosophy, and Cambridge was a heady and delicious place to be. From such desiderata, helped along by cowardice and inertia, are life choices made. Now, twenty-five years later, I'm trying to give an accounting of myself not only to the idealistic adolescent I was but to the political activist I might have become. And the temptation is to turn to my students and say, "I did it for you, because I think that you matter, that it's just not true that the real world starts where the campus ends; because I think that your lives are real lives, and making a difference to them is making a difference in the real world; because what we do together can be radically transformative, not only of you but of the other lives you touch. Please reassure me that I haven't been coopted, that you don't see me either as an irrelevant relic of a failed radicalism or, perhaps worse, as just another liberal infatuated with radical chic. Tell me that I haven't become one of 'them.'"

It's too much to ask. But, worse, it's the wrong sort of thing to ask. It's asking, in part, to be accepted as one of them, to be granted, not visiting privileges in the community they've created, but full membership. And finally, it's incoherent: It's asking to be absolved in the wielding of power I fully intend (and they need me) to go on wielding, asking to be granted the magical combination of knowledge and innocence, power and purity. (In different but related contexts, I think something like this is what white or heterosexual women often ask, with equal inappropriateness and incoherence, of women of color or lesbians. An important difference is that it's at least arguable that, unlike racist or heterosexist privilege, the privileges of academic positions do not always and only serve to advantage those who have them at the expense of those who don't.)

The knowledge and power of which I want to be absolved are, of course, exactly those that students are in school in part to acquire: they are apprenticing for the position of privilege I am finding so compromising. All very well for me to voice my discomfort with the apparatus of academia: I have tenure. The situation is infinitely riskier for those who want to join me there and whose ability to do so can be threatened by their adopting stances that might not only lose them favor with those whose favor they need but, perhaps even more important, cynically alienate them from a discipline and a form of life they want to inhabit, however critically.

II.

When I was in fourth grade a paper I wrote on evolution was turned into the class play, and I got to narrate, as Father Time. I had even then a loud voice and the ability to project to the back of the school auditorium. When, on the day of performance, I was outfitted with a microphone, no one told me I could let it do that work for me, and my voice reverberated down the halls. I didn't know how to modulate it under conditions of institutionally sanctioned amplification, and, nearly forty years later, I still don't quite have the knack.

It's a tricky situation. The school provided the microphone and, so long as I boomed out the lines I was supposed to say, my voice got picked up and carried. But had I decided to deviate from the script (I wrote it, after all, so why not?) and called for a schoolyard insurrection, I'd have had the plug pulled on me pretty quickly. I have now, of course, a great deal more scope for deviating from the script (academic freedom doesn't afford much protection to fourth graders), but it would be foolhardy, especially in the face of the efforts of wealthy right-wing foundations and the academics they fund, not to worry about the health of the relatively friendly environment on which I have come to depend. My own job may be safe, but the conditions that make it possible to do what I take to be the real work of that job are much less clearly so: an institutionally validated women's studies department and feminist research center, a philosophy department receptive to feminist students, and a university that is receptive to adult students with work, community, and family responsibilities, and that has some degree of institutional commitment to multicultural-ism and to gay/lesbian/bisexual studies.

But it is, I find, psychologically easier to focus on the threats to my privilege than on its reality. Even if the microphone can be yanked, the fact is that at the moment it's plugged in, and I have to learn how to speak through it. I have to learn, for example, how to allow for the difference in the weight my words carry. I learned to speak in public with the bravado of the rebel, confident that whatever I said would be filtered through heads cooler, more pragmatic, more conservative than my own before anything was actually done. For the most part, of course, this "confidence" was a cause of anger or despair, since it meant that what finally made it through all those filters would be such a faint whisper as to make little or no difference to the goings-on that had elicited the rebellious words. By contrast, my words today have acquired at least considerable perlocutionary, and in some cases illocutionary, force.[5] I am in a position to make things happen.

From such a position, naughtiness can be at best unseemly and at worst irresponsible. I'm a great believer in naughtiness (having exhibited far too little of it as a child), in part because it helps to keep rules and those who make and enforce them on their toes and a little off their guard. Like the three-year-old's constant demands to know "why," naughtiness presses the limits of the otherwise taken-for-granted, as puns and other verbal wordplay press the limits of intelligibility. Discovering what we can get away with is a good way of figuring out why some things are required or forbidden, of uncovering the hidden stakes behind the rules.

As Barnard prepared me for Harvard in large measure by making me unneedy of the approval of my teachers there, so Harvard similarly prepared me for the world I moved into as a junior faculty member. Confident, not to say arrogant, I adopted a stance of naughty irreverence toward the subject of philosophy, playfully tweaking the nose of this character who worried about the reality of the world beyond that nose, not to mention of the nose itself. The first time I tried it, it didn't work: I found myself among excessively solemn canonical loyalists, and I lost my job. But in the far friendlier environment of the University of Minnesota, I was tolerated, even encouraged. I was, I at least like to think, seriously naughty, responsi-bly transgressive.[6] But then I got promoted to full professor.

---

5. The terms are J. L. Austin's. "Perlocutionary force" refers to the effects one's words can have, for example, to frighten or to persuade. "Illocutionary force" refers to what it is that one's words directly, performatively, do, as when one promises, asks or answers a question, or, with the authority of office, brings it about that, say, a syllabus is laid down, a policy is enacted, or a grade is assigned. See Austin (1962, pp. 98–107).

6. Issues of seriousness and responsibility, naughtiness and playfulness have concerned me since I was a child, when I resolved to become an adult, but never a grown-up. Adulthood meant taking oneself and others seriously, being responsible; being grown-up meant solemnity and the loss of playfulness. I have never, by the way, understood why not taking oneself seriously is meant to be a virtue: However could one trust people who failed to take themselves seriously? (If taking oneself seriously seems to require a suspect metaphysics of selfhood, the problem ought to be with that seeming. The idea that any notion of

Not that I didn't think about it. Part of me was more than happy to stay junior to most of my colleagues—securely tenured, but still somehow a kid. But the role was fitting me less and less well. Not only did I want the respect that came with being seen as what a German colleague once referred to as "internationally reputated," but it did neither feminist philosophy as a field nor the colleagues and students who relied on me for letters of recommendation any good for me to seem to be stalled in the middle ranks. I managed, in fact, nearly to convince myself that I was giving up the psychic freedom of my less-than-fully-senior status for the greater good.

As noble a gesture as this was, the reality is that, in a world filled with injustice, I've succeeded. Leaving aside the more global examples of oppression and exploitation, the academic world nourishes some and starves out others in ways that are hardly models of fairness. I had, ironically, made my career by crafting a critique of that unfairness. So promotion was a replay of the anxieties of tenure: Whom had I betrayed for this to happen? What had I done wrong to be so rewarded? What Faustian bargain had I struck, and when and how was my soul to be collected? Or had it already been, and was I even now doing the devil's work?

The devil? Just whom did I have in mind? The distance between me and those I might be tempted to demonize, at least in the academic arena, had disconcertingly shrunk. And then there's the pesky question of that microphone. The amplifier to which it's hooked up has been getting stronger and stronger, and I have no intention of pulling the plug myself. (I have no illusions about who would grab it if I did: as we've learned in other arenas, simply dumping privilege, even if one can actually do it, does no one one cares about any good.) I can try to use my access to it to give a boost to other voices, but I can't turn it over entirely (for one, if I seriously tried to do that, the plug would be pulled: that we play gatekeeper is one of the nastier bargains radical academics have to strike), and to the extent that it is mine to turn over, that's part of the problem.

These conundrums notwithstanding, there is a lot those of us with access to the various apparatuses of voice-amplification can and should do to democratize that access. But my concern here is how to think in a politically responsible way about my voice when I'm at the mike, and in particular when it's directed to students (rather than on the one hand to administrators or on the other to feminists and others outside the academy whose ally I would be).

One of the ironies in my relationship to students doing feminist work is that insofar as I see them as colleagues—insofar, for example, as I see their work not as student exercises but as contributions to projects we jointly

selfhood that allows for taking oneself seriously is suspect accounts for why so many of the rest of us find certain postmodernists untrustworthy.)

care about—I see myself not only as their teacher but, like them, as a contributor to those projects. That is, I don't think of myself as invisible, like Patsy's parents, nor can I bring myself to hope that I will be invisible to the students I work with. The question about what I'm for is answered in part by my producing, as they do, some of the work that we care about. And, especially in a field as new and as small as feminist philosophy, some of my work will be among the work that constitutes the subject matter of our discussions, the syllabi of our courses. The very strength of their community and the delights of my participation in it become part of the problem: I want to be visible to them, but it's hard to find the ground between invisibility and being the center of attention.

III.

When I was an undergraduate my teachers seemed socially quite distant. (After I got to graduate school it seemed silly to continue to call my undergraduate professors "Miss Larson" and "Miss Mothersill," but I didn't find it easy to switch to "Sue" and "Mary," even though by then the norms had shifted and that's what their current undergraduate students called them.) Thus the seriousness with which they took me philosophically seemed comfortably subjunctive: they were treating me as if I were a philosopher, a colleague, a peer—when obviously I wasn't. It seemed to be how they taught, with a confident expectation that I would grow into the status they subjunctively conferred.

In graduate school the matter was somewhat different. Especially in philosophy there's little reason to be in graduate school if one doesn't aspire to becoming one's teachers' colleague, so being treated that way (the subjunctive being replaced by the future indicative) is simply being treated decently, that is, not as though one's admission were thought to be a mistake. But in my experience, first names or no, the distance remained; it seemed not so much relational (a matter of our roles as teacher and student) as relative (a matter of age and status).[7]

Certainly when Harvard began hiring people for nonrenewable three-year positions ("folding chairs"), those faculty members were much closer to the graduate students: they were younger than some of us, some of them didn't have their Ph.D.s yet, and our community was much easier to feel a part of than that of the senior faculty. On those terms, I am long

7. I'm quite certain that the difference is not one of relative eminence but of the differences in my status and between the two schools. It was a commonplace for Harvard undergraduates to complain that the faculty didn't seem to pay much attention to them, presumably because they were paying attention to the graduate students. The graduate students knew better. There were and are excellent and dedicated teachers at Harvard, including in the philosophy department, but it's not the ethos of the place: another undergraduate commonplace mirrors the perception I shared with my fellow graduate students—that most of one's education comes from other students. Barnard was, and I assume still is, very much a teaching college, however eminent its faculty.

overdue for a change of status, but the reality is that I feel more, not less, a part of the graduate student community than I did before. Part of it is that, unlike my peers in graduate school, who were nearly all in their mid-twenties, the graduate students at Minnesota are of a range of ages, many of them having returned to graduate school after having done other things: like many of the undergraduates there, they are adults, with adult lives and concerns, not in the extended adolescence continuous schooling can prolong.

But their not all being half my age, though it no doubt helps me to feel a part of their community, doesn't explain why I need to. That, I think, goes back to the tenured radical stuff, to my neither wanting nor being able to be in the position either of relatively out-of-the-fray nurturing teacher or of *éminence grise*. If their community is where the action is, it's where I feel the need to be. It would be against my politics (not to mention demonstrably false) to think that the action wasn't there, that they were only in training to do someday what I do now. The irony is that my taking them in this way seriously raises my stakes in their acknowledging me, makes me less willing to recede into the background, to leave a puzzle about what I'm for. I'm reminded uncomfortably of parents who are trying too hard to be their children's friend to be their parent: Is this less a problem in very large families with secure, happy siblings? I don't know.

I have a different sort of concern with women students, especially feminists, who don't find feminist philosophy to be what they choose to do, either because something else simply interests them more or because they find the arguments about the relevance of gender to (at least) most of philosophy unconvincing. Since I used to be in their position, hooked on epistemology and metaphysics, which I confidently believed had nothing to do with gender or with anything else political, I feel I know something of what it's like. But that feeling is an illusion. For one thing, it's hardly helpful to convey the impression (and hard to avoid doing so) that, since I was once where they are, they will someday, when they learn better, be where I am. For another, the center of gravity has markedly shifted. Back when I believed that gender was irrelevant to epistemology and meta-physics, hardly anyone in the Anglo-American philosophical world believed anything else. Today, although most of that world still thinks of epistemology and metaphysics in apolitical terms, there is a strong and vocal feminist presence that both asserts otherwise and claims to have been oppressed by the dominant views. That latter claim is an especially problematic one: it can be unbearable to find out that something one loves has been used as a club (in both senses of the word) to terrorize and ostracize people one cares for and identifies with.

Without the microphone, when I was just shouting into the wind, I could be confident (again, it usually felt more like despair) that no one was going to be seriously affected by anything I said. Now, both because of the force of my words, published or spoken, and because of the size and vigor of the community I helped to form and continue to mentor, women I care about—students I would like to be able to teach—are hurt by what they perceive to be the distance between who they take themselves to be and a picture of women that they find in those words and in that community. If it were a picture I thought were somehow false, I could work to correct it, but that's not the problem. It needn't be false to be problematically coercive, and I don't know what to do about that.

Part of the problem is something that comes up in a number of diverse contexts, namely, a disparity between privilege as it exists within a group and as it exists in the world around the group. One of the points of separatism is in fact to create such disparities, to create contexts in which an identity that is marginal or oppressed in the world at large is central, and in which those whose identity it is have the power to decide how things will go on. Such disparities can cause problems, especially if the group is not strictly separatist, allowing or even welcoming members who choose to ally with, though they don't share, the identity in question (or if the identity that becomes central is a subset of the one around which the group formed, as a feminist group can come to have lesbians as its most central members). The central group members will typically be exceedingly aware of the marginality of the identity that brought them together: the outside world will loom as the frame within which they defend, usually perilously, their space. The others will typically be far less aware of the salience of their privilege in the outside world (it's likely to be relatively invisible to them) and much more aware of their own marginality and lack of privilege within the group.

The problem is particularly acute when central group members are not the only ones to feel marginalized or oppressed by the rest of the world. One doesn't have to be a feminist philosopher or even a feminist (though it helps) to feel marginalized and oppressed by the world of academic philosophy: being a woman is enough. And communities of feminist philosophers are natural places to turn for support, especially when, as in my department or in the Society for Women in Philosophy, such communities are strong and vibrant. But for good reason those communities are likely to have at their centers strong counter-identities that may feel to some more marginalizing than welcoming, be that lesbian or a radically feminist stance toward philosophy.

Like the problems confronting "tenured radicals," these are problems of success—success at changing parts of the world when most of it remains untransformed. I have solutions for none of these problems. My hope is that in raising them I have done something more than whine about things that only the overprivileged have the time for. I do, when it comes down to it, believe that teachers and students inhabit the real world and that what we do with each other matters, and that doing it responsibly is neither easy nor trivial. So the something more I hope to have done is to have contributed to that work by sketching not just a self-portrait but a picture in which some of you will find yourselves—with whatever mixture of relief or discomfort—and others of you will find people whose exasperating behavior may seem a little less opaque.

ACKNOWLEDGMENTS

My thanks to Jane Gallop and to Kathleen Woodward and the Center for Twentieth Century Studies at the University of Wisconsin-Milwaukee for the conference on "Pedagogy: The Question of the Personal" that helped to shape my reflection on the topics of this essay. (That reflection took shape in a somewhat different form on the occasion of my writing the introductory essay to a collection of my papers, published in 1993 by Routledge under the title *Engenderings: Constructions of Knowledge, Authority, and Privilege*.) Thanks to Jane also for her urging that I write up what I said at the conference. Writing in this way "for Jane" is a fascinatingly disconcerting experience, rather as though my editorial superego has been unceremoniously turfed from its office by my id, which has taken up residence there, its feet up on the desk. This essay is also marked by a degree of expansive and reflective distance. I am writing from the charmed space of the Society for the Humanities at Cornell, a place of many temptations and few obligations: it precisely does not "concentrate the mind." My tenure here also allows me the opportunity to explore some of these issues in conversation with, as it were, surrogate colleagues and students, as one can more easily explore familial tangles with someone else's parents or siblings. But my greatest debt is to the members of SOΦIA, back home in Minnesota, as well as to other philosophy and women's studies students there, equally for inspiration and for critique.

Chapter 4

Terminal Moraine

> You can watch people align themselves when trouble is in the air. Some prefer to be close to those at the top and others want to be close to those at the bottom. It's a question of who frightens them more and whom they want to be like.
>
> Jenny Holzer, "The Living Series"

WHITE LIKE US

When I was five or six, I was taken by my parents to a holiday party for progressive activists and their kids at which Paul Robeson was the guest of honor. Upon being introduced, I sang to him. That would have been bad enough (the only tune I have ever been able to carry is "Teen Angel"), but even worse is what I chose (or was prodded—the story does not say) to sing: a song from an album called *Little Songs on Big Subjects*, the chorus of which goes, "You get good milk from a brown-skinned cow./ The color of your skin doesn't matter no-how./ Ho ho ho, can't you see/ the color of your skin doesn't matter to me."

After the party, my parents went into the city for dinner with Robeson. At his suggestion, they went to Longchamps, and my parents worried about whether or not he would be served. As it turned out, Robeson was recognized—as, of course, he had expected—and they were shown to the best table and waited on in ways my parents were certainly not used to. Longchamps was more Robeson's world than it was my parents', but if he thought their solicitude condescending, he certainly gave no sign of it—much as, I am told, he reacted with apparent delight to my off-key assurance that I was deigning to treat one of the towering figures of the twentieth century as my equal.

The song I sang and my parents' protectiveness capture the spirit of the principled, committed antiracism with which I was raised and that motivated my parents and many other whites to support and participate in the civil rights movement of the 1940s, 1950s, and 1960s. Anti-Black racism was a terrible wrong, and white people—especially, for complex reasons, Jewish white people—had a moral obligation to do what they could to help those who suffered from it and to work to end it. Like many other

63

"red diaper babies"—the baby boom children of communists, socialists, and assorted other "progressives" (the umbrella term that at that time separated the serious left from what were derisively referred to as "liberals")—I was pushed in my carriage on civil rights picket lines and marches and carried to rallies and meetings. Our own activism in the 1960s was less a matter of rebellion than it was the carrying on of a family tradition: We were the dutiful children of courageously rebellious parents.

But with notable differences. Unlike some of my acquaintances, I never got drawn into the more romantically revolutionary activities of the Weather Underground; my only brushes with the law involved several unsuccessful attempts at arrest for civil disobedience. But over the years, my politics diverged in various ways from my parents', notably around the rethinking of antiracism that characterized the theoretical and political shifts associated with the Black Power movement and subsequent identity politics. From these perspectives, what is most salient about the song I sang to Robeson is the fact that the milk you get from a brown-skinned cow is white: The message is that, under different colored skin, everyone is really just like us white people.

In particular, Blacks were just like us Jews. My parents were not religious, at least not in any institutionally recognizable way. My mother had been raised in a left-wing, secular milieu, attending a Sholom Aleichem *schul* (a secular Jewish version of Sunday school), at which she studied Yiddish along with Jewish history and literature. My father had been raised in an Orthodox family, but the story in my memory (though not in my mother's) is that as a young man he swore never to belong to a synagogue again after having to pay for a *minyan* to say Kaddish for his father. (A *minyan* is the quorum of ten adult Jewish men required for rituals such as the Kaddish, the prayer for the dead.) My sisters and I were raised with a strong cultural identification with Jewishness, which in our family centered on a commitment to fighting so that others might be liberated, as Jews had been, from the various tyrannies that had enslaved us and continued to enslave others. As the bumper sticker on my car says, "None are free so long as any are oppressed."

The principal Jewish holiday we observed was Passover, for which my father put up a banner on which he had written the words from the seder service that are inscribed on the Liberty Bell: "Proclaim liberty throughout the land." We always invited non-Jews to join our seders, which were filled with discussions of current events, especially those involving liberatory struggles in the United States and internationally. When the cup of wine was put out for the prophet Elijah, we understood that he would not be coming yet: The role of the Messiah he heralded was not to save us from anything but to let us know that we had succeeded at what I later learned to call *tikkun olam*, the healing of the world. "Next year in Jerusalem," the words that close the seder, referred not to the possibility of *aliyah*—moving to Israel—but to the impossible dream that by next

year the world would be healed and, consequently, but only consequently, our Diaspora ended.[1]

My parents were not anti-Zionist, but on the whole, Israel did not loom
large in my consciousness (I have still not been there). From time to time,
to commemorate some occasion or other, we planted a tree in Israel, and
we had relatives living there, one of whom lost two sons in the Six Days'
War, which immediately preceded my wedding in 1967 and lent it an air
of somber celebration. But it was clear that our calling as Jews was here, in
America, in solidarity with those whose lives here had not yet achieved
the success of ours. The displacement of the Diaspora had in my mind less
to do with the destruction of the Second Temple than with the anti-
Semitism that at the turn of the century had driven my grandparents and
so many of their generation from Europe, and that culminated with the
Holocaust and the destruction of Europe as a home for Jews. The ending
of the Diaspora consequently had less to do with a return to Israel than
with an end *both* to the continuing threat of anti-Semitism, which made
the state of Israel an arguable necessity, *and* to the whole range of other
threats that put other groups of people at similar peril. In particular, given
the extent to which many Jewish Americans had come to feel—however
ambivalently—at home in the United States, it was our responsibility to
help make that achievement possible for others, to help make the United
States live up to the words in Emma Lazarus's poem on the Statue of
Liberty, promising the safety of home to those in need of it.

In my suburban, Long Island high school, most of the students in
the honors track were Jewish, although we were a minority in the school.
We jokingly referred to the few Christian students in the program (only
one of whom was Black) as "honorary Jews." A group of us hung out
together, listening to Dave Brubeck, Miles Davis, Joan Baez, and Bob
Dylan and talking about such things as whether the earth might not be a
particle circling the nucleus of some huge atom, until all hours of the night
(specifically, until what my parents—in a gesture toward something like
but not quite a curfew—referred to as "skeighty-eighty o'clock"). We called
ourselves "YID," an acronym for "Youth for Intellectual Discussion," the
self-mocking glibness of which marked our blissfully ignorant distance
from a world of anti-Semitic slurs. The oppression from which we had
been delivered had happened long ago and far away: Adolf Hitler merged in
my mind with the Pharaoh to whom Moses had sung "Let my people go."
History was a dangerous place that had been very bad for the Jews; but that
was then and there. Here and now we were safe, and our obligation as Jews
"never to forget" found concrete expression in a commitment to fighting on
behalf of others who here and now were not safe.

One of my mother's favorite films and books is *Gentleman's Agreement*,
and she alludes to it when she wants to make the point that one ought not to

---

1. On the socialist internationalist culture of *Yidishkayt*, see Klepfisz (1990). On the view of the
Diaspora as not ending with the formation of the state of Israel, see Boyarin and Boyarin (1993).

remain silent in the face of expressions of bigotry. I recently read someone's sardonic comment on the film: that its lesson is that one ought to be nice to Jews because you never know when one will turn out to be a gentile.[2] That is not, of course, the moral my mother draws; but it is telling that the moral heart of the film, and the point of identification my mother urges, is not the Jewish soldier but the Gregory Peck character whose masquerade as a Jew is aimed both at confronting an injustice and at awakening his fiancée to the moral imperative not to remain silent, even when speaking out is socially uncomfortable or even dangerous.

This lesson is at the heart of the moral identity I associate with Jewishness. My own identifications—in films, novels, television programs, and news stories—tend to be not with those who fight injustice on their own behalf, but with those who, from positions of privileged safety, fight on behalf of others. That I grew up with a sense of privileged safety— especially during the McCarthy era—is a source of wonderment to me.[3] Even as native-born Americans, my parents hardly experienced the world as a safe place for Jews. Not only had anti-Semitism been a reality in their New York lives, but also they had been antifascist activists, aware of what was happening in Europe and fully cognizant that it was, in some cases quite literally, our relatives to whom it was happening.[4]

I was conceived two months after my father's return from the War, and when I was eighteen months old, we moved from Brooklyn to Long Island, where I lived for the next sixteen years and where I sang to Robeson, assuring him of my generous color blindness. I want to explore what that story encodes, as well as what it hides and distorts, not just about my own quite particular post-War suburban Jewish girlhood, but about the whiteness of Jews in post-War America and about the complex and diverse meanings of the relationships between Black Americans and their Jewish allies in those years. My guiding image is that of terminal moraine, which is what, geologically, Long Island is.

THEN AND THERE; HERE AND NOW

> Just a few Yiddish words, the very sound of the language evokes
> very strong feelings and memories. So I am determined that
> Yiddish will never be a barrier, as it has been for many Jews

---

2. According to Judith Weisenfeld (in conversation), the remark is attributed to Ring Lardner.

3. I similarly wonder at my having had an immediate sense of entitlement to philosophy, despite being both a Jew and a woman; and I have written about what it meant that the generation of my teachers—overwhelmingly women and Jewish men—gave me the ambiguous gift of empowering ignorance. See chapter 1—a *Festschrift* for one of those teachers, Burton Dreben, of blessed memory.

4. My father—upon enlisting to fight the Nazis—had been posted to the China/Burma/India theater, as an officially designated "premature antifascist," that is, someone whose left-wing political sympathies made him unfit to serve in Europe because of concerns about what would happen when Russian forces met up with the other Allied forces on the eastern front.

whose parents spoke it only *az di kinder zoln nisht farshteyn,* so
the children won't understand.

Irena Klepfisz (on her choice to use Yiddish but not to write in
Yiddish only), *Dreams of an Insomniac*

Somewhere else, the earth lies in narratable formations—the familiar list
of igneous, stratified, and metamorphic. Geologists and paleontologists
can read the mineral and fossil stories preserved in place in the layers of
rock. But sometime in the distant past, a glacier came along and broke
some of the rock-narratives into fragments, called moraine, which it
carried along as it moved south. As the ice age ended, the glacier receded,
leaving a line of "terminal" moraine marking its furthest edge. That
strip of terminal moraine is Long Island, in contrast to Manhattan,
which is bedrock. Significantly, one speaks of living not "in," but "on"
Long Island—or even "on the Island," as opposed to "in the City," which
is, of course, also an island. (Brooklyn and Queens, which are geologically
on Long Island but geographically in New York City, are, in common
parlance, neither on the Island nor in the City.)

To grow up on terminal moraine is to grow up on the unnarratable
fragments of other people's stories. Or so it seemed from the perspective
of those of us who had been brought to or birthed on Long Island because
it was "a good place to bring up children"; in contrast to the City, it was
"safe," lacking in the sort of stories and histories that clashed with the
wide-open possibilities that we were supposed to see ahead of us.[5]

In reality, of course, Long Island had a great deal of history, but it
belonged to other people. Many of the place names are American Indian:
Ronkonkoma, Massapequa, Patchogue, and Montauk; but I do not recall
that our education included learning who or what they were names of, or
which nations lived there or what happened to them. Slightly less obscure
in my mind is the colonial and revolutionary history of Long Island: In the
seventeenth century, Manhattan was not the center of that part of the
world, and communities far to the east, which are now sleepy outposts,
were thriving ports. The town to which my family moved the summer
before I went off to the City to go to college is steeped in revolutionary
history, though what I know of it is anecdotal. Nathan Hale gave his
one life just down the road (in Halesite); and, so we were told, colonists
shipped off a bunch of cattle from our beach to General George
Washington's forces on the other side of Long Island Sound under

---

5. Certainly others whose external circumstances were similar to mine were more susceptible to the
stories that surrounded us and felt the Holocaust as more immediately related to their own lives (in
particular, the *Diary of Anne Frank* played a central role in bringing the Holocaust within our imaginative
scope). I am working on the presumption that my sense of detachment—as though all of history were long
ago and far away—is not just a piece of my own psychology but reflects something more general,
something that speaks to the construction of "Jewish whiteness." I am gambling that some significant
number of readers will find in my stories resonances of theirs.

the noses of the British troops, who were sleeping off a drunken stupor, the consequence of a Christmas party the locals had thrown for them.

But I do not recall knowing anyone (though surely I must have) whose parents, let alone more distant ancestors, had been born on the Island. Nor, for that matter, do I remember knowing anyone whose parents had been born in Europe (though most of my friends' grandparents had been). My experience as a post-War American Jew is very different from the experiences of those who were born here of parents who had fled or survived the Holocaust. The experience for which I am evoking the image of terminal moraine is that of having the ground under one's feet be that of other people's stories, other people whom one may be exhorted to honor—never to forget—but whose lives are neither vivid nor individualized but, rather, fragmented and jumbled, out of place and time.

The move to Long Island was, I think, the move to just such a place, a place where the possibilities of the present and future were unconstrained by history, where anyone could grow up to be anything. Jews of my generation ought to be haunted by history, as those who are the children of survivors typically are, deeply aware of the strenuous efforts to make sure that no one like us was ever born, aware of carrying the burden of all the lives that in fact never were, or that were cut off. But I think something other than the sheer unimaginability of the Holocaust accounts for why—along with, I believe, many if not most who share the relevant parts of my history—I am not haunted, do not perceive the world as personally dangerous, and do not viscerally think of the Holocaust as something that happened to people just like us, not so far away and not so long ago.[6]

Films like *Amityville Horror* and, especially, *Poltergeist* suggest that the suburbs are, in fact, haunted—in *Poltergeist* by the ghosts of those buried in a long-forgotten cemetery over which the town was built, with homes for people who knew nothing of the strangers under their feet. The moral—that history does not stay buried, that what you do not know can hurt you, that the past requires remembering—is one that is deeply familiar to Jews.[7] It is at the heart of the traditional Passover seder—the

6. This sense of inexpressible distance from the Holocaust is not, of course, confined to post-War American Jews. In an interview, Kershaw (1999), the English author of *Hitler, 1889–1936: Hubris*, the first volume of a two-volume biography, says of the Nazi era: "This is not very long ago, and yet it seems to be on another planet." The archiving of survivors' memories is driven in part by the awareness of how hard it is for others really to comprehend the enormity of what happened and the consequent danger that the deniers, having credibility on their side, will win. (See Root (1998), for an argument, based on Hume's remarks on miracles, that we ought to believe what another tells us just in case the improbability that they are lying or mistaken is greater than the improbability of what they are reporting. If their report strikes us as unimaginable, the epistemic weight borne by their credibility is enormous.) The specific, disorienting irony I want to focus on is how this incomprehension figures in the lives of those for whom the injunction never to forget is meant to provide a moral compass and to orient us in the world.

7. It is also the moral of John Sayles's film *Lone Star*, in which history literally comes unburied and needs to be faced—as the Chicana schoolteacher has been urging in the face of Anglo community resistance—before reconciliation and the recognition and embracing of (literal) kinship are possible. The myth such stories play on is a very deep one in American cultural life: Suburbia is a recapitulation of earlier frontier myths of a vast, minimally populated wilderness, whose few inhabitants had no real

knowledge that all over the world, today as for thousands of years, Jews are saying the same words, telling the same story—as well as of post-Holocaust Jewish identity. But the imperative to remember was oddly but understandably muted in post-War suburbia: If we too vividly had in mind what it was we were exhorted never to forget, we could hardly have moved in the world with the sense of entitlement to self-invention that our parents meant to give us in the safety of the suburbs.

FROM VICTIMS TO SAVIORS

Jewish Israeli national identity[8] was forged largely in defiant opposition to the image of the Jew as persecuted victim. In a country of "tough Jews,"[9] Holocaust survivors were an embarrassing presence: a particularly chilling epithet for them was the Hebrew word for soap.[10] But however much Israel's claim to legitimacy might be internally buttressed by appeals to its being the historical, original home of the Jews—to which we all had, biblically, a right of return—in the eyes of the world its legitimacy rested on the need for sanctuary for those who had found themselves turned away from the shores of the countries where they had sought refuge from persecution and extermination. If, in Robert Frost's words (1914), "Home is where, when you have to go there, they have to take you in," the failure of the world to take in the refugees from Hitler was an overwhelming argument for a Jewish homeland. Throughout the many subsequent years of conflict, Jewish American support for Israel has been an odd mix of anxious protectiveness toward a precarious, threatened homeland in a hostile world and pride in the military might of the swaggering *sabra*.

The material, social, and cultural success of Jews in the United States has been the source of deep ambivalence.[11] In a Christian country, with an enduring history of anti-Semitism, that success has inevitably been linked with danger, as it has been at least since the medieval and early modern association of European Jews with usury.[12] (Money-lending

claim to the land. Following a Lockean model, private ownership and forms of government based upon it were what turned space into place. Those places that are suburbs came into official existence as they were "developed." The sorts of instantly fabricated towns of which Levittown is the prototype are in fact referred to as "developments."

8. See Bar On (1994), for the importance of the term "Jewish Israeli," as a contestation of the idea of Israel as a Jewish state, according to which all other Israelis, but not Jews, are marked by modifiers, such as "Arab Israeli."

9. For the articulation of this image, especially as it resonates in the consciousness of American Jews, see Breines (1990).

10. Bat-Ami Bar On informs me that another, possibly stronger, association with soap was with the pale skin derided by *sabras* as associated with urban diasporic life. See Almog (1997, p. 143).

11. Riv-Ellen Prell has explored this ambivalence especially as it has played itself out in the edgy relationships between Jewish men and women. See especially Prell (1999).

12. The social location of such wealthy and powerful Jews—whether in medieval and early modern Europe, in Germany before the Nuremberg Laws, or, to an obviously lesser extent, in the present-day United States—is an example of what I call "privileged marginality." See chapter 8. I use the term to refer

being a necessity but forbidden at that time to Christians, some wealthy Jews became far wealthier under the protection of various courts, even while that wealth and protection marked them as marginal—the clear sign of their refusal to convert to the one true religion—and left them vulnerable to resentment, especially in bad times.) One important strain of diasporic Jewish consciousness has been, since the nineteenth century, a continuing identification with liberatory struggles and an internationalist commitment to social justice; and in the United States, especially in the prosperity after World War II, that commitment became one of the avenues of expression for the ambivalence about material success, a way to deal with the discomfort of being comfortable, as well as a way of distancing oneself from the stereotypes of the Jewish *parvenu*.[13]

Different attitudes about Jewish success—whether Israeli or American—shape our responses to the linked fates of others. In relation to Israel the belief in Jewish exceptionalism has facilitated moral accommodation to the plight of the Palestinians and Israel's responsibility for that plight, helping to rationalize away the parallels of dispossession, while for some Israeli and American Jews those parallels are increasingly, heartbreakingly salient.[14] In the United States, these attitudes have diversely played themselves out in complex sets of identifications and disidentifications with African Americans. The phenomenon of Jewish right-ward defection from the Democratic Party has in large measure been a response to affirmative action, with its supposed echoes of anti-Semitic quotas, and a resentment of those who seemed to need more from the government than the formal abolition of barriers.[15] For Jews on the left, relationships with Blacks have been more complicated, in part because seeing ourselves as the "good whites," antiracist savior-heroes, has been one of the ways of dealing with the ambivalences of success, success that had at its heart the achievement of whiteness (see Berger 1999).

Many, though by no means all, of the barriers that had kept Blacks out of the precincts of white America had also kept Jews out, and the fight to break through those barriers was one of the formative experiences of my parents' generation. The achievement was an ambiguous one: Along with the lowering of barriers came the actual or threatened loss of much of Jewish

---

to forms of privilege that are constructed specifically on the margins and thus carry with them complex amalgams of material and epistemic advantages and risks; another example is the position of tenured academics in a fundamentally anti-intellectual society. One of the defining features of privileged marginality is the particularly fraught relationship of those in that position to others with whom they share the marginality but not the privilege. Consider, for example, the debate over the protection of poorer Jews negotiated by those with relationships to various courts and state powers. See Arendt (1973, pp. 11–53) and Biale (1986, pp. 58–86).

13. On the *parvenu* and the pariah, as well as for the historical background for the situation of Jews as "privileged marginals," see Arendt (1978).

14. See Bar On (1994) for a discussion of coming to full awareness of the bearing of Palestinian dispossession on Jewish Israeli national identity through her friendship with a Palestinian Israeli woman.

15. On the different psychic and social meanings and effects of anti-Semitism (epitomized by the Holocaust) and anti-Black racism (epitomized by slavery), see Thomas (1993).

culture, both secular and religious. Identification with those for whom the barriers still stood became in part an expression of the ambivalence of that loss, including the loss of the solidarity of struggle and the moral clarity of victimization. At the same time, there were the children to think about. Our birth after the War represented the survival of the Jewish people and of Jewish memory, but our lives were meant to be shaped by the confidence that we were among the rightful heirs to the American dream.

Children always pose a dilemma for parents whose commitments or passions would lead them toward lives of instability or risk, but in the case of our parents there were especially poignant—and morally and politically complex—aspects to these tensions, summed up in the notion of safety, one of the prime virtues of the suburbs as a place in which to raise children. The dangers of the city were many, but central among them was the fact that many Jewish neighborhoods were "changing," that is, becoming largely Black.[16] It was difficult to think about "them" whose allies we were as the same "them" whose presence in our old neighborhoods made those neighborhoods unsafe. One "resolution" of the difficulty was color blindness: The neighborhoods were dangerous because of poverty and the attendant problems of crime, alcohol, and drugs; and the appropriate response was integration, especially in education and in housing (in safe, stably integrated suburbs—always, however, more of an ambivalently embraced dream than a reality).

But if the suburbs remained for the most part resistant to racial integration, they did not necessarily feel like home in any deeply resonant sense for many of those who were brought up there and for whose sake the burgeoning communities were being built. From my—specifically middle-class—perspective, feeling at home on Long Island has always seemed like feeling at home in your elementary school—understandable but something to outgrow. When the ground under your feet strikes you as fragmented and haphazard (however comfortably cocooned you might be upon it), you are likely to long for something more "authentic," more substantial, something with more soul—the bedrock of Manhattan, for example. It was urban Blacks—those who lived in the dangerous neighborhoods—not the few who achieved a middle-class integrated suburban life—who filled the imagination of assimilated, rootless post-War Jews, as we exercised one of the ironic privileges of whiteness: the appropriation of cultures of color. The courageously principled participation of Jews in the civil rights movement, some at the risk or cost of their lives, was mirrored by the phenomenon of wanna-be Black hipsters.

The political affiliation of Jews with African Americans was—I want to and largely do believe—a basically, if ambiguously, honorable one. But even as they acknowledge the value and sincerity of Jewish support, most Blacks remember the alliance far more ambivalently than Jews tend to,

---

16. Thanks to Lata Mani for bringing this point to my attention many years ago.

largely because they recognized better than we did both the elements of condescension on our part, our tendency toward white-horsed knighthood, and—especially after the rise of the Black Power movement—our unacknowledged privileging of whiteness as an aspirational ideal. What I want to suggest is that part of what was going on was that for progressive Jews the affiliation served to assuage some of the anxieties of post-War Jewish American life (displaced onto the unstable combination of ideological color blindness with an attraction to the cultural distinctness that flourished in the ghettos we had so recently quit) and to guide the reforging of the moral core of diasporic identity after the formation and increasing stability of the state of Israel.

Furthermore, the contradictions between the imperative to remember and the necessarily hazy indistinctness of our own history—which, had we vividly remembered it, would have made us unable to take up the inheritance our parents had won for us—drew us to the role of savior: identifying with those who were oppressed even as we certified our own membership among the privileged by our ability to offer a helping hand. If we were ambivalent about being at home in America, one way to mitigate that unease was by undertaking to make good on the promises that had drawn our grandparents—the offer of a home to the "huddled masses, yearning to breathe free"—on behalf of those whose ancestors had been brought in chains, centuries earlier, to these shores and to whom the offer of home had never been made in good faith.

BY THE RAILROAD TO BABYLON (NOT QUITE REMEMBERING ZION)

> Baldwin, Freeport, Merrick, Belmore, Wantagh, Seaford, Massapequa, Massapequa Park, Amityville, Copague, Lindenhurst, aaaaand . . . Babylon
> Stations on the South Shore line of the Long Island Railroad

Should we conclude that terminal moraine does not afford a reliable ground for responsible political identity? That such an identity needs to be grounded in the solidity of individual and collective memory, in a nonfragmented, stable narrative? It would be dangerous to draw such a conclusion. Not only are such narratives, for a wide range of reasons, unavailable to many people, but also the conviction that they are necessary leads to bloody, brutal, and brutalizing attempts to secure the ground in which such narratives are believed to be rooted. As Daniel Boyarin and Jonathan Boyarin (1993) argue, a diasporic reading of Jewish identity can help all of us refigure responsible political agency as not requiring a homeland—as even, they argue, incompatible with any homeland that needs to be secured by the force of arms.

What we need, I want to suggest, is to learn how to lovingly tend, as we responsibly stand on, the fragments of our own and each other's narratives.

A broken, scattered past is more, not less, in need of our attention and our recollection: Responsibility lies not in rootedness but in a willingness to take seriously the contingencies of our connections to each other and to the fragments of stories that have turned up under our feet. It is too glib to conclude, from the failure of various foundationalisms, that the whole idea of ground is somehow suspect, or that there is no important difference between terminal moraine and quicksand. There is actual ground under all our feet, and its failure to live up to our demands of solidity does not absolve us of the responsibility to attend to it and to what we do upon it.

What might such exhortations actually, concretely mean? For one, it seems to me that, of the options available for how to be a Jew, especially in the relatively comfortable Diaspora, at the beginning of the twenty-first century, the choice to define oneself in solidarity with those who are oppressed is the most honorable. The other prominent options— militaristic toughness, insistence on our continuing status as victims, or assimilation to the ranks of the privileged—are neither morally defensible nor, in the long run, effective guarantors of the safety they promise. None is really "good for the Jews." A historical reading of the "chosenness" of the Jews suggests that we were chosen for victimization; and the moral and practical faults with those options come from thinking either that we can escape that condition or that we have a preemptive claim on it. We can never be sufficiently tough to keep ourselves safe, and the attempt to do so exacts an unacceptable toll on others. Nor will our claim to special tugging rights on the world's heartstrings protect us from those who choose not to be moved, while defending that claim hardens us to the cries of those who are otherwise harmed, including by us. Adopting the protective coloration of country clubs and the Republican Party will not successfully make us other than Other in a Christian country, but it will make us complicit in the continuing exclusion and marginalization of those who lack our privilege.

If recognizing a liability to victimization as an ineliminable aspect of Jewishness seems unacceptable—as it does to me—the honorable response, I want to suggest, is not to try to eliminate the specific connection between Jewishness and victimization, to make Jews safe in an unsafe world. Even if this were (as I doubt) a prudentially reasonable strategy, the core of what I have learned as Jewishness tells me that it is an immoral one.[17] Rather, if being a potential victim because of who you are (not just because anyone, randomly, could be attacked or killed, but because *people like you are likely to be singled out*) is not okay for the Jews, it is not okay for anyone. Put this way, a world that is safe for the Jews is a world that is safe for everyone: a world in which people are not singled out for attack or mistreatment because they are Black or gay or female or Tutsi or indigenous or Albanian or Palestinian. It is a world in which homes are not defined

17. I have discussed the illusoriness of "safety for the Jews" in chapter 7.

by who is excluded from them, a world in which attentive concern does not stop at some imaginary line, but also a world in which the stranger who has come, for whatever reason, to live among you has a special claim on that concern.

It is equally a world in which those who prosper in the Diaspora have special responsibilities toward those whose homes they live in. To live diasporically is not to live as a tourist or as a guest; one is not on vacation, and one has no home to return to. But the Diaspora is not exile; one is not a refugee, often not even an immigrant, but a native-born child, even of native-born parents, a citizen of this place that is not home.[18] One could even, maybe, grow up to be president. So what does it mean not to be at home?

I have been trying to figure this question out in relation to my not feeling at home in Minneapolis, where I have lived for twenty years, with a wonderful job and friends I love. I say this not because home is New York (I am beginning to think that is not the right explanation). Rather, I suspect that nowhere I was could be home, that the Diaspora is my way of life, that I am that figure, the Wandering Jew, cosmopolitan to the core. Perhaps the appeal of New York is not that it is home, but that it is a place whose meaning is constructed largely by uprooted or rootless cosmopolitans. As bedrock, it will endure, solidly, as people come and go, changing its architecture and its streets—unlike the Midwest, which is, it seems to me, meant for those who are at home there and who, through their labor, change the very shape of the earth beneath their feet.

Though (because?) I am not at home anywhere, there are a great many places where I could live, and many places where I do, in fact, have important pieces of my life; and I move around with ease, among widely scattered friends, but am also comfortable in the presence of strangers—more comfortable at times than I am with those I am close to.[19] Such ease in the world is, of course, the product of privilege. Many who are, in Lugones's terms (1987) "'world' travelers" may come to be extraordinarily adept but are less likely to be at ease.[20] But I need to not overplay the privilege of my ease while failing to acknowledge the value of their adeptness: One of the risks of thinking of oneself as a savior of the less-well-off is that one is likely to miss out on what one could learn through a more interactive relationship; even a conscientious acknowledgment of inequality may leave that inequality intact.[21]

18. For an exploration of the differences between exile and diaspora, see Kaminsky (1999).

19. I explored these issues in Scheman (1992*b*).

20. Binder (2000) addressed the epistemological implications of thinking about movement through actual and imaginative space in her University of Minnesota dissertation.

21. Thanks to María Lugones for calling into question common assumptions about the benefits of privilege in discussion at a meeting of the Midwest Society for Women in Philosophy [SWIP] in Madison, Wisconsin, March, 1999. See Lugones (1991) for a discussion of the ways in which a theoretical embrace of "difference" on the part of white feminists masked a failure to interact with women of color around issues of racism.

More recent work of Lugones is also relevant here. In working on issues of multicultural pedagogy, she has been developing notions of "long" and "wide" selves.[22] Our long selves are our histories: From whom and from where do we come; what were our ancestors doing at different points in history; and how, as their descendants, do we relate to that history? Our wide selves are our relationships to and with other long selves: How and where do we stand in relation to others currently in our various "worlds"; and how are those relationships shaped both by our different, often conflicting, histories and by the material circumstances of our present interactions? To live on terminal moraine (and one way of understanding the "postmodern condition" is that all of us who are in some sense "in" that condition are living on terminal moraine) means that one's long self cannot be tapped by digging beneath one's own feet. One's history is dispersed and survives in fragments, while the real ground under one's feet is made up of the pasts that shape the long selves of others.

We have all become in real, material ways the keepers of each other's long selves, and our ability to recover and remember ourselves is, literally, in each other's hands. Only by undertaking the hard work of responsibility as wide selves, as people who need to learn from and with each other, to figure out how to be not victims and saviors but allies, can we hope to obey the injunction never to forget. I cannot remember my history, lying now under your feet, unless I learn how to take responsibility, with you, for the interactions between us, on the ground, however fragmented, on which we now stand.

ACKNOWLEDGMENTS

Special thanks to my mother, Blanche Scheman, for her critical reading of this essay and her uncritical love of its author, as well as for several corrections of fact, her memory being at the time better than mine.

---

22. I learned about this work at the March 1999 Midwest SWIP meeting; see footnote 21.

PART II

REALITY

The essays in this section explore the "rough ground"—our practices and "forms of life"—to which Wittgenstein urges us to return, the roughness providing the friction that will enable questions to get some traction, ground that will be firm under our feet, firm enough to hold our weight and the weight of any questions we have a real need to ask, including the needs for explanation and justification discussed in Part 1. This firmness has usually been taken by interpreters of Wittgenstein as supporting the satisfaction of those needs, the recognition that *this* is what explanation and justification look like—what we do when we adequately respond to actual, particular queries. But there are times when describing what we do, far from satisfying our questioner, will serve only to sharpen the point of the demand for explanation or justification, notably when those demands are grounded in the experiences of those for whom the friction of the roughness fails to provide traction and enable mobility, but rather bogs them down or trips them up. How, that is, do the structures of intelligibility, which Wittgenstein urges us to find sufficient (to not need qualifying as "merely what we do") seem from the perspectives of those for whom what "we" do is alienating, painful, and incompatible with self-respect?

"Against Physicalism" was written for the "Philosophy of Mind" section of the *Cambridge Companion to Wittgenstein*, edited by Jennifer Hornsby and Miranda Fricker, but the core arguments go back to my dissertation in the mid-1970s. When I was coming up for tenure, in 1992, I needed to demonstrate to my senior colleagues that I had strong, well-argued reasons for turning away from the problems that lay in philosophy's mainstream. Largely through writing "Types, Tokens and Conjuring Tricks," an unpublished distant ancestor of "Against Physicalism," I succeeded sufficiently at that task and turned (or so I thought) to a different set of questions and to problems that arose elsewhere than in philosophical texts. But the philosophical mainstream (or at least some of its major tributaries) continued to draw me in. It kept seeming to me that I had something to say about some of the problems that swirled there—specifically in relation to emerging interest in anti-individualism in the philosophy of psychology (which seemed to me to stop short of the deepest issues)—although I couldn't manage to say any of it in a way that made sense to those whose problems they principally were. And when

I explained what I thought about these core philosophical problems to colleagues outside of philosophy, the responses tended to be overly quick agreement: I seemed to be articulating common sense, even if initially in puzzlingly sophisticated language. (In Wittgensteinian terms, this situation made sense: non-philosophers were not bewitched by the pictures that seemed to me to have such a grip on philosophers. But I believed (and believe) that those pictures are implicit in much ordinary thinking, even if, when one articulates them, only philosophers are willing explicitly to embrace them.)

The influence of Wittgenstein in that paper's arguments is obvious: he famously urges us against taking there to be objects corresponding to all our putatively referring expressions and says of grief, for example, that it "describes a pattern which recurs, with different variations, in the weave of our life." (Wittgenstein 1958, p. 174) Less obvious is the influence of Quine, whose naturalizing of ontology deflates the metaphysical pretensions of attempts to say, quite generally, what there is: on Quine's view, to be is to be among the things our best theory is a theory about, the things that have to exist for that theory to be literally true. (See especially Quine 1969) The singular ('theory') is important: Quine argues for there being a fundamental physics that accounts (at least in theory) for every occurrence at every point in space-time. Such a commitment is common even among explicitly anti-reductionist theorists, who typically appeal to a Quinean distinction between "ontology" (what exists, including real causes) and "ideology" (what we say about what exists). They argue that one ontology can underlie a host of different theories, each of which describes the things that there are in different ways.

Thus—to take the commonest example—it is argued that psychological theories are irreducible to physics, and psychological descriptions are irreplaceable by physical descriptions, but the states themselves that are the objects of psychological theorizing are physical states and all causality is fundamentally physical causality. The aim of "Against Physicalism" is to argue that this way of thinking is incoherent, that in general irreducible theories have irreducible ontologies. I also reject the exceedingly stringent requirements Quine imposes on acceptable theories, arguing that, specifically in the case of psychological states, what matters for "ontological commitment" is rather our commitment to the practices—including explanatory practices—that make those states, and the causal connections they enter into, real.

To the best of my knowledge the arguments in "Against Physicalism" have not been picked up by the philosophers of psychology whose views are the objects of my critique. Part of the reason for that is that I have not tried to publish in the venues in which that work appears, superficially because I have always been working on something that was specifically requested, never on something I wrote first and then submitted. More significantly, although I think the arguments in that paper can be stated in relatively formal, totally nonpolitical ways (as I would need to do to publish in those venues), that is not how I think of them, nor is it why I think they really matter. What seems to me most important is that we become attentive to, and responsible for, the practices that structure our own and each other's lives, the ways we make ourselves and each other intelligible. We need, that is, to take the realm of the socially constructed seriously, meaning that particular things like emotions and beliefs, as well as categories like race and gender, are real because and insofar as we make them so.

"Feeling Our Way toward Moral Objectivity" takes up issues such as these. It was written for a conference at Washington University in 1994 on "Mind and Morals," which aimed at opening a dialogue between ethics and cognitive science. I started from the characterization of mental states as socially constructed—that is, as existing as particular states only in the context of particular social practices—along with a view, which I share with many, especially feminist, philosophers, of the importance of emotions to moral perception and judgment. I argued that, while it might seem that each of these views makes trouble for any conception of moral objectivity, taken together they give us a characterization of objective moral judgment that is both theoretically coherent and practically useful.

What Alison Jaggar (1989) has named "outlaw emotions"—emotions one is not supposed to have—can point to practices that do not stand up to scrutiny, that rely for their perpetuation on general collusion in ignorance: think about the Emperor's New Clothes. Outlaw laughter—or outrage or sorrow—may not initially make sense, or may make sense only to those on the margins, and the work to make it intelligible can reveal the conceptual scaffolding that holds in place both the practices that are the object of the outlaw emotion and the normative unintelligibility of the emotional response. The process of clarification is a spiral, no moment of which is beyond critique: just because an emotional response is "outlaw," there is no guarantee that it is a trustworthy guide to what is going on. But our attention is drawn to what is usually obscured—as the attention of the supplicants to the Wizard of Oz is drawn to the little man behind the curtain—allowing critique to gain a foothold.

The final essay in this section takes this question on explicitly. I wrote "Queering the Center by Centering the Queer: Reflections on Transsexuals and Secular Jews" for two different collections: one on feminist takes on the self and subjectivity and one that followed from a conference that brought together gender theorists with clinicians who worked with children diagnosed with "gender dysphoria." I initially thought I had nothing to say for the latter occasion, mostly because I was stuck in my inability to understand what, specifically, male-to female transsexuals meant when they claimed to be women. The essay began to take shape when I realized that I was finding their claims impossible to understand because I was finding my own claim to be a woman too readily comprehensible.

This way of putting things—finding one phenomenon difficult to understand because of taking some other phenomenon to be obviously comprehensible—is explicitly Wittgensteinian: "We find certain things about seeing puzzling, because we do not find the whole business of seeing puzzling enough." (from his discussion of "seeing as," Wittgenstein 1958, Part II, xi) It is also a clear version of the charge made against white feminist theorists by feminist theorists of color that we were taking ourselves as the standard of what it was to be a woman. Both exemplify the habit of taking oneself to be "intelligibility central": if something makes sense at all, it makes sense here, to me. (In another manifestation of this bad habit, analytic philosophers are taught to say "I don't understand" when they mean "you aren't making sense.") The essay became writable when I attempted to displace myself from the position of intelligibility central with regard to gender, a difficult thing to do. In figuring out how to do it, I was helped by reading and conversing with people whose relations to normative gender construction were less easy (transparent, i.e., invisible) than my own, and in part by looking at what I knew from my own unintelligible location, that of a secular Jew.[1]

The epigraph to that paper is from Jenny Holzer: "Confusing yourself is a way to stay honest." Even better, I suggest, is letting other people confuse you, allowing them to shake your confidence that you know your way around the concepts that structure your life. María Lugones exhorts white women to acknowledge that women of color are "faithful mirrors," showing one of the people we are, and showing that we are many— "something that may in itself be frightening." (Lugones 1991; in Lugones 2003a, 72) The illusion of singular selfhood is like the illusion of singular, unequivocal meaning: each rests on a simplified abstraction from a singular, privileged perspective. To let others confuse me (notably others without my privileges and whose ally I would like to see myself as being) reveals the mechanisms—reveals that there are mechanisms— that hold my identity and the meanings of my words in place, and opens the possibility that I might be disloyal to those mechanisms.

---

1. After writing that essay (and nearly all the others in this collection) I became aware of the work of a group of activist scholars on a project called the Future of Minority Studies. (See Moya and Hames 2000, and Mohanty et.al. 2005) One of their aims in crafting what they call a "post-positivist realist" understanding of group identity is to argue for the epistemic value of identity, as a lens through which the world is made sense of. Drawing on Richard Boyd's conception of scientific realism (Boyd 1981), they argue that it is precisely the role identities play in shaping observation and knowledge that allows for an objective account of identities: as we act more effectively in the world on the basis of our identity-inflected understandings, we get confirmation of the reality of those identities. I have an odd relationship to this project: without my knowing it, an essay of mine from the mid-1970s ("Anger and the Politics of Naming") served as a sort of seed crystal around which Satya Mohanty developed the core theoretical approach of post-positivist realism. But while that essay is frequently referred to as the FMS project develops, their work and my own subsequent work moved along parallel tracks without intersecting until I discovered them a few years ago.

Chapter 5

Against Physicalism

We talk of processes and states, and leave their nature undecided. Sometime perhaps we shall know more about them—we
think. But that's just what commits us to a particular way of
looking at the matter. For we have a definite conception of what
it means to learn to know a process better. (The decisive movement in the conjuring trick has been made, and it was the very
one we thought quite innocent.)—And now the analogy which
was to make us understand our thoughts falls to pieces. So we
have to deny the yet uncomprehended process in the yet unex-
plored medium. And now it looks as if we had denied mental
processes. And naturally we don't want to deny them.
>   Ludwig Wittgenstein, *Philosophical Investigations* §308

When I do not see plurality stressed in the very structure of a
theory, I know that I will have to do lots of acrobatics—like a
contortionist or tight-rope walker—to have this theory speak to
me without allowing the theory to distort me in my complexity.
>   María Lugones, "On the Logic of Pluralist Feminism"

INTRODUCTION

For most contemporary analytic philosophers, the physical sciences are the
lodestone both for epistemology and for ontology; other ways of knowing
and other ways of saying what there is have somehow to be squared
with what physics might come to say. In the philosophy of mind, central
problems arise from the difficulties in accounting for the phenomena of
consciousness (in Thomas Nagel's terms 'what it's like to be' a subject of
experience), and from the apparent intractability (compared, say, to chemistry or even biology) of psychological explanations. This sense that—both
ontologically and epistemologically—something distinctively mental would
be unaccounted for, after physics had accounted for everything it could,
has often been taken to motivate dualism: the mental is left over after
the physical is accounted for just as (though, of course, not nearly so
unproblematically) the forks are left over after the spoons are accounted for.

Feminists have been critical of dualism in part for its implicit if not explicit privileging of the mind over the body and for the misunderstanding of each that results from their being prised apart. Such criticisms remain apt even in relation to accounts that, while metaphysically non-dualist, nonetheless continue to prise the mental apart from the physical, by abstracting such phenomena as memory from their attachment to (better: their realization in) specific, socially embedded bodies. But if dualism has been unappealing to feminists, its usual alternative—physicalism—has seemed to many an unpalatable alternative, in large measure because the sort of attention to bodies that feminists typically urge is not the attention of the scientist to an object of study, but the attention of a subject to her or his own experience, as well as the attention of diversely engaged others.[1]

Feminists' work on topics such as the emotions, the nature of the self and of personal identity, and the relations between minds and bodies can seem irrelevant to the issues that concern physicalists: the starting points, the puzzles and perplexities that call for theorizing, seem quite different. I want to argue that the appearance of irrelevance is misleading: while it is true that feminist theorists are asking different questions and thereby avoiding direct answers to the questions posed in the literature around physicalism, the reorientation of attention characteristic of the feminist questions usefully reframes the problems that vex that literature— problems of accounting for ourselves as physical beings in the world. In particular, what comes to be crucial in accounting for psychological explanation are the ways in which such explanations are irreducibly *social*, a 'problem' to which dualism is an entirely irrelevant response. Understanding our emotions, beliefs, attitudes, desires, intentions, and the like (including how it is that they can cause and be caused by happenings in the physical world) is akin to understanding families, universities, wars, elections, economies, and religious schisms: positing some special sort of substance out of which such things are made would hardly help, nor does it seem metaphysically spooky that there is no way, even in principle, of specifying, on the level of physics, just what they *are* made of. (The university buildings count, but what about the dirt on their floors? If we count the faculty, do we count the food in their stomachs?)

Consider the performance of a piece of music. There is nothing going on *in addition to* the physical movements of the bodies of the members of the orchestra, but there is no way, appealing just to physics, to specify which of those movements are parts of the complex event that is the performance and which are not. What is and is not part of the event has to do with what sort of thing a performance is, what norms and expectations determine what its parts are. For example, the first violinist's coughing is not typically part of the performance, but it certainly can be—

---

1. On feminist accounts of the specifically social nature of the self, see, for example, among philosophers in the analytic tradition, Baier (1985b), Friedman (1991), and Lugones (1987 and 1991).

if, for example, it's written into the score. When it comes to identifying the performance as a cause, there are two very different possibilities. To say, for example, that the performance caused a crack in the ceiling is to say that there are physical events more or less loosely associated with the performance that caused the cracking, but the performance *per se* is not among them (that certain sounds are part of the performance is irrelevant to whether they contributed to causing the crack). If, by contrast, as with the premiere in Paris of Stravinsky's *Le sacre du printemps*, the performance caused a riot, its being a musical performance (something about which the audience had certain expectations) is crucial: in this case the performance *per se* was the cause, but not as a physical event, since it is not one. To say that a performance is not a physical event is not to embrace some odd form of dualism; it is to acknowledge that, from the perspective of physics, the performance is not a particular complex event—one whose (physical) causes and effects we can inquire into—but rather an inchoate jumble of events. Performances are 'socially constructed', meaning that their integrity as particulars is dependent on sets of social practices that make them meaningful wholes.

It is not, of course, at all clear how to relate social explanations to physical ones: the relationships between the social and physical sciences are deeply vexed. But the problems are importantly different from those that have engaged the philosophy of mind, less likely to provoke the a prioristic metaphysical demands that characterize the discussions of physicalism, however empirical those discussions are meant to be. What I want to suggest is this: in explaining ourselves to ourselves and to each other we allude to such things as beliefs, intentions, emotions, desires, and attitudes. Physicalism consists in the claim (specified and argued for in a wide range of very different ways) that, insofar as these explanations are true, the events, states, and processes to which they refer must be identical with or somehow dependent upon or determined by events, states, and processes in or of the body of the person to whom they are attributed. Such a claim is neither required for nor supported by empirical research that shows how it is that, for example, emotional responses are related to changes in brain chemistry. Surely how we act and feel has enormously to do with what goes on in our bodies, but recognizing that fact no more supports the claims of physicalists than recognizing the importance of physiology to the carrying out of the actions that constitute a performance or a riot would support the claim that physiology explains why the premiere of *Le sacre du printemps* caused a riot. The performance as such does not survive abstraction from social context, and neither do its causal powers: its "realness" and its causal efficacy are dependent in part on its being the socially meaningful type of thing that it is. Similarly, I will argue, beliefs, desires, emotions, and other phenomena of our mental lives are the particulars that they are because they are socially meaningful, and when they figure as those particulars in causal accounts, neither those accounts nor the phenomena that figure in them survive abstraction from social context.

Most of those working in the philosophy of mind today subscribe to one or another of the dizzyingly many varieties of physicalism. They share a demand for the mental to be composed of, or determined by, the physical—however differently they work out the details—in some way that attributes to mental phenomena not only continuity with the physical but also the sort of reality that the physical is presumed to have, including independence from our practices of noticing and naming. The failure of such independence, the possibility that much of what we talk about when we talk about our mental lives—our beliefs, emotions, desires, attitudes, intentions, and such—do not exist as determinate physical "somethings", is thought to undermine the possibility of taking such talk seriously, of taking it to be part of a true account of what there is in the world. It is here that feminist discussions both in the philosophy of mind and in seemingly remote areas can shed light, since they lead us to see the importance and the possibility of holding on *both* to the idea that our mental lives are constituted in part by the ways we collectively talk and think about them, *and* to the idea that such talking and thinking are not arbitrary and that the realm of the mental is no less real for being in this sense "made up".

Disputes among feminist theorists frequently take the following form: theorists of type A argue against the appeal to absolute standards of truth or rightness that exist in abstraction from our lives and practices, on the grounds that such appeals reflect a suspicion of plurality and diversity and a disdain for that which is local, particular, contextual, contingent, embedded, and embodied; while theorists of type B argue for the importance of standards of truth or rightness that are independent of what people happen to do or say, on the grounds that what most people happen to do and say—expert discourses and common sense alike—is prone to sexist and other forms of bias, and that we need a more compelling response than simply that we don't like it. Thus arise the debates between universalists and particularists in ethics, essentialists and social constructionists in gender and sexuality theory, empiricists and postmodernists in philosophy of science, objectivists and relativists in epistemology. The tendentious nature of all those labels reflects the divisiveness of the disputes, a divisiveness that obscures the fact that for many of us the disputes are internal to any position we might occupy. They are, I want to suggest, better thought of as necessary tensions, as reminders of the theoretical and political importance *both* of attention to diversity and particularity *and* of non-arbitrary, rationally defensible justification.[2]

One way of characterizing the disputes is as between the suspicion of and the demand for some special kind of thing, which answers to our

2. On the recasting of the central schisms between feminists as fruitful tensions, see Snitow (1989).

needs precisely by being independent of them, by being what it is—Reality or the Good, the essence of something or the measure of an argument—no matter what we might think or do. Such disputes are not, of course, peculiar to feminist theory: they are arguably at the heart of the problems of modern philosophy, where, however, they tend to be treated as purely intellectual puzzles. In their feminist articulations, they reanimate the very practical urgency that gave birth to them—in the turmoil of early modernity, out of the need to ground the claims to truth and rightness being made by upstart rebels against the prevailing standards of a theocratic and aristocratic social order. As part of those struggles it was necessary to articulate new conceptions of the nature of persons and their states, the subject matter of the philosophy of mind. Feminist perspectives at this late stage of modernity throw into relief the historical specificity of those projects of articulation—for example, the field-defining epic struggle between the self as subject of inner experience, abstracted from the surrounding world (even, supposedly, from its own body) and the body as object of scientific scrutiny.

Feminist perspectives shift attention to understanding persons as both bodily and social, and knowledge as interpersonal and interactive. Physicalism then appears not so much false as empty: ontologically, it puzzles over how to establish a relationship—whether of identity or of some form of supervenience (see discussion below)—between what ought not to have been analytically distinguished in the first place; and epistemologically, it concedes to (a philosopher's fantasy of) physics a dominating role even over explanatory schemes explicitly being argued to be non-reducible to it. To reject physicalism is not, as Wittgenstein says, to deny anything—not anything, that is, by way of actual investigation into or explanation of how our experienced lives are shaped by our being the bodies that we are. What is denied is the demand that such explanations have either to underwrite or to supplant the accounts of those lives that rest on appeal to the social practices and norms that make us the persons that we are.

THE DEMANDS OF PHYSICALISM

Jennifer Hornsby (1997), in a series of articles going back to 1980 and collected in her book, *Simple Mindedness*, argues against the ontological foundations of physicalist theses. One of the central targets of these arguments is what she identifies as "mereological conceptions" of the objects in an ontology, according to which relatively big objects can be identified with the unique "fusion" of the smaller objects—their parts—which make them up. John Dupré similarly identifies mereological conceptions as at the heart of what he finds problematic about physicalism (or any requirement of a unified account of diverse phenomena). Both these authors (see Dupré 1993, p. 90; Hornsby 1997, p. 12) see themselves as blocking at some very early stage a frequently unvoiced argumentative move that not only licenses a range of diverse positions but frames the arguments between them. Such a move, if noticed at all, can seem obvious, unavoidable: avoiding it can seem like being committed to something like a soul, a mysterious addition to the physical stuff that constitutes the goings on in and of our bodies.[3]

Supervenience theses most explicitly mobilize this picture, since, unlike other physicalist theses, they typically are mute about actual explanation and insistent on what are taken to be the requirements on the possibility of any explanations at all. Consider the following:

> We think of the world around us not as a mere assemblage of objects, events, and facts, but as constituting a system, something that shows structure, and whose constituents are connected with one another in significant ways...
> Central to this idea of interconnectedness of things is a notion of dependence (or its converse, determination): things are connected with one another in that whether something exists, or what properties it has, is dependent on, or determined by, what other things exist and what kinds of things they are...
> Activities like explanation, prediction, and control would make little sense for a world devoid of such connections. The idea that 'real connections' exist and the idea that the world is intelligible and controllable are arguably an equivalent idea (Kim 1993, p.53; reprinted from Kim 1984).

This paragraph is the start of an essay in which Jaegwon Kim lays out a range of supervenience theses.[4] He goes on to argue for the strongest among them, on the grounds that only it can meet the demands he lays out here. The demands themselves, however, are widely accepted among physicalists, including those who believe they can be met by some form of non-reductive supervenience, much weaker than the reductionism Kim promotes. The paragraph perfectly accomplishes the slide from saying something quite ordinary to being in the grip of a picture, one that leads us to lay down requirements on what the world, or our accounts of the world, *must* be like.[5] The argument is a transcendental one: given that explanation is possible, what *must* be the case? The appeal is to (what is taken to be) explanation *per se*, not to the details of particular explanations or explanatory practices. Later in the same essay, in fact, Kim (1984, pp. 175–76) explicitly argues for the importance of separating metaphysical from epistemological considerations: the mental can be said to be determined by the physical whether or not we ever could be in a position to provide the explanations that determinacy underwrites. The picture (and on

---

3. For an account of and argument for an anti-dualist anti-physicalism, which draws on Dennett's distinction between the personal and the sub-personal, see Hornsby (2000).

4. Kim actually argues in this essay that the positions he calls 'strong' and 'global' supervenience are equivalent, and to be contrasted with (and preferred to) what he calls 'weak' supervenience. He was later persuaded that this equivalence doesn't hold and that global supervenience is, in fact, too weak a principle to be intelligibly defended. See Kim (1993, pp. 82–6; reprinted from Kim 1987). I will discuss global supervenience below.

5. On the laying down of requirements, see Diamond (1991e). On the slide into the problematically philosophical, see Goldfarb (1983).

this point there is wide agreement with Kim) is that physicalism provides the ontological grounds for the possibility of mental explanations, however autonomous or irreducible such explanations might be argued to be.

A linchpin of Kim's arguments (1989) to the conclusion that attempts at non-reductive supervenience are doomed is what he calls the principle of "causal closure": "If we trace the causal ancestry of a physical event, we need never go outside the physical domain." Davidson and Fodor, among many others, explicitly commit themselves to essentially this principle (though they disagree with Kim as to its consequences), and it is one that Hornsby and Dupré, among others, have challenged. I am persuaded by those challenges, but want, for the purpose of this chapter, largely to bracket that issue and focus instead on the question of ontology. In the passage quoted from Kim, he refers repeatedly to "things", as in "things that happen," and at the start of the passage he refers to "objects, events, and facts". For his argument to work, such "things" need to be related in ways that exhibit structure, they depend on and determine each other, their "real connections" are what make the world intelligible.[6] One of my central arguments is that taking commonsense psychology seriously is to be committed *not* to a theoretically vexing ontology of objects (mental events, states, and processes), but rather to practices, explanation among them, and to the nuances of our lives as shaped and made intelligible through those practices.

For Kim, as for some others, notably Davidson, the "things" in question are pre-eminently events, and there are long arguments between them and others as to what it is that events are. Beyond those arguments lies an even murkier ontological swamp—the "states and processes" that usually get appended to the list of mental phenomena.[7] Any physicalist theory is going to have to say something about the ontology of swamp-dwellers— something that provides a way, in theory at least, of individuating the contents of the swamp independently of the norm-laden, interpretive social practices that characterize commonsense psychology. Those "things" have to be individuated in ways that suit their role in the properly physical causal accounts in which they are thought to have to figure if common sense is to be scientifically vindicated. Issues about individuation often slip by, as "the initial move in the conjuring trick", the assumption that mental events, states, and processes are particulars whose nature can be investigated: we can ask what *they* are, whether *they* are identical with

---

6. Here I don't take exception to Kim's use of 'things' *per se*. I myself use 'phenomena' in a way that won't stand up to heavy ontological scrutiny. For the use of 'phenomena' as an ontologically neutral umbrella term, see Rey (1997, footnote 4, p. 13). My own use is even more neutral than his, since he claims neutrality only with respect to the *sort* of phenomenon in question (event, state, process, etc.), whereas I intend to be neutral on the prior question of ontological commitment.

7. Steward (1997) argues for shifting the question of mental causation from that of causal relations between such an array of entities (she argues for reserving that relation to events) and toward an account of causal relevance, which holds among facts and which does not raise the sort of problems, such as over-determination, which have both driven and plagued the philosophy of mind.

or constituted by physical events, states, and processes, and how *they* enter into causal relationships.

When Robert Wilson, in a careful and detailed account of individualism in the philosophy of mind, says that anti-individualist arguments have concerned taxonomic rather than instantial individuation, he is, I think, right. Wilson (1995, pp. 21–25) suggests that one cannot ask whether A is the same as B (a question of instantial individuation) without asking what sorts of things A and B are taken to be (a taxonomic question). Davidson's anomalous monism exploits the idea that the framework of space-time can provide for material objects, and the framework of causation can provide for events, a way of individuating that doesn't depend on any *finer* taxonomizing. That solution is, however, ultimately question-begging, in its assumption that, in particular in the case of events, the presumptively closed and complete system of physical causation individuates all the events that there are.[8] As my example of the performance was meant to suggest, this assumption is deeply problematic, amounting to what Davidson and other non-reductive physicalists are committed to denying—that the explanatory system within which the performance exists as a particular complex event (in terms of which we can make sense of what's part of it and what isn't) can ultimately be reduced to (or otherwise explicated in terms of) physics. If it can't be—if, in general, the discourses with respect to which we understand performances, or our mental lives, can't be systematically connected to physics—then the objects that are constituted in its terms will not be *any* sorts of physical objects, since, with respect to physics, they will have the status not of complex objects but of incoherent jumbles or heaps—certainly not the sorts of things to enter as particulars into nomological causal relationships.

THE USEFUL VACUITY OF GLOBAL SUPERVENIENCE

> Nothing happens in the world, not the flutter of an eyelid, not the flicker of a thought, without some redistribution of microphysical states.
>
>   W. V. Quine, *Theories and Things*

---

8. See Davidson's argument (1980, p. 180) that this is the case. For a similar argument to mine against the idea that token identities can survive the demise of any theory connecting types, see Putnam (1979). Putnam recognized, as Davidson did not, that views about the holistic, normative nature of psychological explanation are incompatible with taking such explanations to be *about* things whose existence as particulars is independent of the practices that ground the explanations. The claim for such independence is often made by separating what Quine referred to as "ideology" from "ontology," a move that proceeds as though in general an ontology—a range of particulars—survives abstraction from a specific way of characterizing what those particulars are, including how those that are complex are constituted. (See the discussion in Rey (1997, pp. 179–80).) The ideology/ontology distinction is, I think, one way of accomplishing the "initial move in the conjuring trick".

...a thesis of such blinding epistemological vacuity as to add
nothing to the thesis of the nonexistence of the immaterial
John Dupré, "Metaphysical Disorder and Scientific Disunity"

Global supervenience, which is frequently criticized as both excessively
permissive and explanatorily opaque, has a role for theorists like Dupré
and Hornsby in making the point that the denial of the existence of
immaterial stuff does not commit one to physicalism.[9] As such it is
proffered not as a positive thesis but as a way of granting the falsehood
of dualism and of articulating the minimal truth of physicalism (so minimal as not to count as physicalism on the terms of most physicalists).
Thus Dupré (1993, p. 91) says: "If one removed from the universe all the
physical entities...there would be nothing left." Global supervenience
has been formalized by John Haugeland, though that is not his term for it.
(He calls it "weak supervenience", which for most authors in this termi-
nologically confusing literature refers to something quite else, involving
a different parameter of variation among theses from the one that concerns me here.) Haugeland's formulation (1982, p. 97) (replacing his use
of 'weakly' with 'globally') is: "K *globally supervenes on* L (relative to W)
just in case any two worlds in W discernible with K are discernible
with L." (K and L are languages, W is a set of possible worlds. For present
purposes let L be the language of microphysics and K be the language of
commonsense psychology.)

Global supervenience captures the idea that if anything happens at all,
something has to happen on the level of microphysics. If everywhere and
for all of time all the microparticles (or whatever microphysics turns out
to be about) were exactly as they in fact are, then nothing *else* could be any
different. What is important to note is just how weak this thesis is. It does
not imply token identities. (Haugeland in fact proposes it explicitly as
an alternative to token identities, which, he argues, fail for cases far
less complex than the mental.)[10] Nor does it imply that supervening
(e.g., mental) events are "determined by" or "dependent upon" physical
events—an implication that is crucial for what most theorists want out of
a supervenience principle and partly definitive of what is meant by
'physicalism'.[11]

The point of calling global supervenience "global" is to stress (what
"serious" supervenience theorists find problematic) that there need be no

9. Hornsby never explicitly endorses any form of supervenience, but I have no reason to think that
she would find global supervenience, as I am understanding it, problematic. She is certainly not committed to Cartesian, or substance, dualism; her argument is that it is a mistake to think that dualism and
physicalism (all events/objects are physical events/objects) exhaust the ontological options.

10. His example is of "wave hits" caused by waves from two directions converging on a bobbing cork
(Haugeland, 1982, pp. 100–01).

11. It is not clear to me how much of what I say Haugeland would agree with. His argument is meant
to show that physicalism does not require token identities, but it is not clear to me what Haugeland means
by physicalism, in particular, whether he appreciates and accepts just how very weak what he calls weak
supervenience is and whether he would argue against any "stronger" thesis.

spatial or temporal contiguity between a difference on the supervening level and a difference in the supervenience base. A difference in my mental state need not be correlated with a difference in my body or in anything near or causally connected to my body,[12] nor must there be a physically describable difference simultaneous with or prior to the mental difference. All that matters is that there be some difference, even if far away and long ago or even yet to come. Such laxity is frequently expressed as a (supposed) reductio: Post (1995, p. 76) calls it ARFL, the "argument from licentiousness". But whether such laxness counts for or against global supervenience ought to depend on what sorts of connections one thinks there actually are. It is a feature, for example, of many of our ordinary psychological terms that whether they truly apply can be a genuinely open question with respect to everything, known or unknown, in the present or the past, but become retroactively settled by something in the future.

It is, of course, precisely features of commonsense psychology such as this that many psychologists and philosophers of psychology will want to "clean up", in part by imposing constraints on what can belong in the supervenience base. But such constraints have nothing to do with avoiding substance dualism and ought to reflect, rather than dictate, ordinary judgments of explanatory adequacy. One may, for example, believe that the best (most explanatory, most nearly true) accounts of love include this feature: that ascriptions of it remain, up to a certain point (as Aristotle argued for happiness) hostage to the future. Up to that point it can be indeterminate, to be settled by how things go on, whether or not one's feelings are really love.[13] And if one thinks that, one will, for reasons having to do with explanatory adequacy, reject a restriction of the supervenience base to the present and past. A common move at this point is to posit some state that, it is claimed, does supervene on the person's current physical state—as, for example, the notion of narrow content was developed to try to deal with arguments about the non-individualist nature of propositional attitudes. But if, as I will argue below, our beliefs, attitudes, desires, and so on are explanatory—have, for example, the causes and effects that they do—in virtue of their being socially meaningful, then such posits will lose their point, which is precisely their supposed explanatory role.

Thus, the "licentiousness" that physicalists deplore in global supervenience—the fact that it licenses neither token identities nor theses of determination or dependency—is part of its appeal—not because anything goes, but because the question of what goes and what doesn't cannot, and

---

12. Thus, the insights of Tyler Burge, Hilary Putnam, and others about the social nature of the content of propositional attitudes goes much deeper than is usually presumed and cannot, for example, be met by appeals to narrow content.

13. For a fuller discussion of this example, see chapter 6. See also Wittgenstein (1967, §504): "Love is not a feeling. Love is put to the test, pain not. One does not say: "That was not true pain, or it would not have gone off so quickly.'"

should not, be settled a priori. Kim (1993, p. 159; reprinted from Kim 1990) charges adherents to global supervenience with accepting it as "a mere article of faith seriously lacking in motivation both evidentially and explanatorily", but as I am appealing to it, it no more requires either evidence or explanatory usefulness than does my non-belief in imperceptible and causally inert fairies. The work that appears to be done by physicalist theses—including reductionism, eliminativism, functionalism, and token identity theses—is actually done by complex and diverse explanations, including explanations that may be locally reductive. We may in particular areas have well-founded expectations for one or another sort of explanation, but those expectations do not rest on, nor are the successes explained by or evidence for, any metaphysical theses such as physicalism in any of its forms. The unmotivated act of faith is, thus, on the part of the physicalists, who not only have boundless and groundless faith in the explanatory powers of some unimaginably remote Future Physics, but who are willing to sacrifice common sense (as well as real science) on its altar, placing ontological requirements on the objects of explanation in advance of working out what those explanations are.

TAKING EXPLANATION SERIOUSLY

> How could human behaviour be described? Surely only by sketching the actions of a variety of humans, as they are all mixed up together. What determines our judgement, our concepts and reactions, is not what one is doing now, an individual action, but the whole hurly-burly of human actions, the background against which we see any action.
>
> Wittgenstein, *Zettel* §167

If we actually look at psychological explanations—in particular, if we attend to the aspects of those explanations that lead functionalists and Davidsonian anomalous monists, among others, to reject the reductionism of type-identity theories—we find that the phenomena that give such explanations their explanatory force cannot be identified with, or be determined by, particular physical phenomena, for two general, related sorts of reasons. First, the anomalousness of psychological explanations entails that the phenomena that figure in them cannot be presumed to satisfy the constraints on being a physical particular, and will, in fact, typically fairly obviously *fail* to satisfy such constraints, however loosely conceived. And second, in many cases in which psychological explanations *can* be seen to rest in some sense on physical goings-on, such "supervenience" is on happenings that are sufficiently scattered and remote in space and time as to defeat any general, substantive claim of determining supervenience. The irreducibility of psychological explanation is inherited by psychological ontology: we have no grip on what the phenomena of psychology are other than whatever they have to be for psychological explanations to be true.[14] In general, our ordinary explanations of human action, thought, and feeling appeal to social practices and norms; and there is no reason to require, and much reason to deny, that our *best* explanations will be compatible with an ontology whose objects' individuation is independent of the social and the normative.

I want to urge an understanding of socially constructed phenomena that has close connections with understandings, such as those of Dupré (1993), Hacking (1986, 1992) and Root (1993, pp. 149–72; 2000), of socially constructed kinds.[15] Such kinds can figure in explanation, even causal explanation. Consider:

1.   Q: Why didn't Alex get a heart attack when she was younger?
     A: Because she's a woman.
2.   Q: Why didn't Alex become CEO of the corporation?
     A: Because she's a woman.
3.   Q: Why does Alex use the toilet marked with a stick figure with a triangle in its middle?
     A: Because she's a woman.

In the first exchange, referring to Alex's being a woman points in the direction of some physiological property that accounts for her having been less at risk of a heart attack. "Woman" need not be a biologically real kind; gender can be (as many feminist theorists have argued) socially constructed, perhaps to be distinguished from sex, which some have argued *is* biologically real. The explanation works by gesturing toward something both causally related to the risk of heart attacks and typically true of those in the social category "woman", though by no means true of all women (like, for example, the currently suspected property in question, namely, the presence of relatively high levels of estrogen). The answer in the second exchange is explanatory, by contrast, because of the social significance of the category "woman"; thus, it might function as a cautionary admonition to a biological male contemplating sex change. Not only does this explanation give us no reason to attribute biological reality to the category "woman", but any biological category that might be proposed would inevitably lead to a "cleaning up" around the edges that would hurt rather than help explanations such as this one (whereas explanations like the first, while useful as they stand, would be helped by replacing the

14. The parallel to Quine's famous dictum "To be is to be the value of a variable" is, of course, intentional. I would argue, however, that psychological explanation cannot be sufficiently regimented to meet Quinean standards for ontological commitment, and that, in fact, there is no good reason to commit ourselves to any particular *ontology* for the mental at all, which is not to say that we don't have good grounds for committing ourselves to the possibility of objectively true psychological explanations.

15. Root develops an account of what he calls "real social kinds," whose realness consists in the ways in which systematic social practices make all those things (typically, people) that fall within the kind interchangeable. He argues that social kinds are relative to times and places, reflecting the variability of the relevant social practices: if, for example, race or gender is real here and now, it is because we make it so.

social category with the relevant biological one, if any). The third exchange is explanatory in a rather different sense. It notes a connection between gender and segregated public toilets, and what exactly is being explained is a matter of what the questioner can be presumed not to know or to understand: it might, for example, explicate the meaning of the international sign for 'women's toilet', or it might be a reply, albeit a somewhat impatient one, to someone who finds Alex's womanhood questionable, perhaps because, unlike the stick figure, Alex does not wear skirts.

Mental phenomena can be real in the same sort of way. Through our social practices we interpret as meaningful bits of experience that may well be related in significant, non-social ways (as people who share a race or a gender will typically be similar or otherwise related in many non-social ways). But those relationships are not such as to constitute particular entities of any sort. That constitution is done by our finding and acting on patterns of salience, interpreting ourselves and each other, and having and acting on expectations formed in the light of those interpretations. As feminists have argued, for example, not just anyone can be angry at any time, since part of what constitutes the pattern that counts as anger has to do with who you are and whom you might be thought to be angry at, about what, and so on (Frye 1983b; Scheman 1980). It was easier not to notice this fact when theorizing was in the hands of those who were less likely to run up against the limits of intelligibility and who, when they did, had little reason to see their failure to make sense as anything other than an idiosyncratic glitch. (Similarly, noticing the social constructedness of gender was greatly helped by the experiences of those, such as transsexuals, whose identities were, according to the biologically naturalized view of gender, literally impossible.)

Consider the following explanations:

1a. Q: Why did her blood pressure shoot up?
     A: It must have been because she got angry.
2a. Q: Why did he fire her?
     A: It must have been because she got angry.
3a. Q: Why do they think she hates men?
     A: It must be because she got angry.

The first and second examples offer causal explanations and would seem to call for an account of her getting angry that indicates how it can cause something in her body, or some piece of his behavior. By analogy with the first set of examples, however, neither 1a) nor 2a) supports the idea that her getting angry is (or supervenes on or is determined by) some particular physical event(s). In 1a) we can adequately account for the explanatoriness of A while taking anger to be a socially salient pattern of behavior, thoughts, and bodily feelings—once we note that the feelings typical of getting angry are correlated with sorts of bodily tension that can cause a rise in blood pressure. Particular emotions are more or less closely associated with bodily feeling (anger more closely than happiness, less closely than rage), and the nature of such associations is one of the ways in which cultures differ in their emotional repertoires, explanations, and styles.[16] What is important to note—just as with explaining the ceiling crack by blaming the performance or explaining Alex's lesser vulnerability to heart attack by her being a woman—is that as we move toward the more physically explanatory account, getting angry *per se* drops out; what matters is the tension, not what the tension means.

In 2a), by contrast, her getting angry (that it's angry that she got) does not drop out of the explanation—any more than the performance drops out of the explanation of the riot or Alex's being a woman drops out of the explanation of her not being promoted. He fired her because of what he took anger to mean and because of his views about its (in)appropriateness for a woman. In Davidsonian terms, we can put the point by saying that the anomalousness of psychological explanation is inherited by psychological ontology. The normative, interpretive element in psychological explanation enters into the construction of psychological phenomena. No more physicalistically respectable phenomenon could play the causal role getting angry plays in this explanation (as getting tense plays such a role in 1a), since abstracting from the social constructedness means abstracting from the context-specific, normatively laden nature of (her) anger, and hence from precisely what makes an appeal to it explanatory.

The third example would not usually be regarded as offering a causal explanation: rather, getting angry (at something like that) is taken by A to be part of what it is to be a feminist. Furthermore, we can argue over whether to count whatever she said and did as anger, as well as whether to count her anger as marking her as a feminist. The patterns we note as salient and what we take them to signify are matters for real dispute, as real and as resolvable as are disputes over causal explanations; and we need an account of emotions and other psychological phenomena that makes such disputes intelligible.

One might ask at this point whether we, the serious participants in the discursive practices of commonsense psychology, are ontologically committed to such things as beliefs, desires, attitudes, intentions, and emotions. Yes and no. No—if by 'ontological commitment' you mean, as Quine meant, that the phenomena in question need to be in the domain over which range the bound variables of a well-regimented theory that we regard as (approximately) true. There is no particular reason to believe (and some good reason to doubt) that the explanatory practices of commonsense psychology will (or should) ever be so regimented. Nor is there reason to think that anything is to be gained by insisting on the role of specifically nominalized explanations: on 'her anger' rather than 'she was angry', on 'his belief' rather than 'he believes', on 'her arrogance' rather than 'she's talking arrogantly'. But yes—if what's at stake (and I do

---

16. Bodily goings-on are taken to be differently significant, to form a more or less central part of patterns that are emotions, in different cultures. See for example Rosaldo (1989, pp. 1–21).

think this is what matters more) is the possibility of objective, true accounts of ourselves and each other, accounts that we can intelligibly challenge and revise, justify and rebut, accounts that actually explain. That sort of commitment requires not theoretical regimentation but seriousness about our roles and stakes in the practices that construct the phenomena to which we are committed.

Thus, far from urging with respect to commonsense psychology something analogous to Moore's "Defence of Common Sense" with respect to physical objects, I am arguing that attention to our practices is needed precisely because what we are presumed to have in common, what "we" do or say is, from a feminist perspective, far from unproblematic. "The common woman", the poet Judy Grahn (1973) told us, "is as common as the best of bread/ and will rise...I swear it to you on my common/ woman's/ head". Feminist writers, artists, and theorists have often valorized common women's lives, including the knowledge that emerges from hands-on engagement with the messiness of daily life, in contrast to the idealizations of science. When we want to urge experts to take us and our concerns seriously, common sense is what is "ours", not "theirs". But appeal to what "we" are supposed have in common, to what "everyone" knows or values, can prove notoriously uncongenial to feminists and our allies. Many of us stand condemned by common sense: our lives are variously immoral, foolish, obscene, misguided, or impossible. Expert discourses of various sorts can offer real or imagined refuge from those condemnations: we may feel on firmer ground casting our lot with "them" than with an "us" that places us on the margins or beyond the pale. We may, for example, be confident that science will reveal the unnaturalness of heterosexist construals of sexuality or the ungroundedness of presumptions of male superiority.

When, however, María Lugones (2003b) writes about the tyranny of common sense, as the expression of what the comfortable can presume to be obvious, in contrast to the improvisations of those she calls "street-walkers", she is articulating a perspective from which science and common sense are, as they are for many philosophers, continuous, one the disciplined extension of the other, both grounded in what we all are presumed to have and to know in common and which, she argues, actually excludes many from the realm of sense-making. Such are the ambiguous resonances of the word that one could even say that being "common" (not, as some would say, "our kind of person") is one way of being excluded from the commons, the space of commonality. The exclusion Lugones describes—from the easy truths of common sense, what all "right-thinking" people know—is the epistemic analogue of the ejection of homeless people from the public library.

Once we acknowledge the ways in which, in Lugones's terms, we "make each other up", set the terms in which we will be intelligible, mark out the patterns of salience that construct the phenomena of mentality, we can ask about who "we" are, how and why we do what we do, who reaps the benefits and bears the burdens of the practices that give our lives the shapes they have, and who has what sort of power when it comes to issues such as these. These are questions that redirect our attention, away from what is presumed to lie under and to underwrite the truths of common sense, and toward the practices through which such truths are constructed.[17]

17. This chapter was meant to be a revision of a paper I wrote in 1983, which haphazardly circulated under the title "Types, Tokens, and Conjuring Tricks". It contained arguments (valid, I still believe, and not all since made by others), mostly via counterexamples, that the anti-reductionist arguments that motivate anomalous monism, functionalism, and substantive supervenience theses in general tell equally against those proposed alternatives. For various reasons I had put that paper aside to pursue what I thought were rather distant interests in interdisciplinary feminist theory. The invitation to contribute to the volume in which this chapter originally appeared (Fricker and Hornsby 2000) seemed the perfect occasion for finally revising it and for making explicit the connections that were coming to seem more and more obvious to me, especially when I belatedly discovered Jennifer Hornsby's and John Dupré's work. As subsequent drafts worked their way through my computer, however, the relationship of the present chapter to its ancestor became sufficiently attenuated as to strain any plausible criterion of identity. I would, nonetheless, like to thank David Golumbia and Lisa Banks for first encouraging me to reenter the philosophy of mind fray; Ernie Lepore for his criticisms of the 1983 paper and for (only partially heeded) advice on updating it; and Louise Antony, Richard Boyd, and especially Georges Rey for pushing me to explain why I professed to believe things that sounded completely crazy. I have presented versions of the present chapter at the University of Toronto, University of London (where John Dupré was my commentator), and Gothenburg and Umeå Universities, and was greatly helped by the discussions, as I was by Michael Root's and Georges Rey's careful critical readings of an earlier draft (though Rey, in particular, may wish to dispute any influence on the current version) and by long conversations with Hornsby, Dupré, and Miranda Fricker. Thanks to the Department of Feminist Studies at Gothenburg for providing a congenial setting for writing this chapter.

Chapter 6

Feeling Our Way toward Moral Objectivity

However diversely philosophers of psychology have thought of emotions, they have mostly agreed on thinking of them as states of individuals. And most moral philosophers have agreed on thinking of emotions as for the most part inimical to the achievement of moral objectivity. I argue in this chapter that both views are wrong and that we can learn something about why they are by looking at how they are connected.

I

Arguing that emotions are not states of individuals can seem merely perverse. My first attempt to do so (Scheman 1983) has seemed so to most philosophical readers.[1] It is, of course, true that we ascribe emotions to individuals and that we speak of individual people as being in various emotional states. But there is a more precise and particular sense of what it is for something to be a state of an individual that I think can be made out clearly, and in this more precise sense, emotions (along with other complex mental "states," such as beliefs, attitudes, desires, intentions, and so on) are not states of individuals. The sense I mean is this: S is a (complex) state of an individual I only if the elements of S are related to each other in causal or other ways that make of S a complex entity independently of I's social context. (My concern will be to argue against this necessary condition; I have no interest in what might be sufficient conditions for something's being a state of an individual, or in any states that might be argued to be simple, such as qualia.)

The ontological distinction I am relying on is that between a complex entity and a jumble or a heap. Complex entities differ from jumbles or heaps in the relationships of coherence among their component parts. There is no way of drawing this distinction in any absolute way, since there will always be relationships to be found, or created, among any collection of entities. Rather, we need to ask whether some collection constitutes a complex object with respect to some particular theory or explanatory scheme (or some set of theories or schemes).

---

1. For an extensive and very thoughtful discussion based on this (mis)reading of the argument, see Grimshaw (1986). For a later attempt, see "Against Physicalism," this volume.

My argument will be that the coherence of emotions and other complex mental states is relative to irreducibly social, contextual explanatory schemes. In abstraction from particular social contexts, there is no theoretically explicable coherence among the behavior and the occurrent thoughts, feelings, and sensations (or whatever else one might take to be the components of an emotion; I have no commitment to this particular list, though it seems to get at what we do in fact point to when we identify emotions and other mental states). The distinction is akin to that between galaxies and constellations. Despite their both being made up of stars, galaxies are, and constellations are not, complex objects with respect to astronomy. The stars that make up a galaxy are related to each other causally and spatially, while the stars that make up constellations are related to each other only against the background of a set of stories about the night sky told by particular cultures on a particular planet; they are not even spatially contiguous except from the perspective of earth.

Emotions, I argue, are constellation-like, not galaxy-like. Their identity as complex entities is relative to explanatory schemes that rely on social meaning and interpretation. Emotions and other complex mental states differ from constellations in depending ontologically on explanatory schemes that have enormous depth and power and that we have every reason to continue to use—unlike astrology. The analogue of eliminative materialism would eliminate constellations from the furniture of the universe—not, I would think, inappropriately. But eliminative materialism as usually understood, which accepts my negative judgment on the possibility of even token identities between mental and physical states, would require that we jettison the explanatory resources of common sense, along with literature and the other arts, not to mention most of psychology, a prospect I find bleakly inhuman, as well as pointless.

It is, of course, true that many genuine states of individuals—diseases, for example—are identified and named only in particular social contexts, but the causal relationships that obtain among the causes and the symptoms are independent of those contexts; they are there to be discovered. There are intelligible questions to be asked about whether some particular pattern of symptoms constitutes a disease, and one important deciding factor is whether, independent of their seeming to be somehow related, they hang together, as, in the paradigm case, by being all caused by the same pathogen. If, on the other hand, the pattern of the symptoms is explicable in terms not of underlying somatic processes but of social salience, then it would be wrong to speak of a disease.[2] What is at issue is not what we call it, or even whether we call it anything, whether we find it interesting or important to name it, or whether its

---

2. There is an extensive literature on what constitutes a disease, much of it concerned with arguing that what is called the "medical model" misidentifies as disease complexes of behavior and symptoms that take their significance from their social context. See, for example, Zita (1988).

cause was or was not "biological" (pathogens can be social; to argue that a set of symptoms is caused by, for example, childhood abuse is not to argue that they do not constitute a disease). What is at issue is whether there is an "it" at all.[3]

This argument, drawn from Wittgenstein, is an explication of what he refers to as "the decisive move in the conjuring trick . . . , the very one we thought quite innocent," since all we have done is to say what it is we intend to look at, that is, "processes and states . . . [we] leave their nature undecided" (Wittgenstein 1953, § 308). What has, surreptitiously, been decided is that these supposed processes and states are complex entities according to some possible theory, yet to be developed. There must, by this picture, be some underlying mechanism that knits each process or state together, some structure for some future science to reveal. But why should this be so? What are we assuming, and what are we precluding, when we make this initial, apparently innocent move? What we are precluding is precisely what I want to suggest is the case: that emotions (and other complex mental "states") are situationally salient, socially meaningful patterns of thought, feelings, and behavior.[4] As such they may well be supervenient on physical facts, but only globally—that is, not only on physical facts in my body and not only on physical facts in the present or even in the past.

Consider, for example, these lines in Shakespeare's *Sonnet 116*: "Love is not love which alters when it alteration finds." There is something paradoxical in the claim—the same paradox as in Gertrude Stein's remark about Oakland: "There's no *there* there." In both cases there is something to point to, though the point of the pointing is to get one to see that there is, in a sense, no *thing* there, that by the standards by which we (more about "we" later) judge such things, this, whatever it might be, just does not count. The "it-ness" is not to be taken at face value: Shakespeare and Stein are urging us to have higher ontological standards, not to confer the dignity of coherence on what we ought, rather, to regard as a jumble or a heap. Jumbles and heaps can be pointed to; they can even be named but paradoxically: to do so is to adopt an interpretive perspective that one does not fully and wholeheartedly occupy. (In Sabina Lovibond's (1983) terms, it is to speak ironically, in inverted commas.) True love, or San Francisco, is "real" not because each has an inner coherence that false love and Oakland lack but because the patterns that lead us to see each as a coherent, complex object are salient from positions in which we wholeheartedly stand.

3. This point is similar to the one Helen Longino (1990, p. 99) makes in arguing for the importance of attending to "the specification, or constitution, of the object of inquiry"; she in turn acknowledges Michel Foucault and Donna Haraway.

4. I argue this claim, concerning all complex mental states, more fully in several of the essays in Scheman (1993*b*) and in "Against Physicalism", this volume.

One might ask, in response to the denial that love that alters is (really) love: "If it isn't love, what is it?" I suggest that "it" might not be anything at all. Not that nothing is going on: rather, all that is going on—all the feeling, all the behavior—may not add up to anything, may not coalesce into a pattern we recognize as significant enough to name. It is as though one started out to choreograph a solo dance and midway through got bored and drifted off into aimless jiggling and sashaying. The dance, had one stuck with it, would have been a "something": in the absence of its completion, what we have is a jumble of movements, not ontologically distinct from the rest of what one is doing, before, after, and during that time. What I call the individualist assumption in the philosophy of psychology is the assumption that whatever we find it significant to name—whatever patterns of feeling and behavior we find salient enough to use in explanations of ourselves and others—must also pick out complex events, states, or processes with respect to some theory of the functioning of individual organisms (neurophysiology, for example). Only the strongest reductionist projects would support such an assumption, since it is precisely the assumption of type/type identities.

There are two things in particular to note about the account of love in Shakespeare's sonnet. One is that it is clearly intended to be normative; that is, we are being urged not to count as love anything that alters when it alteration finds. (And it may well be difficult not to see it as love, especially if the feelings are one's own; one may well feel injured or betrayed by whatever "alteration" seemed to destroy one's love and cling to the sense of the value of what one feels was stolen. Similarly if one is the object of the "love which is not love," one might cling to the idea that one was, really and truly, loved—so long as one was, say, young and beautiful.)

Second, as a normative account, it is potentially and unpredictably retroactive; that is, what seems to be love today might be judged not to be love because of something that happens tomorrow, something that need not in any sense be latent today. We are being urged to withdraw an honorific label from a set of feelings and behavior because of a failure of constancy in the face of change—not that it could not have been love if it failed that test, as though there were something else in which its authenticity consisted, of which constancy were a reliable indicator. Wittgenstein draws our attention to this sort of normativity: "Love is not a feeling. Love is put to the test, pain not. One does not say: 'That was not true pain, or it would not have gone off so quickly'" (Wittgenstein 1967, § 504). What is at stake is less what "it" is than what we are, what we care about, value, and honor, a refusal to be swayed by the intensity of passing feeling. And it makes sense to say this to us only if we are at risk of being so swayed.[5]

---

5. Thanks to Daniel Hurwitz for deepening my reading of the sonnet, in particular, in insisting that the point cannot be that "it" simply is not love.

I want to consider further examples to try to make plausible the view of emotions as situationally salient, socially meaningful patterns of thought, feelings, and behavior, rather than as states that one might discover within particular individuals at a particular time. The point is that it is such patterns (not, for example, physiological causal connections) that make the components of an emotion hang together as a complex object rather than being a jumble or a heap. And, like pattern perception generally, the identification of emotions cannot be abstracted from the contexts in which the relevant patterns are salient.

The first example is drawn from the film *Torch Song Trilogy*, in particular, from the scene in which the central character, Arnold, is at the cemetery with his mother. Arnold is a gay man. He is, in fact, a drag queen by profession. He had a loving, committed relationship with another man, Alan, who was murdered by gay-bashing men in the street beneath their apartment. Arnold has buried Alan in the cemetery plot that his parents provided (presumably for the wife they hoped he would have). He goes to the cemetery to visit Alan's grave with his mother, who is visiting the grave of her husband, Arnold's father. Arnold's mother looks over at Arnold at his lover's grave and sees him reciting the Jewish prayer for the dead, and she asks him what he is doing. He says he is doing the same thing she is, and she replies in outrage that no, he is not: she is reciting Kaddish; he is blaspheming his religion. She finds it outrageous that he might take himself to be feeling grief, as she is feeling grief, and to have felt for Alan love, as she felt love for her husband.

That is, she looks at what Arnold is feeling in the context of Arnold's life and sees something quite different from what she felt in the context of her own life. Sure, she thinks, he goes through these motions, says these words, even feels these pangs and aches, but they do not add up, hang together, or amount to the same thing as they would in the context of a proper marriage. (His feelings are no more grief than his saying those words is reciting Kaddish. To her they are equally meaningless jumbles.) Arnold, however, looking at his and her feelings, perceives the patterns differently from how she does; he weighs differently the similarities and differences, in the contexts of his and her lives, and ends up seeing the same feelings of love and of grief. It is the burden of the film, with respect in particular to a heterosexual audience, to persuade us to accept Arnold's mode of pattern perception and to reject as narrow-minded and heterosexist his mother's refusal to find in his actions and feelings the same valued coherence she finds in her own.[6]

A second example is drawn from popular songs, of which there are an enormous number, that couple love with potentially violent jealous possessiveness. In songs going back at least to those that were popular in the forties, one of the commonest themes, along with the "somebody done

6. I discuss this example more fully in chapter 8.

somebody wrong" songs, is the idea that love, in particular that which a man feels for a woman, must be reciprocated; she has no choice but to reciprocate it, and her turning her affections elsewhere is a possibility that, because what he feels is love, he cannot allow. Her simply failing to reciprocate his love may, in fact, constitute the "wrong" that he takes her to have done him.

Songs like this are interesting and important to think about, in particular because of the current controversy over the words in so-called gangsta rap. If we are going to take seriously the influence of popular song lyrics, we need to focus at least as closely on those that have filled the mainstream airwaves as on those that come from subordinated populations. What is it that we are doing, in particular, when we call the complex of sentiments in those popular songs love? We could, alternatively, pathologize this complex of feeling and attitude and behavior. We could call it something like "possession dementia" and enter it into the next edition of the *Diagnostic and Statistical Manual of Mental Disorders*. Or we could simply fail to see any "it" there at all. Valorizing and pathologizing are equally ways of bestowing coherence, however much we may believe that we are merely pointing to something—an emotion or a disease—that exists independent of our interest in it. The consequences of the elision of our interpretive activity in favor of a supposedly helpless recognition of "love" are, of course, disastrous, both because of the male behavior that is thereby licensed and because of the compliance it exacts from women who believe that such congeries *are* love, believe that it is something to be valued and honored.

On a socially constructionist account of emotions, as María Lugones argues (1987, 1991), we "make each other up," at least insofar as we set the parameters of intelligibility. We determine which patterns of feeling and behavior will count as love or grief or anger or whatever else. We also more personally and directly make each other up, as we help or hinder each other in seeing new or different patterns. For example, I have argued (Scheman 1980) that the central character in that paper, Alice, was helped by other members of her consciousness-raising group to see a pattern of depression, odd outbursts of impatience and pique, and a general feeling of undefinable malaise as anger. We can sharpen each other's pattern perception in the face of various kinds of resistance or fear.

Often, as is likely in this case, we will come to regard a particular pattern (Alice's anger) as so striking, once we come to see it, that a fully realist vocabulary is apt (she *discovered* she was angry). Speaking this way amounts to placing our interpretive activity in the background, taking it for granted, treating it as part of common sense. There is often, of course, good reason to do this, as others will have good reason to challenge it. What is important to note is that such challenges ought not to succeed if all they do is point out that Alice's anger is visible as such only if you stand *here* and look through *these* lenses. The response to that is, "Yes, of course, and what anger is any different? Do you have a problem with standing here, with looking through these lenses?" The answer to that question may well be yes: we cannot make judgments without standing on some ground or other, or see without lenses (even if only those in our eyes), but we need to be ready, when concretely challenged, to argue for the rightness of the choices we make, even those we may not have recognized as choices until someone questioned them.

For example, in the story I tell, the other women in the group spoke of their own anger, in the contexts of lives not unlike hers, and Alice's not regarding them as moral monsters or as wildly irrational helped, along with an evolving political consciousness, to create the background against which she could similarly see herself as angry. What goes on can be described as a kind of crystallization. And there is, of course, all the difference in the world between unacknowledged and acknowledged emotions. Once we acknowledge a significant pattern in our feelings and behavior, we are in a position to act differently. There is also all the difference in the world between the discovery of anger and its creation, especially its inappropriate creation, as some would argue that Alice was brainwashed by feminist antifamily propaganda.[7] I do not want to deny that there is such a difference, but there are no formal grounds—no grounds less contested than feminism itself—on which to base a judgment about which it is.

Conversely there is the possibility of justifiably chosen disavowal of feeling. For example, one can take as infatuation rather than as love feelings one judges to be inappropriate, feelings that, given how we think of ourselves as moral beings or as socially situated in the world, we think it would be better for us not to have. Or we could work toward overcoming prejudicial fears and antipathies by thinking that those feelings are incompatible with the people we take ourselves most fundamentally to be. We do not take ourselves simply not to have such feelings; rather, we redefine them. In the first case—redefining love as infatuation—we are likely to downplay the "it-ness" of what we are feeling, to fragment our responses, to attach them to various features of the situation, rather than letting them all cohere around the person we are trying to "get over." In the latter case—transforming judgment into phobia—we might rather focus on whatever coherence we can find not in the situation but in our history; we might choose to see as coherent, caused pathology what we might have been inclined to regard as situationally differentiated responses. Locating the explanatory coherence in ourselves, not in the objects of our judgment, is a central piece of identifying, for example, our own racism or homophobia.

How we do all of this shifting in pattern perception depends enormously on the interpretive resources, the encouragement or discouragement of those around us. Centrally, it depends on whom we take "we" to

---

7. A much more subtle objection to the role that I give others in the identification of feelings (and a persuasive argument for serious attention to the inchoate) is explored in Campbell (1997).

be—those with whom we share a form of life, whose responses we expect to be congruent with or touchstones for our own. Sympathy and empathy—feeling with and for each other—are therefore not just matters of response to independently given emotional realities. Rather, they change the context of experience and the context of interpretation. In so doing, they change the emotions themselves, frequently in ways that do not work by causing any changes in behavior or in immediate felt experience; such changes can, for example, be retroactive. A characteristic theme of Henry James's novels and novellas, for example, is the way in which subsequent events can utterly change the meaning of what someone felt and did—can, for example, make it true, as it was not before, that one person loved another. (I am thinking in particular of *The Golden Bowl*, *Wings of the Dove*, and "The Beast in the Jungle.")

II

The second argument is for the necessity of emotions to moral judgment. One of the reasons for this necessity has to do with the importance of moral perception to moral judgment—that is, much of the work of moral judgment is done in how we perceive a situation, what we see as morally relevant or problematic. Probably the moral theorist for whom such perception is most obviously central is Aristotle, for whom practical wisdom consists largely in this ability to perceive the salient features of a situation. But equally, if less obviously, for Kant, perceptions of salience are necessary to determine what the appropriate maxim is, that is, the one we need to test against the requirements of the categorical imperative: of all the ways I might describe what I am considering doing, which description best captures what might be morally problematic? (Do I ask if it is permissible to say something pleasing in order to make someone feel good, or do I ask if it is permissible to lie in order to make someone feel good?) Moral perception is arguably also important for utilitarians: everything I do potentially affects the pleasure and pain of myself and others, but not everything I do is appropriately subject to the felicific calculus. Any usable utilitarian moral theory is going to have to distinguish between actions that are and actions that are not morally problematic, and their having consequences for someone's pleasure and pain cannot be a sufficient ground. What is sufficient, however, presumably will have centrally to do with what those pleasures and pains are likely to be; in coming to an accurate description of what is morally salient about a situation, we need to be sensitive to the relation of our possible actions to the emotions of ourselves and others.

Emotions play various roles in moral epistemology, in helping us come to adequate moral perception. The first is that emotions partly constitute the subject matter of moral epistemology; that is, how I and others feel is often part of the morally relevant description of the situation. Furthermore, such descriptions are always given from the perspectives of emotional complicity. For reasons related to my first argument, these are not disinterested perceptions; they are, rather, the perceptions of people who are, at the very least, part of the background against which the emotions being described get the salience that they have.

The second role of emotions in moral epistemology is that of an epistemological resource. One of the clearest statements of this point is Alison Jaggar's (1989) discussion of what she calls "outlaw emotions": emotions that, according to the hegemonic view of the situation, one is not supposed to feel. Women, for example, are not *supposed* to be angered by whistles and catcalls as they walk down the street. We are supposed, rather, to feel flattered by them. One is not *supposed* to feel anger at certain kinds of jokes—sexist, racist, and so on—in certain social settings. Feelings such as these, which one is not supposed to have, are, Jaggar argues, often the best sign that there is something going on in the situation that is morally or politically problematic.

Outlaw emotions can work quite effectively against the phenomenon of gaslighting, a phenomenon that the poet and essayist Adrienne Rich (1979c) has described, whereby we undermine our own and each other's perceptions. Something is going on that leads us to feel an outlaw emotion—for example, sexual attentions or sexual joking in the workplace that feels creepy and uncomfortable. We can be told and can learn to say to ourselves that we are being overly sensitive, prudish, or whatever else, and we thereby undercut the possibility of there being a critical edge to those emotions. A way of working against gaslighting is to take outlaw emotions seriously, as epistemic resources pointing us in the direction of important, often morally important, perceptions.

One way of putting this point is that unemotional perception is problematically partial, especially in its failure to include outlaw perceptions. The effect of ignoring or bracketing our emotional responses will frequently be that we gaslight ourselves into a failure to notice and learn from importantly critical perspectives, as we perceive only along the hegemonic lines of sight. (The problem is not confined to what we might think of as the context of discovery; it is not just that we are less likely to notice a wrong, but from a perspective uninformed by the relevant outlaw emotions, we will not acknowledge it even when it is pointed out to us. That is what gaslighting is about: a systematic biasing of the contexts of both discovery and justification.)

As Jaggar notes, not all emotional responses, not even all outlaw emotional responses, are valuable in this way. There is, I suspect, nothing to be learned from the annoyance some people feel in the face of having it pointed out to them that their behavior, including their choices of words, contributes to forms of social subordination. The defensibility of making such responses "outlaw"—that is, not how people are "supposed" to feel—rests in part on there being nothing to be learned from taking them seriously, nothing we do not already know about resistance to having one's privileges challenged. There may, of course, be much to learn from the fact that people do feel these ways, but the feelings are not themselves valuable epistemic lenses.

Much of the current dispute about "political correctness" can be seen as disputes about which responses ought appropriately to be seen as out-law—not, that is, *outlawed*, if that even makes sense, but regarded as inappropriate, as epistemically unreliable. It follows from my first argu-ment that any talk of emotions is deeply and pervasively normative, so there is no escaping such judgment of appropriateness, or any way of circumventing the politically tendentious nature of the judgments we make. Nothing simpler than attention to the specificities of a particular case will settle the question of what sort of epistemic weight we ought to put on a particular emotionally informed perception. Again, what is at stake is the identification of an appropriate "we" and our own, possibly problematic or partial, frequently critical, at times ironic, identification with it. Outlaw emotions can, for example, draw our attention to the dangers of excessive rigidity and a passion for purity, even with respect to values we wholeheartedly endorse. (Such was, of course, the original intent of the term 'political correctness'.)

III

I have been arguing that (1) any descriptive account of emotions is necessarily social, including normatively—that is, both generally and in specific cases, moral judgment enters into a descriptive account of our emotions—and (2) our emotional responses to situations and to each other necessarily inform the moral judgments that we make. I argue now that this circularity is benign and that it facilitates rather than under-mines the possibility of the objectivity of moral judgment (and for that matter, the objectivity of the ascription of emotion, though it is moral judgment that I will focus on here).

In order to make this argument I need to explain what I mean by objectivity. I want to take as the motto for this account a quotation from Wittgenstein (1953, § 108): "The axis of our examination must be rotated, but about the fixed point of our real need." What is our "real need" with respect to objectivity?[8] I suggest, especially with respect to the objectivity of moral judgment, that the need is for moral knowledge that is "commonable," that is, stably sharable across a maximal diversity of perspectives. Can moral knowledge be objective in this sense? (Alterna-tively, one might ask the question: is moral *knowledge*—as opposed to moral opinion—possible?) I can see no reason why it should not be, but we need to consider the conditions of its possibility—that is, the condi-tions of the possibility of moral judgment that we have good reason to

8. For a fuller discussion of the question of objectivity, see Chapters 1 and 11.

believe will be stable across a maximal diversity of perspectives, that will remain in place and not be upset when the situation is looked at from perspectives different from those that have informed it heretofore.

The usual problems with respect to objectivity—that is, the reasons people who believe in its possibility think that it is difficult to obtain—are conceived of as problems of partiality defined as bias. Seeing the problem in this way leads to such things as ideal observer theories or other theories couched in terms of desirable forms of ignorance. Factual knowledge may need to be maximized, but following the dominant epistemology of empiricism with respect in particular to emotions (which takes it as necessary insofar as possible to bracket them), the emphasis is on an epistemology of parsimony. We need to bracket off those influences that are taken to be problematic, where "problematic" means in practice "likely to produce diversity of opinion."

But we could see the problem rather as one of partiality defined not as bias but as incompleteness. That is, a judgment we have arrived at seems acceptable to us, but we cannot be sure that someone will not walk through the door and say, "That looks wrong to me"—and that in the face of that challenge we will either agree right off that their claim has standing against our consensus or be persuaded eventually to change our initial assessment of it or of them as mad, ignorant, romantic, childish, or whatever else. If this is the way that we think of the problem, then what we need is not an epistemology of parsimony, guarding us in advance against the possibility of objections, but rather an epistemology of largesse.[9] We need to be expansive in who constitutes the "we" whose judgments and critical input help to shape the knowledge in question.

One way of addressing our "real need" with respect to objectivity is to ask what reason we have to believe that something we think we know will not be shaken by criticism coming from a yet unforeseen perspective. The best answer is that we have no reason to believe that. Our claim to objectivity rests precisely on the extent to which our practice makes such critique a real possibility. Rather than being able to argue in advance that no effective criticism could be forthcoming—because we have managed methodologically to anticipate and defuse it—we stake our claim to legitimacy, that is to objectivity, precisely on our record of having met actual, concrete criticism and thus earning the trust that we will do so in future. Objective judgments are more, rather than less, defeasible. What makes them count as knowledge—rather than, say, a working hypothesis—is their having come out of and been subjected to the critical workings of a sufficiently democratic epistemic community.

---

9. I am indebted here to the account in Longino (1990) of objectivity as primarily a characteristic of scientific practice, rather than of theories or whatever else result from that practice, which practice is objective insofar as it embodies the conditions of effective critique, so as to take into account the essential role played by values. Presumably no one would argue that moral knowledge should be value free, but the problems of how to characterize objectivity in the face of diversity are not dissimilar.

Largesse is not, however, the whole story. Not all voices are or should be equal. Not all perspectives afford usefully different vantage points. Not all criticisms should lead us to change our minds. The mistake of empiricist epistemologies—epistemologies of parsimony—has been to put faith in formal general principles of exclusion to erect a *cordon sanitaire* that would serve to discriminate a priori between those influences on belief that are appropriate and those that are not. But certainly in the realm of moral knowledge, as in any other knowledge that concerns human flourishing and harms, such faith is misguided. (Feminist philosophers of science and others have argued, persuasively, I believe, that it is misguided even in the "hard" sciences. See, e.g., Longino 1990.) Discrimination—between the crackpot and the reasonable, the bigoted and the spiritedly partisan, the intolerant and the upright, the subordinated margins and the lunatic fringe—is both necessary and unavoidable. But nothing less substantive, less political, less controversial than fully messy engagement in the issues at stake, in the real differences between us, in the concrete ways in which various "we"s are constituted, will enable us to make these discriminations in ways that do not beg the very questions they are meant to decide. Emotions, in particular, can be invaluable epistemic resources as often as they can be biasing distractions, and there is no way of formally deciding which is the case.

I want to discuss briefly one particular role of emotions in achieving moral objectivity. The principal barrier to the actual achievement of objectivity is power, that is, the ways in which hegemonic social locations are constructed and others are marginalized, silenced, or distorted. The thinking of those who occupy positions of authority and privilege is problematically and systematically parochial. The knowledge claims that we produce, whether moral or factual, are in need of critical examination from the standpoints of the subordinated. The reason for such critique is one Marx articulated in his discussion of ideology, and it has been developed by feminist standpoint theorists. (For an overview and critical discussion of this work, see Harding 1986, 1991.) To see the world from the perspective of privilege is to see it through distorting lenses that produce views that naturalize or otherwise justify the privilege in question. Those who are privileged are not doomed to view the world only through those lenses, but it is at the very least unlikely that learning to see differently will come about without the experience of listening to and learning from those who are differently placed—an experience not likely without conscious effort. Preempting or stigmatizing those other voices is a central strategy of the ideology of privilege: either we think we already know what they have to say, or we think we have reasons for rejecting in advance the possibility that what they say will be of value.

María Lugones (in a talk at the University of Minnesota) gave a very interesting example of this sort of critique by looking at the moral virtue of integrity defined as singularity of subjectivity and of will, including a direct connection between one's will and one's actions. (For a related discussion, see Lugones 1990a.) From the perspective of the subordinated, there are two things that are evident. One is the visibility of the meant-to-be invisible facilitation provided by various kinds of social structures that step in and enable the intentions of the privileged to issue in actions that appear to have been done in a straightforward, direct, unmediated fashion. Marilyn Frye (1983d) gives an illuminating example of this phenomenon when she suggests we see patriarchy through the analogy with a play that proceeds thanks to the invisible labor of stage-hands (women) who are not meant to be seen. The play of patriarchy is disrupted—revealed as a play—when women stop looking at the play and at the actors and start looking at each other.

The second thing that, on Lugones's account, becomes evident from the perspective of the subordinated is the necessity on their part of various sorts of ad hoc devices compensating for the meant-to-be invisible facilitations provided to the privileged by the social structure. Consider, for example, the ways in which language typically allows the privileged to say directly and straightforwardly what they mean. Part of the reason that it is so easy to ridicule attempts at bias-free language reform is that it really is awkward and graceless to avoid, for example, using the masculine as though it were generic. What we should learn from this discovery is just how pervasive and pervasively debilitating the biases in our languages are, how much they are set up to make some able to navigate smoothly while others systematically founder on jagged assaults to their self-esteem or engage in constant tacking against the wind in order to avoid them.

Similar situations arise in the realm of action. The privileged can (apparently) directly and straightforwardly do what they intend ("apparently" because we are not supposed to notice the assistance they are receiving, the ways in which all the paved roads are laid out to go where they want to go). The subordinated are driven to constructing various Rube Goldberg devices—in the realm of discourse, circumlocution; in the realm of action, manipulation. That is, everything that they do to make things happen, all the bits and pieces, are both patched together in a makeshift fashion and are also glaringly evident. They are "devious," not "straightforward," or so it seems from the perspective of privilege.

The articulation of such critical perceptions and their entry into the moral conversations of the privileged require what Lugones (1987) refers to as "world travel," and various things go into effecting it. One is the cultivation of relationships of trust; another is the willingness of the privileged to acknowledge others' views, including others' views of *them*; another is the evocation and the articulation of outlaw emotions and their acknowledgment as an epistemic resource; and a final one is attention to how we make each other up, especially across lines of privilege, how we create the possibilities of meaningfulness in each other's lives.

A crucial piece of such epistemic work is to transform dismissible cynicism and rage on the part of the subordinated into critique and transformation. As long as people feel effectively shut out of the procedures of moral conversation, they are likely to respond, if they respond at all, with global cynicism and inchoate rage, which are too easily dismissible, rather than with focused, specific, and intelligible critique, which has the possibility of being transformational. The work of creating a context in which this articulation can occur is in part the task of the more privileged, as it is the structures of privilege that have set the problem, and it cannot be solely up to those who are subordinated to take on the remedial education of those who continue to benefit from their subordination.

The progress toward moral objectivity is thus in the form of a spiral: as we become better at the forms of emotional engagement that allow the emotional resources, in particular, of those whose perspectives have been subordinated, to become articulated and to be taken seriously by themselves as well as by the relatively privileged, then the terms of the descriptive apparatus for our emotional lives shift, which then allows for even more articulation of emotionally informed perceptual responses, and so on. What appeared to be a problematic circle is in fact a spiral, and if we have defined objective judgments as those that we have good reason to believe have been subjected to effective critique, existing in contexts that allow for the future possibility of further critique—that is, judgments that we have good reason to believe are stable across a wide range of different perspectives and that will shift, if they do, not capriciously but intelligibly—then it follows that the social constructedness of emotions and the ineliminable role of emotions in moral judgment work together in order to provide the possibility of moral objectivity.

Chapter 7

Queering the Center by Centering the Queer

Reflections on Transsexuals and Secular Jews

Confusing yourself is a way to stay honest.

Jenny Holzer

Twentieth-century liberatory activism and theorizing have lived with and on the tension between two visions: For one the goal is to secure for the marginalized and oppressed the relief from burdens and the access to benefits reserved for the privileged, including the benefits of being thought by others and oneself to be at the center of one's society's views of what it is to be fully human. For the other the goal is to disrupt those views and the models of privileged selfhood they underwrite—to claim not the right to be, in those terms, fully human but, rather, the right to be free of a stigmatizing, normalizing apparatus to which one would not choose to conform even were one allowed and encouraged to do so. Struggles in the arenas of race, colonialism and imperialism, gender, class, and sexuality have all, in varying ways and to differing degrees, in different times and places, been pushed and pulled, shaped and molded, formed and deformed by the tensions between these two visions.

Among the perquisites of modern Eurocentric privilege are socially supported expectations that one can and will conform to certain norms of selfhood: One will be a person of integrity—whole and of a piece, some-one to be counted on, stable and steady; one's beliefs, attitudes, and feelings will be explicable and coherent; one's actions will follow straight-forwardly from one's intentions; one will be simultaneously solid and transparent—a block of unclouded substance.[1] (That the very wealthy and powerful are often allowed, or even expected, to be creatures of unpredictable caprice and inexplicable temperament is the exception that proves the rule: The acquisition and in most cases the maintenance of privilege are matters of discipline, so that flamboyant flouting can be a

---

1. As this description of privileged subjectivity indicates, I am deeply indebted in my thinking about issues of identity, subjectivity, and integrity by reading, listening to, and talking with María Lugones for fifteen years.

sign that, by one's own efforts or by the inheritance of the efforts of one's ancestors, one is so securely privileged as to be able to let the discipline go. In short, part of how one flaunts one's privilege is by acting as though one need do nothing to continue to earn it.)

As María Lugones has argued (in a talk at the University of Minnesota)[2], such an ideal of integrity is not as straightforward as it may seem. The direct, unmediated route from intention to action that is one of its hallmarks is typically more apparent than real: We are taught not to see the elaborate collaboration provided to the privileged by a compliant social structure. By contrast, the necessary survival strategies of the oppressed make these marks of full, moral humanity unobtainable: Manipulation, deviousness, fickleness, and other stigmata of less than fully straightforward, solidly transparent subjectivity can be the signs not of defects of character but of the only available ways of getting by in a hostile world. If the straight roads are ones that require tolls one cannot afford to pay, and if they are laid out not to go where one needs to, then one has no choice but to find alternative routes, routes that snake around the roadblocks thrown up by those who have no interest in your getting anywhere you want to go.[3]

Among the coherencies that philosophers from John Locke to Derek Parfit have put at the criterial heart of personal identity is the continuity of memory. Such continuity marks what it is to be the same person throughout time, thus to be the bearer of responsibility, the maker and receiver of promises, the recipient of trust. From a wide range of causes—notably including childhood abuse—memory is subject to distortion and even erasure, making it difficult for those who have suffered such a loss to fashion a sufficiently coherent narrative of themselves to be credible. (At the extreme, such abuse can lead to the literal fracturing of the self: One of the distinguishing features of multiple personality disorder is the failure of memory across at least some of the different personalities—A has no recollection of doing what B did.)

Insufficiently noted by philosophical theorists of personal identity is the role of the memory of others in constituting selfhood. It is not just that we are the persons we remember ourselves as being: We are equally, for better or worse, the persons others remember us as being.[4] The others around us may be loving or arrogant,[5] thoughtful or careless, with their memories of us; and we can be grateful or resentful or both for being held in their memories, for being continuous with the persons they remember us as being. Persons who are forgotten or not well remembered—if those

---

2. For fuller working out of these ideas, see Lugones (2003a).

3. See also Hoagland (1988 and 2001) for the related argument that what is read as incompetence or unreliability on the part of subordinated people is often, in fact, sabotage.

4. The role of others in "holding us in memory," especially when we are, for a range of reasons, unable to hold ourselves, has been a central theme in the work of Hilde Lindemann (Nelson). See especially Nelson (2001) and Lindemann (2008).

5. Frye (1983c) discusses the distinction between loving and arrogant perception.

in whose memories they might have been held are dead or gone, absent-minded, or uncaring—are seen and often see themselves as diminished. And some, in order to be the persons they are becoming, or believe themselves always to have been, need to detach themselves from the memories of those who would hold them too firmly in mind, trapping them in selves that no longer fit, if they ever did. They need to reinvent themselves, to live without the coherence of a shared, remembered past.

One could argue at this point (especially with regard to the role of memory), as adherents of the first vision would, that the picture of privileged subjectivity is not in itself a problematic one: The problem is in its exclusivity. Nor are wily survival strategies inherently admirable, as much as we may admire those who manage by means of them to survive: Surely people often have to do things to survive that they would far rather not have to do. We need, on this view, to be careful not to romanticize oppression by celebrating the character traits it breeds.

Adherents of the second vision would counter that we equally ought not to celebrate ideals of humanity that have been realized literally on and through the bodies of others to whom those ideals have been denied. Privileged subjectivity is not some neutral good that just so happens to have been scarfed up by an unscrupulous few. Rather, it is a form of subjectivity well suited to unscrupulous scarfing up, that is, to a view of oneself as naturally meriting a far larger than average share of the world's benefits and a far smaller than average share of its burdens—as having, in Marilyn Frye's (1983c) terms, the right to graft onto oneself another's substance. The privileged self, on this view, is not only engorged but also diminished: It has split off and projected onto those same others the parts of itself deemed too messy or embarrassing to acknowledge. Its seamless integrity is achieved by throwing out all the parts that don't quite fit, secure in the knowledge that one can count on commandeering sufficient social resources not to need a fully stocked, even if incongruously jumbled, internal tool kit (See Anzaldúa 1987, Sherover-Marcuse 1986, and Miller 1984). Even memory works in some ways like this: The coherent remembered narrative, shared with others who hold us in mind, is an artifact of privilege in terms of both what it contains and what it omits. People do not remember everything that happens to them, and culturally available story lines help give shape to the stuff of some lives (make them "memorable") while leaving others gappy and jerky. Narrativity *per se* may be humanly important, but we have no access to narrativity *per se:* What we have are culturally specific narratives, which facilitate the smooth telling of some lives and straitjacket, distort, or fracture others.

Resistance to the disciplining apparatus that defines privilege (even the "privilege" of full humanity) can take a romantic outlaw form, lived on what are taken explicitly, defiantly, to be the margins, shunning, insofar as possible, what is acknowledged as the center. Alternatively, in ways that will be the focus of this chapter, resistance can take the form of challenge to the stable cartographies of center and margin. Such resistance aims to cloud the transparency of privileged subjectivity, making it visible, and visibly "queer," by revealing the apparatus that goes into normalizing it. The status of the "normal" can, that is, be problematized, rather than either aspired to or rejected—or replaced by some competing normalizing picture.[6] I want to explore the possibilities for what I call "queering the center" by looking at two specific normalizing apparatuses: heteronormativity and what I call "Christianormativity."

1

As David Halperin (1995) argues in a discussion of Foucault,[7] heteronormativity is productively slippery: A large part of its power comes from its deployment of two mutually incompatible discourses—that of (biological) normality and that of virtue. Heterosexuality, as both unremarkedly normal and markedly virtuous, is privileged indirectly: Not itself a site of inquiry, it is constructed by implicit contrast with the equally mutually incompatible characterizations of homosexuality—as sickness and as crime or sin. Arguments against one mode of stigmatization tend notoriously, in the maze of heterosexist (il)logic, to buttress the other: So, for example, arguing that gay men and lesbians don't choose their sexuality reinforces the view of that sexuality as sick, whereas arguing that gay men and lesbians show no more signs of psychopathology than do straight people reinforces the view of their sexuality as chosen and culpable.

Heteronormativity constructs not only sexual identity but gender identity: In order properly to regulate desire it must divide the human world unambiguously into males and females (For the best known articulation of this claim, see Butler 1990). The discourses of queerness are marked by specifically gender transgressiveness, by a refusal to allow gender to remain unproblematized in a struggle for the rights of same-

---

6. (a) The norm-flouting I have in mind here has a political meaning at odds with that of privileged eccentricity, but the two are not always easy to distinguish, especially when class privilege accompanies, for example, a stigmatized sexual identity. The risks and costs of being "out" vary enormously, and some forms of politically progressive transgression can be more easily available to those who are otherwise comfortable and safe. Alliances between those who do not have the choice to pass, for whom strategic inventiveness is required for bare survival, and those whose transgressions are more a matter of choice are precarious—at risk on one side from the need for protective coloration that can be read as overconformity, and on the other from the possibility of playfulness that can be read as unseriousness. The responsibility for establishing trusting alliances is not, however, equally shared: Nancy Potter (1994, 2002) has argued that the burdens of creating trust properly fall disproportionately on the relatively privileged. (b) 'Problematize' is a word that has gotten something of a reputation as a piece of theory-jargon. I think the reputation is undeserved, as I know of no other noncumbersome way of referring to just this activity, which is a crucial one for any liberatory theorizing: the rendering problematic (questionable, in need of explanation) of some phenomenon taken to be transparent, natural, in need of neither explanation nor justification.

7. Halperin also draws on Eve Sedgwick's (1990) discussion of the productive incoherence of heteronormative and homophobic discourses.

gendered sexual partners. Such transgressiveness can also be found in some feminist, especially lesbian feminist, attempts to redefine women (or "wimmin" or "womyn"), as something other than not-men. That is, such feminist attempts recognize both that the gender divide is predicated on the sexuality of heterosexual men ("women" = sexual objects for heterosexual male subjects) and that the male/female gender dichotomy is actually a male/not-male dichotomy (see Frye, 2000).[8]

There is a striking similarity between the heteronormative representation of the homosexual and the representation of the Jew in what I call "Christianormative" discourse. Analogously to the androcentrism of heteronormative gender, Christianormativity purports to divide the world into religions (all presumed to be like Christianity except for being mistaken) while really having only two categories: Christian and not (yet) Christian. The Christian model of religion misrepresents many of the indigenous cultures that Christians have evangelized, just as heteronormativity misrepresents what it is to be a woman. Like homosexuals, Jews are not only misrepresented but abjected by the normative scheme, not properly caught in its classifications. Since the start of the Christian era Jews have been defined by their closeness to and knowledge of Christianity, just as homosexuals are defined by their closeness to and knowledge of gender difference: In both cases there is a perverse refusal/inability to act on the knowledge they all too clearly have.

On the one hand, the Jew is the quintessential (potential) Christian: Christianity is a matter not of birth but of choice; the paradigmatic Christian is a convert—originally, and most naturally, from Judaism.[9] On the other hand, the Jew is indelibly marked on her or his body: An extraordinary range of body parts have been taken in anti-Semitic discourse to mark Jews (Gilman 1991). Jews are both profoundly culpable for continuing to deny the divinity of Jesus and unable, no matter what we do, to shed the racial heritage of Jewishness.[10] This contradictoriness, as

8. Through a misreading of history and of theorists still very much alive, this connection is typically unacknowledged by queer theorists, for whom 1970s lesbian feminism exemplifies the sort of "essentialism" queer theory sets itself against.

9. In a liberal Christian society, such as the present-day United States, there is a presumption of Christian identity that works much like the presumption of hetero-sexuality: People are given the "benefit" of the doubt and assigned, in the absence of positive counterevidence, to the privileged category. Nor, as Jacob Hale has pointed out, is the privilege that comes of being born to Christian parents easily shed, especially since the alternatives to it that most occupy the American imaginary are racialized: Even if the question "Are you a Christian?" is typically about faith, the presumption of Christian identity is usually not. (The racializing in the U.S. of non-Christian identity has massively increased after 9/11, with the racialization of an otherwise incoherent group of people—those taken by mainstream Americans to be Muslim, Arab, or both, some of whom—Sikhs or Indian Hindus, for example—are actually neither. Note added in 2010.)

10. As Lisa Heldke has reminded me, there is a common way of resolving this tension, by dividing Jewish identity in two—the religious component and the racial or cultural component. The resolution doesn't work, in part because it simply pushes the problem back by one step: What is the relationship between the two "components," and how are we to characterize the second—since on any plausible notions of race or culture, Jews belong not to one but to several or many? (The problem was literally "pushed back" by the Nuremberg Laws, by which the Nazis sought to racially classify the Jews: Jewishness

in the case of heteronormative discourse, is productive: It grants to Christians the simultaneous statuses of natural (the way humans are meant to be, the default state for humanity) and especially virtuous.[11] Literally, of course, Christianity is not supposed to be biologically natural, as heterosexuality is, but it is part of most Christian orthodoxy to believe that everyone is loved by Jesus in the way he loves Christians: What is called for is acknowledgement of that love, not the earning of it. Heterosexuality can be seen similarly, as part of essential human nature, so that homosexuality counts as the willful denial of one's true self, just as Jewishness counts as the willful denial of God's love.

Heteronormativity and Christianormativity both have, in addition to their dichotomizing aspect, a universalizing aspect: They both imagine a world of sameness, even as they continue to require not only objects of desire (proselytizing or sexual) but also abjected others. The emphases, on maintaining difference or striving toward sameness, may differ, but the tensions between the two animate both discourses. Although Christianity is officially universally proselytizing, there is reason to believe that Jews play a sufficiently important role in the Christian imaginary that if we didn't exist, they'd have to invent us; and certainly assimilating Jews have met with less than full cultural acceptance, often being stigmatized precisely for conforming to the norms of Christian society (see Prell 1992). Heteronormativity officially envisions a world of only heterosexuals, while similarly requiring the homosexual as a negative definition of normality; and, as Daniel Boyarin and Natalie Kampen have persuaded me, even the gender dichotomy itself contains a universalizing moment alongside the more obvious, official emphasis on ineluctable difference. Although men don't typically proselytize women into sex change (that women are important to the male imaginary seems clear), there is a strong current of mono(male)-gender utopianism, both in Pauline Christianity (see D. Boyarin 1994) and in Enlightenment thought. (Notably, in both cases, the body is meant to be transcended: It is in our minds, or our souls, that we are all really men.)

2

The inconsistent conjunction of sin and sickness, nature and virtue, that characterizes heteronormativity and Christianormativity strikingly (but unsurprisingly) characterizes modern Western conceptions of subjectivity.

was defined in terms of religious observance in the grand-parental generation [Pascale Bos, personal communication].)

11. Putting the matter this way highlights the fact that Christianormativity and Christianity are no more the same thing than are heteronormativity and heterosexuality: In both cases there are particular histories of ascendancy to centrality, which histories need to be told in tandem with the complementary histories of the corresponding stigmatized identities.

The clearest statement is perhaps Kant's ([1785] 1969, Sec. 2). The rationale for the categorical imperative—the answer to the question of why it ought to motivate us—is that only by seeing ourselves as bound by it can we see ourselves as free. Our noumenal identities, if expressible at all, are expressed through duty; the alternative is being determined by inclination—that is, by natural forces no more expressive of our freedom than are any other causal determinations. Virtue may be impossibly difficult to realize, but it is in an important sense natural, not imposed from outside. Kant is left with the problem of accounting for culpable wrongdoing: If acting freely is always acting morally, how can we hold someone responsible for acting badly? The problem is at the heart of Kant's account of the nature of morality and agency: If he allowed the possibility of acting freely in a way that didn't accord with the categorical imperative, he would have to answer the moral skeptic, who challenges the motivational charge behind the categorical imperative. The question of why we should do what duty commands would be a real one and, in Kant's terms, unanswerable, if freely, rationally, we could do otherwise. So the person who heeds not duty but inclination (who might be all of us, all of the time) is not only immoral but (contradictorily) unfree.

Epistemologically, as well, the emphasis has been less on the positive difficulty of obtaining knowledge than on the negative challenge of avoiding error—from Descartes' emphasis on resisting assent when ideas are less than fully clear and distinct, to the positivists' emphasis on the error-producing dangers of subjectivity. Both morally and epistemically the knowing subject is characterized as both generic (normal, universal) and as especially virtuous. The connection is in a sense unpuzzling: As a matter of fact most people most of the time won't be thinking in the manner argued to be the correct one, thus inescapably raising the question of what makes such thinking correct. What is it about those who do think in the privileged ways that makes their thought right for all the rest of us? The distinctively modern (i.e., liberal) answer to that question cannot be that those people are in some way special, with the authority to do the important thinking for the rest of us. Rather, they have to be seen as us— all of us—at our best, where "best" means simultaneously most natural (uncorrupted, healthy) and normatively most excellent. The two have to go together in the absence of anything other than "natural" for normative excellence to refer to.

One can, therefore, see the naturalizing moves of much of twentieth-century analytic philosophy, with its characteristic problems of theoretically justifying normativity claims, as rooted in the fundamental project of liberalism—what I have elsewhere referred to as "democratizing privilege" (Scheman 1993c, p. 77). That oxymoron reflects the tension between the universalistic theories and the inequalities that theoretically ought not to exist, especially those that are uncomfortably correlated with the supposed irrelevancies of race and gender or the supposed anachronism of class. In the absence of anything to account for inequality other than what people actually do—and can properly be held responsible for doing—the accounting has to be in terms of the wrong—or at least the less than optimally right—behavior of those who fail to prosper, without there being any independent, non-question-begging way of characterizing "wrong" or "right." The coupling of the apparently contradictory discourses of nature and virtue (or sickness and sin) are the inevitable result of the need to maintain a normativity that cannot speak its name.[12]

In the work of many philosophers, notably Descartes, there is nothing to mark those who exemplify the norms—in his case, by thinking properly—from those who don't: We are all equally capable of careful and of sloppy thought. Other philosophers, notoriously Kant ([1771] 1960, p. 81)—who thought duty and obligation meant nothing to women—have been less egalitarian: It is only some among us who actually have the capacity to reason in the ways supposed to be generically human. The rest of us have been marked by the odd conjunction of moral turpitude and natural incapacity that are taken to characterize the homosexual and the Jew. We have, that is, been characterized as constitutionally incapable of instantiating what is nonetheless supposed to be the essence we share with more privileged humans. Their generic status and the privileges that go with it require that we be essentially like them, whereas the terms of our exclusion, resting as it does on what we are, not on anything we may do, requires that we be essentially different from them.

Those of us so marked have variously struggled against such stigmatization, most often using the tools of liberalism: We have denied our alleged natural incapacity and claimed an equal share in humanity's essential attributes. Thus, for example, Jews have sought civil emancipation, gays and lesbians have sought civil rights, and women have sought equal rights: In all cases the argument has been made that howsoever members of these groups differed from the already-fully-enfranchised, such differences were of no importance when it came to the status in question, typically that of citizen. Given the distressing hardiness of racism, anti-Semitism, sexism, and homophobia, it has been easy for liberals to argue that doing otherwise—asserting the relevance of difference, however socially constructed; resisting offers, however genuinely goodwilled, of acceptance into the ranks of the same—is political suicide.

I do not want to minimize the truth in this argument, nor to dispute the goodwill of those who make it, but it does have the logic of a protection racket, as noted (by Peterson 1977) in relation to the discourse around male violence toward women: There are afoot very bad

---

12. For reasons much like these, David Halperin (1995) has called heterosexuality "the love that dare not speak its name" (i.e., that dare not name itself as one sexuality among others, needing, like them, to explain itself). Thanks to Diana Tietjens Meyers for pointing out that the discourses of normality and of virtue are not contradictory if normality is read in a normative way. The contradictoriness comes in when that normativity is occluded, camouflaging undefended, possibly indefensible, claims about excellence—when, that is, we are not supposed to be able to ask: "Says who?" or if we do, the answer is: "Nature."

people who will do you grave harm, and your safety lies in availing yourselves of the protection we offer. What makes the offer suspicious, no matter how sincere and empirically grounded, are the connections between the protectors and those who pose the danger. Protection is problematic when one's protectors benefit from one's acceptance of the terms on which that protection is offered—feminine docility in the case of protection from male violence, and acceptance of the paradigmatic status of the privileged in the case of protection from racism, anti-Semitism, sexism, and homophobia. As women are supposed to acknowledge needing men, those who are "different" are supposed to acknowledge the "honor" of being regarded as essentially the same as straight white middle-class Christian men.

The disputes currently roiling college campuses concerning "multiculturalism" illustrate the normativity of the paradigmatic. The deepest challenge of multiculturalism is to the paradigmatic centrality of the privileged: From whose vantage point is the world most accurately seen? Whose art and literature set the standards of aesthetic excellence? Whose experiences represent generically human encounters with life, death, the natural and social worlds? Shifting the center with respect to questions such as these—shifting which work is taken as most interesting, innovative, significant, worth supporting and encouraging (so taken by those who set curricula, give grants, make decisions about hiring and tenure and promotion)—has nothing to do with freedom of speech or academic freedom; but it is so profoundly threatening to those whose placement at the center has seemed to them a fact of nature that, faced with such shifts (which are, to date, minuscule), they are convinced, I suspect in some cases sincerely, that their rights must be being violated. Similarly, one finds the conviction, probably also in some cases sincere, that the shifting of norms means the abandonment of the true ones, those that can seem to come from nowhere only so long as they come from an unchallenged center, at once privileged and universal.

The liberal strategy is to leave unchallenged the paradigmatic status of the privileged, but to argue that it does not in theory, and ought not in practice, entail the exclusion or even the marginalization of others: The others are, in all the respects that ought to matter, essentially the same as the privileged. If this argument were a good one, then shifting in the other direction ought not to matter: It ought to be unproblematic to put at the center some groups previously relegated to the margins, to say not that black people are just like white people except that their skin is darker, but that white people are just like black people except that their skin is lighter.[13] But, as the near hysteria around "political correctness"

---

13. The specific example is Elizabeth V. Spelman's (1988, p. 12), and she makes the general point especially well. See also Sarah Hoagland's (1988 and 2002) refusal to take up the question of whether or not women ought to have equal rights, since it presupposes the rights of men as the unquestionable norm against which women need to stake a claim.

indicates, such shifts are hardly unproblematic: Being the standard of comparison is a very big deal, no matter how liberally others are deemed to measure up to it.[14]

For the remainder of this chapter I want to work at "queering the centers" of heteronormativity and Christianormativity by juxtaposing two subject positions, neither of which makes sense in the respective normative terms: the transsexual and the secular Jew. The juxtaposition is in part fortuitous: I am a secular Jew, and I have for some time been trying to figure out what that means; and, as a born-female feminist, I have been pressed to understand the experiences and perspectives of those whose attempts to deconstruct gender have an embodied literalness absent in my own life. Furthermore, living outside the norms exacts disruptions of memory and integrity for transsexuals and secular Jews significantly more than for homosexuals and religious Jews. With such experiences at the center, I want to ask what it is to live an intelligible and admirable life—what the structures of subjectivity look like from perspectives other than those of normalizing privilege. The question is an explicitly transcendental one: It starts from what I take as the fact that such lives are lived, hence livable, and asks after the conditions of that possibility.[15]

My hope is that starting from the intelligibility of the normatively unintelligible can serve to uncover the problematic assumptions that make secular Jews and transsexuals incoherent, assumptions that sustain both the status of the normatively coherent (including, in the case of gender, me) and the larger hierarchies in which those identities are embedded. I want to argue that placement at the intelligible center is always a matter of history, of the playing out of privilege and power, and is always contestable. One reason for the contestation is to lead us beyond the impasse between the two visions with which I began—both of which, as usually understood, tacitly accept the structures of normalization, whether by claiming one's rightful, central place in them or by defining oneself as outside of or marginal to them. Relocating the gaze to a place of normative incoherence can help to destabilize the center, upsetting the claims of those who reside there to that combination of naturalness and virtue that characterizes normativity.

---

14. For an excellent discussion of paradigm case reasoning and its role in the maintenance of privilege (as well as its difference from "essentialism"), see Marilyn Frye (2000).

15. Marcia Hagen (in conversation) drew my attention to the historical specificity of the unintelligibility of secular Jewish identity, by pointing out the persistence in Canada, for one generation more than in the United States, of a vibrant secular Yiddish culture. My discussion is grounded in post–World War II U.S. culture, where the terms that governed assimilationist possibilities joined with the memory of the Holocaust to make impossible the thinking of Jewishness in anything like racial terms. And, in the American imaginary, religion was the only remaining possibility. (I wonder if the centrality of distinct Québecois identity, however problematic, to Canadian thinking helps to provide conceptual space lacking in the United States.)

3

As our (modern Western) world is now, failure to conform to the norms of gender is socially stigmatizing to an unbearable extent: To be human just is to be male or female, a girl or a boy or a man or a woman. Those who cannot readily be classified by everyone they encounter are not only subject to physically violent assaults but, perhaps even more wounding, are taken to be impossible to relate to humanly, as though one cannot use the pronoun 'you' with anyone to whom one cannot with total assurance apply either 'she' or 'he.' Those who are not stably, unambiguously one or the other are, as Susan Stryker puts it (1994, p. 240), "monsters."[16] In such a world, boundary blurring carries psychic costs no one can be asked to pay, and the apparently conservative gender-boundary-preserving choices (surgical, hormonal, and behavioral) of many transsexuals have to be read in full appreciation of what the real options are.

One need not downplay the oppression of women to acknowledge that a certain sort of privilege, one essential for social validation as human, attaches to being located squarely on one side or the other of the gender divide.[17] Those of us who, as stably female-gendered feminists, would choose to see that boundary blurred to oblivion need to learn how to see and be seen as allies by those whose lives it slices through. The work of blurring that boundary is being taken on by a growing number of theorists and activists who are variously resisting the imperatives of gender conformity, including the imperative that transsexuals move decisively from one side to the other (see, e.g., Bornstein 1994, Feinberg 1999, Gabriel 1995, Stone 1991, and Stryker 1994). To the extent that the social construction of gender is against the interests of all feminists, it ought to fall to those of us who occupy positions of relative safety and privilege to complicate our own locations, to explore the costs of our comfort, and to help imagine a world in which it would be safe to be non-, ambiguously, or multiply gendered.[18]

16. Thanks to Jacob Hale for stressing the importance of this point. The monster Stryker (1994) has most particularly in mind is Frankenstein's, but the figure of the monster—as "unnatural" because created, a "creature"—is central to her discussion of what she calls "transgender rage." See also Feinberg (1993) for a harrowing and moving portrayal of the experiences of a "he-she," and Frye (1983c) for a discussion of the extent to which gender ascription shapes our responses to each other.

17. Analogous work is being done around race and the experiences of those who are not readily racially classifiable—in particular, those of mixed race (see, for example, Camper 1994 and Zack 1995). There are, of course, enormous differences: Miscegenation provides an all too easily imagined answer to the question of how someone "came to look like that," and looking and otherwise seeming more white is more a matter of privilege for people of color than looking and otherwise seeming more male is for women (though in some circumstances the former can be more problematic and the latter more privileging than is usually acknowledged).

18. Being "stably female-gendered" is not an all-or-nothing thing: The dividing line of gender slices through at least the edges of many lives. In our culture's terms, as a feminist and a philosopher even I may not be a best paradigm case, and certainly many others are even less so—notably lesbians, who are routinely told, and often, especially as children, believe, that they are not "real women." And certainly not all feminists share the desire to end gender as we know it—one may, for example, be more concerned to fight for the recognition of one's identity as a woman despite one's gender-role nonconformity or one's

My own gender identity has never been a source of confusion, nor have I puzzled over what it means to say that I am a woman, and this certainty has been untouched by my increasing inability to define gender.[19] My certainty is partially grounded in my relatively easy conformity with heteronormativity: As theorists as diverse as Catharine MacKinnon (1990) and Judith Butler (1990) have argued, sexual identity, particularly as it is shaped within the structures of compulsory heterosexuality, grounds, rather than depends upon, gender difference. My questioning of heterosexuality (including my own), along with the other norms of gender, came rather late in my life (after adolescence) and in communities that tended toward an empirical stability (if not essentialism) concerning who women were: Lesbians, for example, were woman-identified and woman-loving, not "not-women."[20]

I was, therefore, initially puzzled by how to understand the claim of (most) male-to-female (MTF) transsexuals to be women—how, that is, to make their claims (their lives and experiences) intelligible.[21] My inability

less than stereotypical appearance. My appeal here is to those feminists who do share the desire to radically transform the meaning of gender, if not to eliminate it altogether, and who have the privilege of at least sufficient gender conformity to, for example, use a women's restroom without being hassled. Obviously, the challenge will be different depending on one's circumstances: I'm addressing most directly those who, like me, have lived close enough to the center never to have directly experienced the knife-edge of the gender divide.

19. I share this confusion with many if not most feminist theorists. Kessler and McKenna's (1978) book played an important role in moving us away from the premature sense of intelligibility expressed in the sex/gender distinction of most 1970s feminist theory. As I will argue, this confusion is entirely appropriate at this point in history: We have good reason to distrust *any* conceptually coherent account of gender.

20. (a) Jacob Hale (1996), in a discussion of Monique Wittig's claim that lesbians are not women, provides a subtle and complex (Austinian) analysis of the diverse meanings of "real woman", along with a persuasive argument that any understanding of gender or sexuality has to proceed by way of an understanding of the margins: It is in the experiences and perspectives of those who inhabit the boundaries that the contours of a contested conceptual space are articulated. I have, of course, been surrounded by sophisticated discussions about the ways in which women are not born but made, and made specifically by patriarchy for its ends—but underlying those discussions has been a virtually untouched dualism dividing those who were slated to be made into women from those who were not, along with a sense of the centrality of that constructed identity even for those who in many ways rejected it. (b) The impetus to explore these issues came largely from an invitation to a conference on "Sissies and Tomboys," held on February 10, 1995, at the Center for Gay and Lesbian Studies, City University of New York Graduate Center. I was invited by the organizer, Matt Rottnek, whose confidence that I did, despite my skepticism, have something to say about these questions, led to my beginning to pull these thoughts together. I was enormously helped, in preparing for the conference, by several of the programs (including Leslie Feinberg's plenary address) in "Differently Gendered Lives: A Week of Programs About Transgender and Transsexual Experiences," sponsored by the University of Minnesota Office of Gay, Lesbian, Bisexual, and Transgender Programs, and held on campus from January 28 to February 3, 1995.

21. Sarah Hoagland (1988) and Jan Binder (personal communication) have helped me to see the political implications lurking in questions of intelligibility: Who has to make themselves intelligible to whom, in what terms, for what reasons, against what forms of resistance, with what resources? Heteronormativity requires for intelligibility that one be one gender or the other: But some transsexuals are beginning to resist this requirement, in particular as enforced by "medical, psychotherapeutic, and juridical institutions" that police the gender boundary (Stryker 1994, p. 252), and hence no longer to identify as women (or men), plain and simple (Bornstein 1994; Stone, quoted in Gabriel 1995; Stryker 1994; Jacob Hale, correspondence; Susan Kimberley in discussion at the University of Minnesota conference).

to understand seemed to come from the fact that, despite my own unshakeable sense of being a woman, there was nothing I could point to as constituting my gender identity when I abstracted from a lifetime of unambiguous gender ascription on the part of others and an unambiguously female body. Surely, it seemed to me, if there was something independent of social role and body that male-to-female transsexuals could recognize as their gender identity, I should be able to find whatever it was in my own sense of identity—but there simply didn't seem to be anything like that there. (I was reminded of Hume's inability to find in himself a substantial Cartesian self.) Whatever they meant when they said they were women, it didn't seem to be what I meant. What, then, did they mean? And how, to put a Wittgensteinian spin on the question, were they able to mean it?

For various reasons, reinforced by Leslie Feinberg's eloquent politics of solidarity (1999 and in her plenary address to the Minnesota conference, see fn 20b), I found myself moving away from the feminist suspicion that lay behind that puzzlement, a suspicion that tended to see male-to-female transsexuals as men, with typical male arrogance, claiming female identity; and female-to-male (FTM) transsexuals as self-hating, male-identified women. Those analyses singularly failed to fit the people whose voices I was hearing and reading, especially those who were seriously concerned about being allies in feminist struggles. Nor did those analyses fit with a commitment I thought I had to the deconstruction of gender (in reality, not just in theory).

Yet even with the motivation of solidarity, I still just did not understand. But that motivation—and the political thinking it engendered—did lead me to what it ought not have taken me so long to see: I was keeping to myself the position of unproblematized, paradigmatic subject, puzzling over how to understand some especially recalcitrant object. To put it in Wittgensteinian terms, I was finding one sort of phenomenon to be maddeningly opaque because I was taking another sort of phenomenon to be transparent. I couldn't understand the gender identity of transsexuals in part because I thought I understood my own—or, more accurately, could take it for granted, as not in need of understanding. (Wittgenstein suggested that part of the reason we were hopelessly puzzled about how it was possible to figure out what other people were thinking and feeling was that we thought there was nothing to figure out in our own case.)[22]

The very overdetermination of my gender identity, the congruence of body, socialization, desire, and sense of self—the fact that everything pointed the same way—was what made it hard to see what was going

---

22. Not only my Wittgensteinian philosophical bent ought to have alerted me sooner to what I was doing, since it was precisely what feminists of color had accused white feminists of doing: taking for ourselves the position of the paradigmatic, making of others objects of investigation and knowledge. (note added in 2010)

on, hard, in fact, to see that anything was "going on" at all.[23] I am (unlike very many diverse nontranssexual women, who for all sorts of reasons do not conform in so many particulars to the norms of femaleness) so close to the paradigmatic center that I am in a very bad position to see how the apparatus works, to get a feel for how diverse forces could push and pull one in different directions. I may not like the forces that construct gender identity, but their tugs on my body and psyche tend more to hold me in place than to unbalance me: I don't know them, as others do, by the strains they exact in the attempt to stand erect. Clearly what I needed to do was to problematize my own gender identity.

Easier said than done.

4

By contrast, I don't have to work at finding my Jewish identity problematic. Unlike my gender identity, my Jewishness, though a central and unquestionable part of who I am, is a puzzle to me. Not only, as with gender, can't I define it, but I can't figure out what it means to say of me that I am a Jew, nor what I might be conforming to in order to count as one. Although I have no doubt about it, or about its centrality to who I am, I am genuinely puzzled about how to understand it—and, unlike my gender, it does seem to need to be understood. That is, although the ways I live gender make its operations unproblematically transparent to me, as invisible as the air, the ways I live Jewishness are maddeningly opaque. But opacity, of course, is also visibility: Again, in Wittgensteinian terms, what seems to get in the way of seeing clearly is what we need to be looking at, and recognizing as what we need to know. In my case there is a rich set of mostly familial experiences that inform my sense of Jewishness, in ways that link it with my rationalism, my respect for science, my judgmentalism, my sense of humor and irony, and (most centrally) my passionately internationalist, socialist sense of justice. But my awareness of how less-than-fully shared these commitments are among Jews, along with the absence in my life of a community that takes these as constitutive even of one way of being Jewish, makes such experiences, and the identity they ground, seem not to be an answer to the question of what I know about myself when I know myself to be, specifically, Jewish.[24]

23. Aside from being a feminist, a philosopher, and an adult-onset bisexual (and having loved math and logic), my only major failures to conform to the norms of femaleness are that I have never been pregnant and I am not a mother. But I managed to leave those options at least hypothetically open until this summer, so never confronted the implications for my inclusion as a "real woman." I am writing the final draft of this chapter while recuperating from a total hysterectomy, surgery that removed not only the possibility of pregnancy but the internal organs most definitive of my femaleness. The timing is coincidental, but suggestive.

24. Irena Klepfisz's (1990) account of her experience of a vanishing Yiddish culture in New York helped give me a sense of what it would be like to have a community-based sense of secular Jewish identity.

Nowadays in the United States, the questions to which "Jewish" is the correct answer are almost always questions about religion. Being Jewish here and now is one identity in a contrastive set that includes Christian (with all the subsets thereof), Buddhist, Muslim, and so on. Forms of Christianity, most centrally forms of mainstream Protestantism, are the paradigm cases of religions in the United States, so Judaism is distinguished by its most noteworthy distinguishing features from a Christian perspective: Its adherents go not to church but to synagogue or temple, and they go not on Sunday but on Saturday or on Friday night. If you're in the hospital (one place you're likely to be asked your religion) and take a turn for the worse, they'll send for a rabbi, not for a priest, minister, or pastor. For some Jews this religious way of thinking about what sort of identity Jewish identity is may work reasonably well (though I think even for observant Jews there has been a problematic "Christianizing" of identity in, for example, the moving of religious observance for all family members from the home to the synagogue). But it makes no sense at all to secular Jews like me (as, for different reasons, I suspect it makes no sense to Buddhists, among others).

I don't have a religion: I'm a life-long atheist on increasingly principled moral grounds; I know very little about Jewish religious observance and feel comfortable with less; and though I know I had religious ancestors, among them my paternal grandparents, what I share with them, as with other Jews, does not feel to me to be a religion. Religion is rather what estranges me from many other Jews, for much the same reason as it estranges me from Christians and others: I am nonreligious, even anti-religious, about as deeply as I am Jewish.

But I am Jewish. No one, actually, would dispute this, even though many people would insist on misrepresenting it. So far as anyone knows (albeit, as is the case for most European Jews, this is not very far), I have only Jewish ancestors, and that settles it. Were I to deny that I was Jewish, I would be accused (rightly, I think) of self-hatred, of internalized anti-Semitism. As I was growing up I was told (apocryphally, perhaps—my mother's source was the film *Gentleman's Agreement*) that Einstein said he would consider himself Jewish as long as there was anti-Semitism in the world, and certainly by the definitions of anti-Semites I am Jewish. That is surely part of it: Disaffiliation is dishonorable.

But that isn't—or shouldn't be—all there is to Jewish identity, even for the most secular. Surely, it seems, the Nazis and their ilk ought not to be the arbiters of our identity. What is it I know about myself when I know that I am a Jew?

As with questions about gender identity, part of my questioning comes from trying to understand someone who claims to share this identity with me but who seems clearly not to have it in the same way that I do. In the case of Jewish identity my questions have concerned converts—in particular, converts to Judaism.[25] In Christianormative terms, individual faith and knowledge are at the heart of identity, and conversion to Judaism is a religious process, governed by rabbis and requiring large amounts of religious instruction. The consequence is that converts to Judaism are intelligible as Jews in a way that I am not. Christianity is quintessentially a religion for converts: Being born a Christian may make you one in the sense that you are part of a Christian community, but to be a "real" Christian you have to acknowledge for yourself the place of Christ in your life, and being born to a Christian family merely makes that more likely. Similarly, converts to Judaism know a lot more about Judaism as a religion than I do, which also makes them more intelligible on Christian terms: One can't be a real Christian if one is ignorant of creedally appropriate interpretations of scripture, for example. If it is hard for me to understand how one can be a woman other than by being born female, it is all too easy to understand how one can be a Jew having been born something else. But that's not how I am a Jew.

Problematically, the Jewishness of converts is intelligible, even to me, in a way that my own is not, since theirs, unlike mine, fits the conceptual framework of Christianormativity. Part of that framework is that there be a definite "there" there, typically involving confirmation (as it is called) by a designated authority. And part of my problem is that, were I required to submit to such confirmation, I would surely fail. The rabbinical authorities charged with deciding who will get to become a Jew decide on grounds that have no connection to my own Jewishness. I am not, of course, required to be so confirmed: Those same authorities, specifically as they interpret the Israeli Law of Return, would unquestionably include me (having a Jewish mother is sufficient). But even so, their authority feels irrelevant to me. Rabbis are religious authorities, and my Jewishness is not a religious identity.

Contemporary Jewish thinking is deeply concerned with what it is to be an authentic Jew: In particular, there are those who deny the possibilities of authentic nonreligious identity after the Holocaust, or of authentic diasporic Jewish identity after the founding of the state of Israel[26]

---

25. As in the case of gender, I respond differently to people who "go the other way," who give up the identity they share with me for another: female-to-male transsexuals and Jewish converts, especially to Christianity. I feel abandoned, as though someone I thought was "on my side" had gone over, if not exactly to the enemy, then to the class of others who historically have oppressed us. I'm learning, largely through listening to and reading Leslie Feinberg and, more recently, reading and corresponding with Jacob Hale, to think and feel differently about FTM transsexuals, but it is harder for me to accept Jews who convert to Christianity. The difference, I think, is that although it is no part of sexism to get women to defect and become men (not, at least, in this world and in bodily form; see Boyarin [1994] for an argument that Pauline Christianity does envision women's becoming spiritually men), it is at the heart of orthodox Christianity to get others, most especially Jews, to defect and become Christians. If there is anything I think is essential to Jewish identity in Christian cultures, it is the resistance to Christian proselytizing. At the very least, a convert can be held accountable by Jews, as an FTM transsexual can be held accountable by women, for conscientiously dealing with newly acquired Christian—or male—privilege.

26. Natalie Kampen has pointed out to me the importance of the idea of authenticity to Jewish identity, and the relation to similar discussions concerning, for example, black or Chicano identity. The

(Goldberg and Krausz 1993). And though no one would deny that I am a Jew, there are many who would question the authenticity of my Jewish identity, who would claim that as a Jew I have obligations I am turning my back on. I, too, am tempted to make similar claims on others: It seems to me profoundly un-Jewish to be a Republican or to oppose affirmative action or, for that matter, to oppose the rights of Palestinians to self-determination. Unlike the rabbis, I have no power to enforce my claims, but what is it that grounds my making them: What do I mean by them? What am I doing in attempting to police the boundaries of an identity I find unintelligible? And how might figuring that out help me to understand my temptations to police the boundaries of an identity I find all too intelligible?[27]

5

When I bring the murkiness of my Jewish identity together with the suspicious transparency of my gender identity, one question that suggests itself is: Who cares? To whom does it matter, and why, that I have the identities that I do, and that I do or do not share them with certain others? Another, related question is: Who gets to decide, and on what grounds? How are some people counted in and others out? These are, I think, better—more useful, more practically pressing—questions than the ones I started with, namely: What can a transsexual mean when she says she is a woman, and what can I mean when I say I am a Jew?

One way of framing the shift from the earlier questions to the later ones is by way of a Wittgensteinian account of why the earlier ones seem so intractable. The focus on what we mean (rather than on what we do and why, as though we can answer the one without the other) usually leads to one of three possibilities, or to an oscillation among them. The first is some form of privileged access essentialism: Femaleness or Jewishness is just there, an abstractable part of one's overall identity, a definite, discernible something. Aside from the well-known problems both with privileged access and with essentialism, a serious problem with this approach, from my perspective, is that it leaves me out: If being a woman

concern revolves around a subordinated community's fears in relation to the dominant community: for example, that those members most acceptable to the white or Christian world will be assimilated, while the others are increasingly stigmatized. It is an understandable response to such (realistic) fears to accuse the more "acceptable" of being inauthentic; but, as María Lugones argued in a talk at a Philosophy, Interpretation, and Culture (PIC) conference at Binghamton University (in April 1994), it's misguided and self-defeating, reinforcing the oppressor's logic.

27. Thanks to Diana Tietjens Meyers, Lisa Heldke, and Jacob Hale for pointing out to me that, in earlier versions of this chapter, I had (repeatedly, even after being warned) succumbed to these temptations. Rather than claim finally to have overcome them, I would note here that such lapsing into the perquisites of privileged subjectivity is not only a demographic but an occupational hazard, and the effort to give up identity policing needs to be an ongoing one. (This chapter may be finished, but its author is a work in progress.)

or a Jew consists in a particular inner state, knowable independently of the body or the history one happens to have or of how one is regarded by others, then I fail to be one. And though I am willing to consider forgoing paradigmatic status, I do think any definition of either women or Jews that simply leaves me out is quite likely to be wrong.

The second possibility is expert essentialism. On this view, such identities are complex and not necessarily introspectively accessible, but, by exercising some combination of scientific and legislative authority, experts can make determinations. This view does in fact capture much about current practice. There are in both cases experts who are in the business of making such determinations, though, as I've argued above about Jewishness, they do so in ways that I and many others find troubling. The situation is even clearer when we look at the experts who determine gender, especially as this is done in the case of transsexuals.[28] The physicians and psychiatrists who have had the authority to decide who is "really" gendered differently than they are biologically sexed have tended (though this is changing, as transsexual activists are gaining some influence with the medical establishment) to reinforce precisely the gender stereotypes feminists have attempted to undermine: To be a woman in their terms has meant to be feminine. There has also been (though this too is changing) a conflation of gender and sexual identity: A real woman is supposed to be heterosexual.

Also, curiously, in the case of gender, though not in the case of Jewishness, the experts insist on the inbornness of gender identity, even when it is discordant with biological sex. Those who would convert to Judaism do not have to demonstrate to the rabbis that they have "really" been Jewish all along—one can quite openly be a convert. But, as Kate Bornstein (1994, p. 62) sardonically notes, the only way to be a "certified" transsexual is to deny that you are one—that is, to convince the doctors (and agree to try to convince the rest of the world) that you are and always have been what you clearly are not, namely, simply and straightforwardly a woman (or a man). Since you cannot have had a history that is congruent with such an identity, you are left without a past (Feinberg 1999). As I argued above, it is not only in our own memories but in the memories of others that our selves take shape, and the institutionalization of transsexuality functions as a theft of selfhood, in making a transsexual life not only closeted but literally untellable, incoherent.

The theft is premeditated, carried out with malice aforethought. The illusion of the naturalness of sex and gender requires that we not see what the magician is up to before the impossible being—a newly born adult man or woman—emerges from beneath the surgical drape. Our

---

28. For a discussion of another site of expert determination of sex/gender, that of sex-assignment at birth in cases of genital ambiguity, see Kessler (1990): Feminist suspicions about the phallocentrism of the sex/gender system are reinforced by her argument that the determining factor for sex-assignment is the presence or absence of a "good-enough" penis.

(nontranssexual) comfort requires that we fail to acknowledge transsexuals as such, seeing what the surgery and the hormones and the scripted behavior intend for us to see: a "natural" man or woman. If the illusion fails—perhaps because those who "rise up from the operating tables of [their] rebirth . . . are something more, and something other, than the creatures [their] makers intended [them] to be" (Stryker 1994, p. 242)—we respond to the affront to that comfort by seeing the transsexual as, to quote the term Stryker uses and appropriates, a "monster."

"The transsexual body," as Stryker points out, "is an unnatural body. It is the product of medical science. It is a technological construction. It is flesh torn apart and sewn together again in a shape other than that in which it was born" (1994 p. 238). But so are the bodies of women who attempt to stave off aging by multiple plastic surgeries. So, especially since my hysterectomy, is my body. And none of us, for reasons as natural and unnatural as the full complexities of our lives, is the shape we were when we were born. We are all creatures, as Stryker (1994, p. 240) reminds us, in the face of our unwillingness to remember, not just in our mortal corporeality but in the constructedness of our psyches and our bodies. The illusion of the naturalness of bodies and psyches that conform to the dictates of heteronormativity is maintained when identity boundaries are policed by experts committed to keeping their work under wraps. Even when the experts are facilitating the crossing of sex and gender boundaries, they do so in ways that attempt to do as little damage as possible to the clarity of the lines: They may be crossed, but they are not to be blurred.

A third possibility for how it is that an identity can be claimed—privileged access voluntarism—has, in the face of the inadequacies of the other two, seemed very attractive, especially to some transgendered people. On a privileged access voluntarist account, one is, a woman if one says one is, and the claim means whatever one takes it to mean: It is not up to anyone else to tell me whether or not I am a woman, nor is there some particular essential property I have to have in order to be one; being a woman might in fact mean something quite different to me from what it means to you. The problem with this picture is that, in appearing to give the individual everything, it in fact gives nothing at all. As Wittgenstein has argued, meaning cannot be a private matter: A word means what it does not because I have joined it in my mind to an idea or an image (as Locke would have it) but because there exists a set of social practices in which I participate, in terms of which I can get the meaning right or wrong. Allowing that 'woman' means whatever anyone who applies it to herself takes it to mean gives the freedom of self-naming at the cost of there being any point to the activity, any content to the chosen name, any reason for saying that one is a woman, rather than a man—or, for that matter, a car or a chrysanthemum.[29]

---

29. See Nelson (2002). Also, Leon J. Goldstein's chapter, "Thoughts on Jewish Identity" (especially p. 81), in Goldberg and Krausz (1993), similarly rejects the coherence of the idea of Jews as simply self-identifying. For a Wittgensteinian argument against the metaphysics of privileged access, see Chapter 1.

In practice, of course, naming oneself a woman is neither capricious nor unconnected to cultural meaning, even if, for some people—as Kate Bornstein suggested in a radio interview—what is really intended is that one is not a man, in a world in which there are simply no other conceptually allowable alternatives. On this view at least some MTFs are—or would be if conceptual space allowed—not women but something else altogether. It will also be true that for those transsexuals who do think of themselves as women, the associations with womanhood that seem especially resonant may well be idiosyncratic, and there is no reason why they cannot pick and choose among them—why, that is, transsexuals should not have the same freedom as born women to embrace some aspects of womanhood and vehemently reject others. But once we drop the idea that there is a specific something (knowable either internally or to experts) in which being a woman consists, while holding onto the idea that there has to be some substantive, shareable content to the assertion, we have moved toward my second set of questions, those concerning who cares and who gets to decide.

The shift to this latter set of questions hinges on seeing meaning as something that we do, not something that we discover, as the introspective essentialist would have it. Both the expert essentialist and the privileged access voluntarist seem to recognize this fact, but in different ways they obscure the practices involved—the latter by making those practices empty, and the former by granting to experts a problematically unquestionable authority. To take seriously the idea that meaning is something we do is to raise questions about who "we" are and why and how we do what we do; it holds us accountable for how we mean what we say.[30]

I know myself to be a woman and a Jew because of how I was named at birth: Neither of them seems to come from anything that I have done. But what do I now do when I take these identities to be in this way given, and what is my role in maintaining systems that identify people at birth? Such a role can seem quite troubling. Susan Stryker experiences rage at the moment of "nonconsensual gendering" (in which she sees herself as complicit) at the birth of her lover's daughter: "A gendering violence is the founding condition of human subjectivity; having a gender is the tribal tattoo that makes one's personhood cognizable. I stood for a moment between the pains of two violations, the mark of gender and the unlivability of its absence" (1994, p. 250). The complexity of her rage is in that dilemma: It is not as though, in the world we know, one would better treat a child by withholding gender, since, in the world we know, one would be withholding personhood.

---

30. The metaphysical underpinnings of the idea that social classifications (such as race and gender) are the real products of social actions—in other words, that constructivism is compatible with realism—are being developed in detail by Michael Root (see Root 2000).

Recognition of the oppressive nonconsensuality of natal gendering need not obviate the significance of the feminist insistence on the specific oppressiveness of female, in contrast to male, gendering, although emphasizing one rather than the other has led to political and conceptual conflict. Such conflict has emerged in the political antagonism between (some) transsexual women and men and (some) feminists, especially (some) lesbian separatists, conflict that emerges in differing understandings of the meaning of "women-only" spaces. As Sarah Hoagland has reminded me, separatists were concerned with the creation of new meaning within self-defined spaces, not with the boundaries that marked off those spaces: Attention circulated within lesbian space, rather than being focused on those on the outside, following Marilyn Frye's (1983*d*) definition of lesbians as women whose attention was drawn to other women. Furthermore, as Anne Leighton pointed out to me, many lesbians, especially separatists, were more than ready to acknowledge transsexuals as such, as (another species of) "impossible beings."[31] Nor, of course, is "woman" a category lesbian separatists have had any particular fondness for, let alone any desire to maintain the clarity and distinctness of. Self-identified women, I am told, have never been asked to submit to tests aimed at "proving" their womanhood as a condition of entry to "women-only" spaces such as the Michigan Women's Music Festival. Why, then, the battles over the inclusion in such spaces of (those who identify as) MTF transsexuals?

The interpersonal politics of such encounters are complex and surely not to be resolved by an armchair observer. But, aside from echoing Kate Bornstein's (1994) admonition that lesbian separatists are hardly the most politically savvy choice of adversary for transsexuals (and vice versa), I would like to introduce a possibly helpful piece of terminology to get at what I think separatists have in mind when they use such problematic terms as 'womyn-born-womyn' to exclude MTF transsexuals. A major reason for the existence of separatist space is to engage in the activity of self-naming and self-creation, and it is clearly inconsistent with such an aim to allow the definitions of the heteropatriarchy to determine who is to be allowed in. (The use of 'womyn' indicates that the identity in question is specifically not the one with which one was labeled at birth, whereas the people to whom it is intended to apply are precisely those who were so labeled.) But separatism exists against the recognition of the Adamistic

---

31. One of the best articulations of what it is to be an "impossible being" is, in fact, Marilyn Frye's, in her *tour de force* essay "To Be and Be Seen" (1983*d*)): In the logic of patriarchy, it must, she demonstrates, be impossible to see women as lesbians see them. That she starts this essay by quoting Sarah Hoagland on the conceptual impossibility of lesbians further reinforces the point that lesbian separatist suspicion of MTF transsexuals need not rest on an essentialist or biologistic account of who women are. Both Frye (1988) and Hoagland (1988) are clear on the constructedness of female identity and on the inextricability of that construction from the subordinating projects of male domination. They are also both insistent that the focus of lesbian attention is on other lesbians, not on the borders that might be taken to define either "lesbian" or "woman." (See, especially, Hoagland's [1988, p.70] refusal to define "lesbian" in part because of her refusal to engage in what she takes to be the diversionary activity of boundary marking.)

assumption that men have a natural right to name anything they deem worth naming, and of the fact that wresting that supposed right from them requires vigilance. It also starts from the recognition of the specific harms that flow from the natal ascription of femaleness in a misogynist world. To get at the importance of these concerns, I suggest the term 'perinatally pinked', which refers to the condition of having been named female around the time of birth: by chromosome-testing or ultrasound visualization beforehand, by visual inspection at birth, or by surgical "correction" shortly after birth (see Kessler 1990).[32] Separatist space (and other feminist practices that recognize the separatist impulses that inform even non-separatist-identified female self-assertion; see Frye 1983c) can be seen as a space of healing from having been perinatally pinked, and from living in a world in which being so marked makes one a target for subordination and abuse. Being in the company of others who, like one, were perinatally pinked, and creating collectively with them the affirmative identity of "womyn," is for many separatists of the utmost importance to their survival in such a world. That MTF transsexuals were not perinatally pinked is a simple statement of fact, and it in no way diminishes the oppressiveness of their experiences of gendering— nor, importantly, does it preclude separatists' support of their claim to inclusion in the category of women. That category is one that operates in heteropatriarchal space—the space that requires unambiguous gender-ascription for intelligibility—and in such space many lesbians are natural allies in the struggle to fight the harassment (or worse) that targets those who visibly fail to conform to gender norms.[33]

32. 'Perinatally pinked' suggests, of course, another meaning, one that in this context demands at least acknowledgment: as a description of the circumcised penis of the Jewish male. For discussion of the ramifications of this way of inscribing Jewishness on the male body—that is, in a way that can be read (cannot but be read?) as feminizing—see D. Boyarin (1995), who in turn quotes Geller (1993) quoting Spinoza to this effect.

33. (a) Many thanks to separatists at the Fall 1995 meeting of the Midwest Society for Women in Philosophy—especially Marilyn Frye, Sarah Hoagland, and Anne Leighton—for helping me to understand a separatist point of view on the dispute between MTF transsexuals and separatists, particularly focusing on admission to the Michigan Women's Music Festival. They are not responsible for 'perinatally pinked', nor am I certain of whether they would agree on its usefulness. I've been helped in understanding transsexual women's arguments against their exclusion from the Michigan festival by reading letters and articles in several issues of TransSisters, especially Issue No. 7 (1995), and of Transsexual News Telegraph. (b) It was also helpful to read in both publications about the controversy over the exclusion from the New Woman's Conference of pre-or nonoperative MTF transsexuals. The argument is made that it is a conference for those who share a very specific experience: that of having "lived socially as a man at some time, . . . currently living socially as a woman, and [having] had genital surgery that resulted in making her genitals appear more female than they originally were" (TransSisters 7: 11). In that same issue, both a letter writer, Riawa Smith, and the editor, Davina Anne Gabriel, suggest, what was apparently decided on, that the conference should change its name to reflect better just whom it is intended for, rather than using a name ("New Woman") that others feel an equal need and right to claim. (c) As with my suggestion about 'perinatally pinked', the idea here is that different people will find that different parts of their complex identities and histories are especially salient and, in particular, define a space of safety and refuge—of home, in one of the senses of that loaded word; and that such identities and spaces are vitally important but, as Riawa Smith echoes Bernice Johnson Reagon (1983), not to be confused with the space of activist politics, even as they make such politics possible, by providing a space both of refuge and of wild imagining.

If heteronormativity requires natally ascribed gender as the sign of intelligibility, Christianormativity tends to make the natal ascription of identity unintelligible. Abstract individualism, a distinctively Christian view of persons, views group identity as properly a matter of choice, and as subordinate to one's unmarked humanity in constituting identity (see Lafer 1993). In practice, of course, individuals are hardly unmarked at birth, and not only by gender: The obvious additional natal mark is race, and, as argued above, all sorts of deviations from normality get labeled inborn. But identities thought of as inborn are seen not as a matter of group membership but as traits inhering in individuals. Group membership is meant to come later, and to be chosen. So the only intelligible way to be born a Jew is if Jewishness can be seen as a "trait," or a cluster of traits—a ground of intelligibility that anti-Semitic discourse has been only too happy to provide.

But what if we resist the dictates of Christianormativity on this point, and insist on the intelligibility of being born a member of the Jewish people? Can we find in such an exercise a way of thinking that makes better sense of what it is to be born a male or a female (see Boyarin 1994), where one criterion for "better sense" is the greater intelligibility of those who come later to dispute the gender membership into which they were born?

One thing to note is that Jewishness would not be the sort of identity it is if some people were not born into it: It is in this way not (or not just) a religious identity. Being born Jewish is not the only way to be Jewish, nor is it necessary for born Jews to be thought of as more authentic or "real" Jews than converts (though often they are). What is true is that born Jews have certain histories that converts do not, though it is important to keep in mind just how diverse those histories are, including not only the wide range of different experiences of Jewishness but also the possibility of not knowing for most of one's life that one is Jewish: Discovering that one is means discovering something about one's own history. (You may, for example, have been born to Jewish parents and adopted by Christians and discover your Jewishness when discovering your birth parents. Note that in the reverse situation, it would be wrong to say that you would discover you were Christian.)

Part of the difficulty involved in thinking about Jewishness is acknowledging the importance of history, along with group identity. Ignoring or theoretically deconstructing the role of history—of the given, the unchosen—leads to the sort of arrogating voluntarism I discussed above. The denial of the relevance of the body and of history (often, confusedly, in the name of anti-essentialism) also seems to me to be both masculinist and Christian, insofar as both those discourses privilege the mind over the body, the chosen over the given.[34] That some of us confront some of

34. Having had these thoughts rather inchoately for a long time, I was excited to find them developed in scholarly detail in Boyarin (1994), where he discusses the implications of Paul's proclaiming

our identities as ineluctable, as constitutive of who we are, as something about ourselves we cannot change, is to say something about how certain experiences are socially constructed; it is not to be committed to essentialism.

To speak of Jewishness as paradigmatically unchosen has, of course, an additional reasonance, since to be Jewish is to be "chosen." That is, it is God who gets to do the choosing; one is chosen whether one chooses to be or not. Jewish atheists are in general a peculiar breed: We are given to having deeply disputatious relationships with the God we don't believe in, often centered on just what He had it in mind to choose us for. My own sense is that we were chosen to be canaries. Just as one sends canaries down mines to see if the air is safe to breathe—if it will kill anything, it will kill a canary—so Jews are, over the long run, a good test of the oppressiveness of a social environment (at least in those parts of the world where Jews have historically lived). Sooner or later those who are committed to ideologies of domination and subordination will reveal themselves as anti-Semites.

Thus, the quintessentially Jewish injunction that "none is free so long as any are oppressed" is for Jews a literal truth, no matter how hard individuals or groups may work at denying it, whether by assimilating within a Christian culture or by militarizing the state of Israel: A canary on steroids is still a canary. Affluent conservative American Jews may think that their interests lie in opposing affirmative action and other efforts to undo anti-black racism, but they are mistaken. The Black-Jewish alliance of the civil rights era may have been romanticized, but it had its roots in a deep truth: Racists are also anti-Semites, and Jews have no business consorting with them, even if they allow us into their subdivisions, universities, and country clubs. Our mortgages, degrees, and membership cards will not make us safe: The world will not be truly safe for the Jews until it is safe for everyone, and we forget that at our peril (See chapter 4).

A consequence of this notion of chosenness is that power is a misguided and ultimately ineffective response to danger.[35] Precisely because one cares about an imperiled identity, one has to resist the temptation to protect it with fortified barricades. Thus, one can think of conversion to Judaism not in the context of Rabbinic law (although for those for whom religious faith is at the heart of their Jewishness, chosen or otherwise, Rabbinic law will be something to engage, perhaps, as it has always been engaged, disputatiously) or of the intricacies of the Israeli Law of Return, but in the terms Ruth used in following Naomi: "Thy people shall be my people."

in Galatians that "[t]here is neither Jew nor Greek; there is neither slave nor freeman; there is no male and female. For you are all one in Christ Jesus."

35. See Boyarin and Boyarin (1993), to which, along with conversations with Daniel Boyarin, I am deeply indebted for pulling together these ideas.

Conversion to Judaism is more like marrying into a family than it is like conversion to Christianity, including analogous problems around the policing of families by, for example, the social and legal restrictions of marriage. A notion of family that broke free of such restrictions would function like the notion of "my people" that Daniel and Jonathan Boyarin (1993) call "diasporic"—nonpoliced, not shored up by apparatuses of institutionalized power. Belonging to such a family or a people would mean being related in some complex amalgam of chosen and unchosen bonds to a group, some of whom are born members, others of whom are, we might say, "naturalized."[36]

The term is both precisely right and deeply wrong. It is deeply wrong in its association with citizenship, that most quintessentially state-regulated of identities.[37] Its very suggestive rightness lies in its making evident the fact that "natural" is something one can become (there is a process that produces it), and in its marking a contrast that distinguishes collectivities that at least some members are born into from those that are wholly chosen. Being a born member of such a collectivity is, importantly, a matter of genealogy—that is, of history, not of essential traits: There is no suggestion that the whole shebang (the *ganze megillah*) is anything other than a social construction. A further important feature of such collectivities is that one shares one's membership in them with others with whom one would not choose to be associated and whom one cannot expel.

What happens when we bring these reflections on Jewish identity to the questions about sex and gender identity as raised by, specifically, MTF transsexuals? If we push the analogy, the fact that there are born women is constitutive of the category "woman," just as the fact that there are born Jews is constitutive of the category "Jew." What counts, of course, is not who one's parents (or mother) are but how one is enrolled into the sex/ gender system at birth. The category "woman," however, can also include variously "naturalized" members, where naturalization has to do with a deeply felt identification with at least some (and almost certainly only some) earlier members, a feeling that one is in some sense "like them." (When identity is officially regulated, those who are not officially natur-alized have the status, as it were, of undocumented aliens—an apt description of not-officially-certified transsexuals, caught in a position in which they are unable to acquire usable driver's licenses or other forms of identification (Feinberg 1999).) Such identification has to be acknowl-edged by at least some earlier members, as one cannot become a Jew without the acknowledgment of at least some already-Jews, though not necessarily by all of them, and not necessarily by born members (see

36. Thanks to Michael Root for suggesting the use of 'naturalized citizen' in the context of thinking about transsexual identity change. Judith Shapiro (1991, 259–60) makes similar use of the term.

37. See Boyarin and Boyarin (1993) for an argument that the particularism of Jewish identity is morally defensible only if *not* coupled with state power.

Kasher 1993). Those who are "naturalized" women are no less women than those who are born female, though the category would not be what it is were no one born into it.

An important disanalogy is that conversion to Judaism tends to be much more a matter of choice than does sex or gender change, and conversion may well have been preceded by a long period of quite comfortable identification as, say, Christian. The disanalogy marks a deep difference in how different identities work: One need not be recognized as Jewish or non-Jewish in order to be intelligible, and we have the conceptual space to narrate a history that goes between them.[38] But the disanalogy reflects aspects of gender practice that we might want to think about changing: That is, thinking about sex/gender identity as more analogous in these ways to Jewish identity might help us to imagine a less oppressive way of "doing gender." The experiences of transsexual people tend to be quite different from the experiences of converts to Judaism—but that may be due to aspects of our sex/gender system that could be imagined otherwise.

There are, I think, other advantages to pushing this analogy. It is less constraining of identity than are the operations of those who expertly police the gender divide: The significance of natal assignment is not to pick out the "real" women from the others but, rather, to note that there would be no categories of the sort that genders are if some people were not assigned to them at birth. There would, that is, be no such thing as a woman to believe that one was if there were not people who were assigned female at birth, just as there would be no such thing as Jewishness to convert to if there were not people who were Jewish from birth. (Again, the same is not true of Christianity.) To deny this conceptual role to natal assignment—to think of gender as more like Christianity, as a system of categories that people sort themselves into based on their own self-identifications—is to ignore the ways in which, as a matter of historical fact, no less real for being contingent and alterable, gender is socially constructed and, hence, the ways in which it functions in people's lives. (Part of the quarrel of lesbian separatists with transsexuals is a disagreement about how gender works. For many separatists, gender is a social imposition that places them in a threatened category: women are created as the objects of misogyny; whereas for many transsexuals gender is an inner identity that needs to be asserted in the face of social mislabeling. I want to suggest that both these conceptualizations are too restrictive to get at all the complex ways in which gender works, though each captures an aspect of gender that is, for some purposes, especially salient.)

---

38. See Gordon Lafer (1993) for the suggestion that traditionally Jewishness was much "deeper" and more connected to what made one socially intelligible. Also, as Diana Tietjens Meyers has reminded me, it is Judaism, the religion, to which converts convert, leaving that murky identity—"Jewishness"—still murky. It is both unclear and, in some communities and families, a matter of real dispute as to whether or not one can "become Jewish," and, if so, just what that means.

Whether or not, or to what extent, the sex/gender system is disrupted by the gender experiences of transsexuals depends on the extent to which those experiences are thought of as paradigmatic. The irony is that in order to support transsexual claims to clear, stable, and unambiguous gender identities, those identities must themselves remain marginal. Only a system that takes natally gendered persons as paradigmatic—that maintains the illusion of the normality of "natural" gendering—can have the solidity to ground *anyone's* unambiguous gender claims. The more important it is for transsexuals to claim a stable and unproblematic gender, the more conceptually dependent they are on their own marginality, as rare exceptions to a fundamentally natural dichotomy. The extent of this importance varies enormously from person to person—as it does for nontranssexuals. But it is a feature, surely alterable, of present-day Western cultures that stable and unproblematic gender identities are expected of everyone—so that those who resist claiming and enacting one such identity live the perilous lives of "outlaws." A sex/gender system in which, by contrast, not only natal members are paradigmatic, in which paradigm status can be shared with transsexuals, would be much more like the system that underwrites Jewish identity: full of ambiguity, unclarity, and vagueness. (In the *Philosophical Investigations* Wittgenstein tried to disabuse us of the Fregean conviction that ambiguous, unclear, vague concepts were not concepts at all: Having been so disabused, we can contemplate the possibility that we have reason in some cases not just to tolerate but to prefer ambiguity, unclarity, and vagueness.)

It is also, I would argue, an advantage to the analogy that it highlights the differences between the relationships of MTF and FTM transsexuals to the born members of their respective genders. Analogizing specifically womanness with Jewishness (an exercise that has, of course, a long and exceedingly complicated history) draws attention to anti-Semitism and misogyny as parts of the social world in which those categories have meaning and in the light of which they are lived. It helps us make sense of the particular anxieties felt by some Jews and some women about the possibility that core definitions of those identities will shift if the boundaries are not policed; and it can help, if not to allay those anxieties, at least to suggest that they are counterproductive. So long as I have no say (and given what sort of category "woman" is, I can have no say) about whether Margaret Thatcher is a woman, it avails me nothing politically to try to keep Kate Bornstein or Sandy Stone or Susan Stryker from being one. Ironically, it is the fact that some people are born women that provides one of the strongest arguments against attempts to police the boundaries of womanhood.

The analogy also shifts the question What is it to be a woman (or a Jew)?—as though there were something there, in me, to be discovered—to, instead, How did I get to be one? How was I claimed or assigned? How was I chosen—by whom and for what? And, having been chosen, to whom do I have what responsibilities, with whom is my fate tied and how? Conversion to Judaism is not, like conversion to Christianity, a matter between an individual and God or an individual and an institutionalized church. It is a matter of joining a "people," of coming to share their history, and their fate. An MTF transsexual may be no more a feminist than Phyllis Schlafly, but she is no more immune to sexism and no less accountable for her failure to identify with the struggle against it.

Such accountability will mean different things to different ones of us and different things to each of us at different times. But one thing it always means is a recognition of and active resistance to the misogyny and anti-Semitism that are part of the inherited histories and contemporary realities of women and Jews. (And a failure of accountability is a moral failure, not an identity test: One has failed to be, in this instance a good person, not a "good Jew" or a "good woman," still less a "real" woman or Jew.) Resistance entails not just fighting the attacks but, equally, refusing the benefits that are advertised as coming with closeting, silence, collaboration, or disaffiliation. I would regard it as profoundly dishonorable to pass—as there is frequent occasion to do—as an "honorary" man or Christian. The emphasis is on the "honorary": It is no dishonor to be taken to be a man or a Christian; what is dishonorable is to let stand the implication that one is therefore more worth respecting than if one were a woman or a Jew. (As a woman currently monogamously involved with a man, I regard it as dishonorable to pass, in this sense, as a heterosexual, which is rather different from identifying as a bisexual.)[39]

Resistance is connected to solidarity, which is a matter of identifying *with*, rather than *as* (Diamond 1993). As such, it can bind different groups rather than divide them, but typically it does primarily bind groups—and individuals, insofar as they are members of groups. Daniel Boyarin (1994, p. 257), in his deeply suggestive articulation of what he calls "diasporic identity," makes this point: Such identity is particularist but not isolationist. (See also Boyarin and Boyarin 1993) As nonhegemonic others (he has in mind primarily, of course, diasporic Jews), we live in larger, diverse communities to which we are deeply bound and to which we are responsible in part as a condition of our group identity. Solidarity, identifying with, is at the heart of the Passover seder, and in some traditions, such as the socialist ones of my family, the celebration of the liberation of "our people" is inseparable from a rededication to solidarity with all the continuing liberation struggles in the world. Similarly, I think, AIDS has

---

39. Thanks to Jacob Hale for pressing me on the need to think about passing as a man from the perspective of an FTM transsexual. What is important, as he pointed out, is grappling seriously with the male privilege that one acquires. What counts as the avoidance of "honorary" status is not always clear. For example, if I teach my classes and attend meetings on the high holy days, I am in effect setting myself apart from those "other" Jews who won't conform to the "normal" (i.e., Christian) calendar; but it feels dishonest to stay home, since neither synagogue attendance nor any other way of specifically marking the new year has any place in my life. Is it a matter of solidarity not to treat those days like any others in support of those faculty, staff, and students who—in the face of lack of cooperation or understanding—do observe the holidays?

come to play a role in lesbian identity, not because lesbians are at particular risk of HIV infection—which, course, they are not—but as an expression of solidarity with gay men who are, a solidarity that is at once "natural" (grounded in shared resistance to homophobia) and conscientiously chosen: My sense is that AIDS-related politics has greatly increased the numbers of lesbians who identify with gay men, and that lesbian identity has, as a consequence, been reshaped. Whom one identifies with is inseparable from what one identifies as.

6

I have (despite my recurrent temptations) no real interest in policing the boundaries of either womanhood or Jewishness, nor is it a job I want anyone else to do: Both identities are better left undefined—or, more strongly, incoherent and confused. If the meaning of identity, like the meaning of anything else, is a matter of the practices that shape it, then it would be both intellectually mistaken and politically unwise to give either of these identities more clarity and coherence than are warranted by their structuring practices. And those practices are a mess—a jumble of oppression and resistance, history and imagination, drudgery and heroism: If meaning is use, 'woman' and 'Jew' have been and continue to be put to such a dizzying variety of contradictory uses that any coherent account of either would have to be untrue. Furthermore, and importantly, it may well be incoherent identities, those that do not fit into the available taxonomies, that bear particularly liberatory potential. María Lugones (1990b) has been articulating this vision in, for example, arguing for the embracing of "multiplicitous" identities lived across worlds and in what, following Victor Turner, she refers to as "anti-structure—places of creative liminality" (see also Lugones 1994).

What does that leave us with as a way of finding identity intelligible? Family resemblance, for one: Male-to-female transsexuals or Jewish converts see in my identity—or the identity of some other women or Jews, born or not, perhaps very different from me—a variation of what they feel or want themselves to be; they look at some of us and see kin. (Talk of family is notoriously dangerous, as white feminists are reminded about the talk of "sisterhood," and as Jacob Hale has reminded me again. But, aside from its Wittgensteinian implications, I think it's worth engaging with—carefully. It helps to remember that family resemblance, like any other form of resemblance, is only very weakly transitive; and one thing we know about relatives is that they can cause us to be related to people we cannot imagine having as kin. But, imagine it or not, we do.) What I see when I look back is not a simple matter. I may look at a MTF transsexual and see not a woman but a man who, with stereotypically masculine arrogance, claims both the right to define what it is to be a woman and the right to take anything he wants, even if it's my identity.

Increasingly, this is not what I see, and the change has to do both with my looking more carefully—seeing, for example, the ways in which the oppressiveness of gender affects those who inhabit its unnameable borders at least as much as it affects those who live near the center of the female side—and with a growing feminist consciousness among transsexuals.

Part of being careful about the use of familial imagery involves displacing its role as a primary site of heteronormativity. Using the family in counter-normative ways is one sort of response to the reactionary deployment of family rhetoric: Rather than rejecting the family (as image or social arrangement), we can "queer" it. David Halperin (1995) proposes 'queer' as a term not for a particular identity, constructed, as all identities are, by complex amalgams of normalizing and stigmatizing practices, but for positionality: as a flexible strategy of resistance to the practices of heteronormativity.[40] Such flexibility is suggested, he argues, by the flexible illogic of heteronormativity: It is strategically better suited than any affirmation of, say, positive gay identity to slipping over, under, around, or through the stigmatizing net. Queer identity, so conceived, is a slap in the face to the illusory "straightness" of heterosexuality, an illusion maintained by diverting attention away from those who are supposed to be the unmarked "normals" and toward the crafty maneuvering of those who try to live lives they can respect in the face of contradictory imputations of sickness and sin.

The question of who is queer (along with the related question of whether queer is a useful and appropriate identity for gay men and, even more controversially, lesbians) has taken on some of the controversy that surrounds questions about who is a woman or who is a Jew. With the ascendancy of queer theory in some parts of the academic and cultural worlds it has become chic to be queer, and many gay men and (perhaps) more lesbians have felt that their identities—and, more important, their histories and struggles—were being ripped off.[41] As Halperin puts it, in a caveat: "Lesbians and gay men can now look forward to a new round of condescension and dismissal at the hands of the trendy and glamorously unspecified sexual outlaws who call themselves 'queer' and who can claim the radical chic attached to a sexually transgressive identity without, of course, having to do anything icky with their bodies in order to earn it" (1995, p. 65).

I want to argue for the claiming of queer identity as an important liberatory strategy—in part because of the challenge it poses to the paradigmatic status of privileged subjectivity—while maintaining the tension between the boundary-shiftiness of queerness and respect for the

40. For a related discussion of positionality as a way of thinking about identity that escapes essentialism without becoming empty, see Alcoff (1988).

41. For discussions of related phenomena, see Zita (1992) on "male lesbians," Boyarin and Boyarin (1993) on "the jew" [sic], and Kaminsky (1993) on exile.

historically and personally specific experiences of those who have "found themselves" (with the mix of activity and passivity that term implies) in identities whose boundaries they encountered as given and fixed, whether as a matter of internal certainty or of unyielding social decree.[42]

The symbolic appropriation of marginalized, oppressed, or stigmatized identities is the flip side of the expert policing of identity boundaries. The policing of boundaries requires definitive statements of who is or is not a "real" Jew or woman or homosexual, whether in the name of valorizing and defending the category or of keeping those in it from getting out. Symbolic appropriation often displaces those who have been thus defined—who may, in part because of such policing, regard those identities as central to their senses of self—in favor of others whose nonliteral (i.e., nonbodily) identifications become what it is to be a "real" Jew or woman or queer. Some male Jungians talk this way about their anima, and it is the suspicion (no doubt in at least some, though I suspect not many, cases well founded) that this attitude characterizes MTF transsexuals that is behind much of the feminist resistance to acknowledging MTFs as women. Daniel and Jonathan Boyarin (1993) have explored the phenomenon of the (lowercase) "jew": the outsider and nonconformist in the European imagination—the *real* Jew, realer for not being confined by a limited and limiting history.[43] There are good reasons to resist this symbolic appropriation of identity, even as it seems to be made possible by—and positively to further—the breaking down of confining definitions.

But there are equally good reasons for encouraging creatively playful, politically serious border transgressing on the part of those who could, given what seem to be the facts about them, safely reside on the more privileged side.[44] Adrienne Rich, writing in the 1970s, articulated a conception of lesbian identity that has affinities with queerness, and it met with similar resistance (see Zita 1981 and the discussion in Rich 1986). Rather than focusing on the specificities of the experiences of some women, Rich wrote about—and to—the lesbian in every woman: "It is the lesbian in us who is creative, for the dutiful daughter of the fathers in us is only a hack" (1979*a*, p. 201). The "lesbian continuum" encouraged any woman to find and identify with her own rebelliousness against heteropatriarchy (Rich 1986). The concern of Rich's critics was that such expansiveness drew attention away from the radical core of

---

42. The arguments here are related to those concerning how to think about racial identity: There are both scientific and political reasons to argue that race is unreal, but doing so obscures the histories and in many cases the antiracist politics of those whose lived experience of race is very real indeed. See, for example, DuBois (1966), Appiah (1986), and Outlaw (1992).

43. Daniel Boyarin (1994, 224ff.) is explicit about the parallels between this erasure of the specificity of Jews and "the post-structuralist deconstruction of the sign 'woman'."

44. In a video performance piece entitled "Cornered," Adrian Piper (1988) confronts presumptively white viewers with the challenge to acknowledge that, at least by the terms of the "one drop rule," many of them, especially those whose ancestors came to the U.S. many generations ago, are actually black, and to consider claiming that identity.

lesbian identity—an embodied erotic connection to other women. Rich wasn't advocating the position I referred to above as privileged access voluntarism, so the problem isn't that "lesbian" becomes contentless; rather it's that the specific transgressiveness of lesbianism is lost if the sexual is downplayed. The dispute is over which practices will be taken as constituting the language game, and, consequently, which family resemblances will emerge as salient.

It was Rich's strategy—as it is the strategy of queer theorists—to be expansive about the practices that constitute lesbian identity, in part as a means of destabilizing those that constitute heterosexual identity. Such destabilization is not just conceptual: Heteronormativity (akin to Rich's notion of compulsory heterosexuality) functions in part through the quotidian complicity of those who cannot imagine—or desire—an alternative. Similarly, in poems such as "Transcendental Etude" and "Sibling Mysteries," Rich (1978) reminds women of mother/child eroticism and of the unnaturalness of abandoning a woman's body for a man's: She is "queering" (women's) heterosexuality, in a way similar to Michael Warner's (1993) discussion in the introduction to *Fear of a Queer Planet*. Queerness is not meant to contrast with straightness so much as to displace it, to reveal its inherent contradictions and instabilities. Thus, queer readings of canonical texts are not attempts to demonstrate that some hitherto believed-to-be-straight author was really gay but are, rather, subversions of our reading practices, disruptions of our imputations to authors of the sort of straightforward, transparent integrity that characterizes privileged subjectivity.

Other theorists have urged the privileged to find in themselves the shreds and patches of transgressive identities. María Lugones (1987) suggests that "world"-travel—the movement into a social world in which one is marked as other, something the oppressed and marginalized have to do for survival—can be embarked on "playfully" by those among the privileged who have the courage and the loving commitment to learn how they are seen by those in whose eyes their privilege marks them as other. Sandra Harding (1991, p. 288) urges those who are privileged to learn to think out of "traitorous" identities, conscientiously disloyal to their privilege. Daniel and Jonathan Boyarin (1993) suggest diasporic identity as an alternative to nationalist identity: a history- and body-laden sense of identity (a sense that these particular others are "my people")—is viable (nonracist) only when it is uncoupled from state power.

Strategies of "queering the center" will vary as the identities in question are variously constructed, policed, and transgressively lived—in particular, as one or the other side of the oxymoronic natural incapacity/willful refusal construction is dominant. Womanhood and Jewishness are illustrative of these differences. Part of heteronormativity is the assumption that gender is not chosen but "natural": given and immutable, either inscribed on the body or, even if in some "deviant" cases at odds with it, set one way or the other at a very early age. As I noted above, the medical control of transsexual experience has served to reinforce, rather than to undermine, the fixity of gender. In the face of this rigidity, it can be liberatory to blur the boundary (both by straddling and by openly crossing it), to argue for the ways in which gender is neither definite nor fixed. Doing so need not, as many feminists have worried, undermine the intelligibility and efficacy of feminist politics, for which the undeniable reality and oppressiveness of sex/gender systems, however historically mutable or even arbitrary, are grounds enough. It can also be important to claim the power of self-naming, including the power of boundary setting. But the "selves" that do the naming need not be confined to those who in the dominant view of things count as women: A politics of solidarity can underwrite transgressive boundary *marking*, as well as blurring or straddling.

Jewishness, on the other hand, is aberrant in a Christianormative culture in being paradigmatically a matter not of choice but, as Daniel Boyarin puts it, of "genealogy" (1994, 236–246). From a Jewish perspective, postmodern anti-essentialist arguments can sound suspiciously Protestant, resting, as they often do, on the idea that any identity at all is "nothing but" a social construction, and that taking oneself to be anything as a matter of birth is bad faith. Furthermore, the conflation of givenness (i.e., the denial of voluntarism) and essentialism is a mistake, as is the opposition between givenness and social construction: Jewishness is no less socially constructed for being heritable.[45]

It is important, I think, to assert Jewishness specifically as an identity that is paradigmatically not a matter of choice—that is, to resist not only the assimilation of individual Jews into Christian culture but the assimilation of Jewish identity itself. (The term 'Judeo-Christian' is an example of such assimilation: Not only does it amalgamate Jewishness with Christianity, but it makes Jewishness out to be the larval form, important not in its own right but as a precursor to Christianity.) Concerning gender and sexual identity, I would argue that, although a case can be made for more body-based, less voluntaristic conceptions than are currently popular in gender studies, given the fit between such a view and that of heteropatriarchy, the dangers probably outweigh the benefits. But, tentatively, I have suggested that some ways of thinking about Jewish identity can provide a helpful model for breaking the hold on us of the rigidities of gender identity, by providing a middle way between the supposed dichotomy of either unproblematically natural or ungrounded and arbitrary.[46]

---

45. These are among the clarifications being developed by Michael Root.

46. After completing this chapter I encountered a paper of Jonathan Boyarin's (1995) in which he makes a similar argument, by way of a specifically Jewish intervention into a dispute he stages between Charles Taylor and Judith Butler concerning identity. I have also just begun to learn about the emerging conversation among Jewish feminists concerning the nature of Jewish identity: As with other identities, it is helpfully articulated from its own, in this case gendered, margins. (See Peskowitz and Levitt 1988.)

There is no single answer to the question of whether an explicitly, flexibly constructionist, or a historically given, body-based view of identity is more politically progressive. (I am assuming, of course, that in some sense there is no "fact of the matter" that questions concerning categorization do not admit of nonstrategic answers: That is, on the metaphysical level, I am assuming some version of social constructionism.) It depends on who is asserting what sort of identity when and where and why, in the face of what other sorts of assertions, especially those that have authoritative standing. My suggestion is that here and now there are good reasons to queer the centers of both heteronormative and Christianormative discursive practices and that such queering can proceed by way of exploring the ways in which some of us live as impossible beings, emphasizing those aspects of our lives that render us impossible: the shape-shifting of the transsexual and the unchosen givenness of the secular Jew. Against the normative backgrounds of essentialized gender and chosen religion, such emphases move the two identities onto a shared middle ground of complex—and normatively unintelligible—mixtures of givenness and choice.

In these ways and others—in articulations of *mestizaje* (see Anzaldúa 1987) or exhortations to become "world"-travelers (Lugones 1987), and in diverse invocations of trickster subjectivities (see Haraway 1991, p.199; Gates 1988)—the experiences of variously marginalized people provide alternative models of subjectivity, less seamless and transparent, less coherent and solid, than those of privilege. Each of them is grounded in the specificities of the experiences of historically particular groups, but all suggest that taking such experiences as paradigmatic of the human can both shatter the illusions of the naturalness of privilege and offer ways out of the constraints of its normativities. The point is not to generate legions of chic lesbian or mestiza or black or American Indian or Jewish wannabes, but to offer alternative, variously queer, provisional paradigms in relation to which each of us tells our own, shifting stories. The issue, then, is not who is or is not really whatever, but who can be counted on when they come for any one of us: The solid ground is not identity but loyalty and solidarity.

ACKNOWLEDGMENTS

Many thanks to the challenging audiences for earlier drafts at the University of Minnesota and at meetings of the Canadian and Midwest Societies for Women in Philosophy and of the American Academy of Religion, and, especially, to Lisa Heldke, Diana Tietjens Meyers, and Michael Root for their extensive comments. Unfortunately, those comments were interesting and provocative, and the result is a denser, more complex chapter and not, as they intended, a clearer one. The largest portion of the blame for the density and complexity, however, lies with Daniel Boyarin and Jacob Hale, who have between them done a wonderful job of confusing me.

PART III

TRANSGRESSION AND TRUSTWORTHINESS

The essays in this section begin an investigation into how we might engage in the work of transformation: how do theorizing and, specifically, the discipline of philosophy look different when attention is focused on the "real needs" of those who are engaging in them or of those whose allies we would be? How can—and should—we use the philosophical "we" after rejecting the spuriously generic "we" of privileged subjectivity? What need do we have for, and how can we fashion usable versions of notions like objectivity, or even a common language?

"Forms of Life: Mapping the Rough Ground" was written for the *Cambridge Companion to Wittgenstein*. It is my most sustained elaboration of the idea, alluded to in earlier sections, that the ground of our ordinary practices has a variegated topography, and that such variation allows for different perceptions of "what we do," including some that articulate critique both radical and grounded. Theorists of the margins, of closets, diasporas, and other locations of (in Patricia Hill Collins' formulation) "outsiders within" (Collins 1986) exemplify these possibilities: the proof of the possibility of radical, grounded critique is provided by actual examples of it.

As a reading of Wittgenstein, that chapter aims in part to counter readings that commit him to some combination of relativism and conservatism, although not by ascribing to him a radical political stance that would have been anathema to him. It is, I suggest, no accident that no clear political stance at all can be gleaned from his writing, which—early and late—is driven by an unease in his relationship to anything that might be considered home, any actual ground to stand on. The minimal metaphysics of the *Tractatus* is supposed to guarantee my connection to the world—the world just is my world—while the *Investigations* famously urges us to bring our words back home, as though it were only philosophy that led them, and us, astray. But since in his own life Wittgenstein vacillated between romanticizing and scorning any of the possible homes he might have claimed, it is, I suggest, odd to ascribe to him a comfortable relationship to the homes to which we are to bring our words. This essay most explicitly makes the case for one of the overarching themes of the volume: it is in the unspoken gap between the right words and the words we can intelligibly say that we can find and claim the space to articulate various discomforts with "home" and begin to imagine alternatives.

"The Trustworthiness of Research: The Paradigm of Community-Based Research" is firmly rooted in practice. It is co-authored with two women—Catherine Jordan, a pediatric neuropsychologist and Susan Gust, a community organizer—who had for about ten years been collaborating in a project involving University of Minnesota faculty and community members in exploring strategies for dealing with the problem of childhood lead poisoning. My involvement came as I began a three-year term as an associate dean in the Graduate School with a particular interest in the ethics and politics of research. The three of us organized a conference for university researchers, funders, and community activists on the challenges and promises of collaborative research, out of which grew an initiative we called GRASS Routes ('GRASS' stands for Grass Roots Activism, Science, and Scholarship). The paper, written from each of our distinctive perspectives, summarizes what we learned through this work, and makes a case for the greater trustworthiness of community-based participatory research. GRASS Routes and the projects we planned were interrupted by my co-authors' taking on responsibilities that grew directly out of our work together: Cathy is the Director of the Consortium on Children, Youth, and Family at the University of Minnesota, and Susan has been active in local and national community health activities and currently serves on the board of Community-Campus Partnerships for Health.

"Epistemology Resuscitated: Objectivity as Trustworthiness" is a more theoretical approach to questions about the trustworthiness of research, and it grows out of various projects I was engaged in while I was in the Graduate School, as specific as disputes between Native Americans and University researchers working on wild rice (most recently, deciphering its genome), and as general as the social role of especially public, land grant universities. The paper was motivated in particular by the "science wars" of the 1990s, especially by the charges by scientists and others on the political left that feminist philosophers of science, along with variously post-modern cultural theorists, were undermining objectivity and hence the ground on which political critique needed to stand. Barbara Ehrenreich, one such critic, was scheduled as a plenary speaker at a conference on "Engendering Rationalities" at the University of Washington, organized by Nancy Tuana and Sandra Morgen. I was scheduled to speak after her, and I wrote the paper in impassioned defense of my colleagues in feminist philosophy of science, from whom, as an epistemologist, I had learned so much. Unfortunately, a burst eardrum from a flight a week earlier and lingering congestion prevented me from attending the conference.

Even though I didn't get to deliver it, the paper bears the traces of its highly polemical origin. It takes up the themes of "Non-Negotiable

Demands" in asking what we really need from objectivity, and answers the question in terms of what I call "epistemic dependency," moving the site of epistemology from grounding individual knowledge (in perception, memory, rationality) to navigating our dependency on others for most of what we need to know. I argue that objectivity just is whatever makes epistemic practices, agents, communities, and claims trustworthy—a complex, robust, practice-grounded notion that enables us, for example, to chart a course between abject acceptance of experts' claims and cynical rejection of them, a course that makes our dependence reasonable. A core argument of the paper is that taking objectivity seriously means that institutions that train, socialize, accredit, and monitor expertise (notably research universities) need to embrace and demonstrate a commitment to social justice. Those who defend and insist on more traditional, apolitical conceptions of objectivity are, I argue, trapped in a fantasy of hard-headedness, brandishing talismans that do no work, that are, in Wittgenstein's terms, "gears that move though nothing moves with them,"

The most recent of the essays collected here, "Narrative, Complexity, and Context: Autonomy as an Epistemic Value," was written for a volume in bioethics that brought together theorists and reflective clinicians whose work was connected to Margaret Urban Walker's moral theory. The editors, Hilde Lindemann and Marian Verkerk, along with Walker, brought groups of contributors together to explore not only the ethics but also the epistemology of naturalized and narrative bioethics, that is, bioethics grounded in the specificities of practice and in the stories told by the different participants in those practices. My chapter's subject is explicitly autonomy, specifically the autonomy of patients and, especially, of subjects in biomedical research. As typically addressed, notably in the context of therapeutic or experimental procedures, autonomy is regarded as something the patient or subject has, prior to and independently of interactions with the clinicians or researchers, who are obligated not to violate that autonomy—an obligation typically discharged by obtaining informed consent. What is standardly lacking is any sense that subjects' autonomy might be relational or that clinicians or researchers have any positive interest in fostering it.

The chapter joins the ethical, epistemological, and ontological themes that wind through the volume. The core idea is that everything is what it is because of how it fits into the world around it, how its structure shapes and is shaped by its relationships to other things. Knowing something thus involves knowing about those relationships, learning from the diverse others enmeshed in them, and crediting their diverse perspectives. Central to the acquisition and exercise of autonomy is the ability to articulate how things look from where one stands, and to have that articulation taken up by others, to be regarded as a contributor to knowledge about oneself and about the world one is in. And central to responsible knowing is a commitment to listening to the objects of one's knowledge and to the various others with which that object is in relationship. Specifically, the autonomy of patients and research subjects is epistemically valuable and relationally evoked. In general, the abstraction from context that is involved in bringing an object of knowledge into the laboratory or the library needs to be coupled with a commitment to re-engagement.

Chapter 8

Forms of Life: Mapping the Rough Ground

> Recognizing what we say, in the way that is relevant in philoso-
> phizing, is like recognizing our present commitments and their
> implications; to one person a sense of freedom will demand an
> escape from them, to another it will require their more total
> acceptance. Is it obvious that one of these positions must, in a
> given case, be right?
>
> (Cavell 1969*a*, p.57)

I "NEITHER SUPER-IDEALIZED GUIDANCE NOR CAPRICE"

> We have got onto slippery ice where there is no friction and so in
> a certain sense the conditions are ideal, but also, just because of
> that, we are unable to walk. We want to walk: so we need
> friction. Back to the rough ground!
>
> (*PI* §107)

Terry Eagleton, in his script for Derek Jarman's film, *Wittgenstein*, takes
up Wittgenstein's image of the "crystalline purity of logic" in contrast to
the "rough ground" of what we actually say and do (Eagleton 1993, p. 55).
A young man, we are told, dreams of "reducing the world to pure logic," a
dream he succeeds in realizing in a world "purged of imperfection and
indeterminacy, like countless acres of gleaming ice." That world, perfect
as it is, is uninhabitable: "he had forgotten about *friction*." As an older
man, he "came to understand that roughness and ambiguity and indeterminacy aren't imperfections—they're what make things work." He dug
up the ice to uncover the rough ground, but, "homesick for the ice, where
everything was radiant and absolute," he was unable to live on the rough
ground, and he ended up "marooned between earth and ice, at home in
neither."

The image of the ice as, precisely, home is Eagleton's and Jarman's, not
Wittgenstein's; but, as I will argue, there is something oddly right about it,
and, taking it seriously, we can ask: Why does the place of perfection and
purity seem like home, rather than like an alluring, exotic locale? Why
would an inability to stay on the rough ground manifest itself as an

inability to feel at home there, rather than as, say, aesthetic dissatisfaction? What is Wittgenstein urging himself and us to return to when he urges us back to the rough ground, back to what we say and do, and why might such a return fail to still the urges that sent us off in search of the perfection of ice? Why does it seem to us, as it continues to seem to Wittgenstein, that in turning away from the ice he "means to deny something" (*PI* §305)?

One important thing Wittgenstein can seem to be denying us is, precisely, ground to stand on, if among our concerns is the possibility of casting a critical eye on the world we inhabit. When he writes that "what has to be accepted, the given is—so one could say—*forms of life*" (PI §226), what—so one could ask—is the force of this "has to"? If, as Wittgenstein wants to lead us to see, it is only against a background of shared practices and shared judgments that doubt can be intelligible, (how) can we register, let alone argue for, disapprobation of a form of life, whether it be one in which we are enmeshed (making our attempted critique self-refuting) or one to which we are alien (making our critique, referentially, off the mark)? In either case, it would seem, we fail to say anything that is both about the form of life in question and critical of it.

Conundrums such as this have a place not only in Wittgensteinian exegesis. The question of where one can stand to obtain a perspective on a set of practices that is simultaneously informed and critical is a deep and central question for political theory, and it arises with special urgency in the context of disputes about "multiculturalism." Is there some privileged point, available perhaps through the resources of reason, from which diverse practices can be neutrally surveyed? Or are all perspectives necessarily partial, in both senses of that word, and all judgments colored by the lenses through which they are made?

It has been argued, most pointedly by J. C. Nyiri, that Wittgenstein provides a way of responding to these puzzles, not by providing such critical ground, but by persuading us to do without it. On this reading Wittgenstein is at once theoretically pluralist and practically conservative (Nyiri 1982, 1986). We are, on this account, tragically misled if we attempt to step outside of the practices in which we are engaged in order to provide a justification of them or, worse, to argue for their reform. It is certainly true that Wittgenstein was deeply distrustful of the employment of practice-transcendent reason ("a medicine invented by an individual," Wittgenstein 1967a (*RFM*) II-23) in the attempt to shape changes in forms of life. One can, to go further, connect this distrust with his remarks, in relation to purely philosophical theorizing, about taking language on a holiday, detaching it from its everyday employment in the futile hope that, detached from quotidian dross, essential truths will be revealed. Time and again, he draws us back to the dross: there, where everything looks at once too mundane and too multifarious, is what, if we could only recognize it as such, would be what we seek.

Yet time and again, the interlocutor voices his—and our—sense that that cannot be all there is:

> Here we come up against a remarkable and characteristic phenomenon in philosophical investigation: the difficulty—I might say—is not that of finding the solution but rather that of recognizing as the solution something that looks as if it were only a preliminary to it. "We have already said everything.—Not anything that follows from this, no, this itself is the solution!"... The difficulty here is: to stop. (Z §314)

One might say that our difficulty is our inability to recognize home when we are in it: we are in the grip of a picture akin to the fantasy of having been left as a foundling on the doorstep of our putative parents, banished for mysterious reasons from our true, incomparably grander, home and birthright.

But it is not only a philosopher's taste for the crystalline purity of ice that might lead one to think that home was another sort of place than here. The rough ground, that which lies beneath our feet, may be problematic for quite other reasons. It is one thing to speak of bringing our words home from the (non)places to which philosophers had tried to drag them when what we do, what we are inclined to say, the practices that shape the senses of our words, are relatively uniform and unproblematic—as they are, for example, in the sorts of cases Wittgenstein uses in his discussions of rule-following, counting, and the like. Our resistance to accepting that we do what we do, our temptations toward the ice, seem different, however, less specifically philosophical in the sense Wittgenstein wants to problematize, when the temptation to seek other homes for our words is prompted by a sense that our relation to what we do is somehow troubled: in the name of *what*, if not what's *really* the case, can we mount a critique of what we say? "'So you are saying [Wittgenstein's interlocutor accuses him] that human agreement decides what is true and what is false?' It is what human beings say [he replies] that is true and false; and they agree in the language they use. That is not agreement in opinions but in forms of life" (*PI* §242).

Wittgenstein's emphasis on agreement is important, since he aims to break us of the conviction that no amount of concordance in human practices could effect reference or truth, that such things cannot be a matter of what we do, that it must always be a possibility that we, all of us, do it wrong, that our words and sentences misfire in their attempts to hit the target of reality. But the emphasis on agreement can mislead us into thinking of Wittgensteinian forms of life as internally homogeneous, leading to what Stanley Cavell has dubbed the "Manichean" reading of Wittgenstein on rules (similar, he points out, to Carnap's distinction between "internal" and "external" questions) (Cavell 1969a, p. 47). On such a reading, one is either inside or outside of a language game, the contours of which are arbitrary, and, if inside, one just does what "we" do; if outside, one is clueless—not a participant, and certainly not an intelligible critic.

But it is not just clumsy readings of Wittgenstein that can lead to this impasse. There is the temptation, centrally a concern of Wittgenstein's, voiced as frequently as any by his interlocutor, to think that our options are, in David Pears's words "either super-idealized guidance or caprice" (Pears 1988, vol. 2, p. 488). That is, the "Manichean" reader of Wittgenstein is importing into his or her reading of Wittgenstein exactly the philosophical move it was his aim to cure us of the felt need for, the move, that is, away from taking our practices as either adequate to our demands of them or, if inadequate, then immanently and empirically revisable, in favor of a search for "super-idealized guidance," thought by such a reader to reside in those practices themselves, sublimed and transcendentalized.

Wittgenstein writes that "the real discovery is the one that makes me capable of stopping doing philosophy when I want to.—The one that gives philosophy peace, so that it is no longer tormented by questions which bring *itself* in question" (*PI* §133). It might seem that what would allow one to stop would have to be a sense of quiet (peace), a sense that one's questions had been either answered or dissolved. But there's no need to take Wittgenstein in this way—it could just as well be that what stops, what is given peace, is, specifically, philosophizing, not because quiet takes its place, but because what has seemed a philosophical problem becomes something else (Schulte 1986, p. 62). We can come to identify our sense of dis-ease with what we do as calling not for a repudiation of human practice in favor of something independent of it, but for a change in that practice, a change that begins with a politically conscious placing of ourselves within, but somewhere on the margins of, a form of life.

The Manichean reading will keep resurfacing (as it does for Wittgenstein himself) so long as such a shift, from the philosophical to the political, does not or cannot occur—so long, for example, as one remains closeted. The closet works rather like children's attempting invisibility by placing their hands over their eyes: the hope is that I will not be seen as who I am if I refuse to acknowledge, perhaps even to myself, that I see the world from the location of that identity. So long as I give my reports on how things seem ventriloquistically, from the imagined vantage point of a more authoritative, because more generic, subject, my actual location may go undetected. In this sense, anyone can be closeted, even, or especially, the privileged, since no one actually occupies the position of the wholly generic subject.

What Quine refers to as "the pull toward objectivity" (Quine 1960, pp. 5–8) is precisely this sort of ventriloquizing, and for him—as for Sabina Lovibond in her discussion of what she argues is Wittgenstein's realism (Lovibond 1983, pp. 58–62)—it is of the essence of our talk about the objectively real world that we do experience and succumb to this pull. In one sense I agree, but it will be the burden of this paper to argue that a fully robust realism requires us not to ventriloquize prematurely, but, rather, to recognize when more is to be learned from a careful account of how things look from *over here*, when the fictive point that serves as the locus of the objective gaze encodes not what we all have in common but the interests of privilege that have come spuriously to be accepted as universal.

I want to argue, that is, that the epistemic resources of variously marginal subject positions provide the ground for a critique of "what we do" that rejects both the possibility of transcending human practice and the fatalism of being determined by it, but that those resources are not available to someone who is unwilling or unable to stand on that ground.

For complex reasons that it is far beyond the scope of this paper to explore, Wittgenstein himself was so unwilling or unable. He was, by chance or choice, intellectually and socially marginal. He was not trained as a philosopher, and he resisted both the professional normalization of his own life and work and the possibility (since actualized) of such normalization on the part of those who would follow him. He lived most of his life outside of his native Austria and never gave up the idea that there might be somewhere he could feel at home, although he was certain it could not be in Cambridge, which was where he mostly lived and worked. He was also, in some sense of the words, Jewish and homosexual, but neither was an identity he could straightforwardly claim: insofar as either could have provided him with a vantage point marginal to forms of life of the Europe of his day, with which he was profoundly disaffected, such possibilities were wholly unacknowledged.[1]

An explicitly political reading of Wittgenstein, one that starts from somewhere on the margins with an articulation of estrangement from a form of life, although alien to his personal sensibilities is, I want to argue, both responsible to his later work and illuminating of it. Such a reading can, furthermore, provide us with a map out of the thicket of the seemingly endless disputes between various forms of objectivism and relativism—disputes that stem from the idea that justification is either absolutely grounded in bedrock or wholly capricious.

When we think we are faced with a forced choice between the extremes of objectivism or relativism, it is because we are in the thrall of a picture whose hold on us Wittgenstein aims to break with his calls to attend to what we do. What he expects us to find is that justification is a practice we engage in with particular other people for particular reasons, to lay to rest particular worries—and that sometimes it works. If we have reason to believe that it "worked" prematurely or suspiciously, we can reopen it, raise new worries, and lay them to rest—or not. But there is no response to the claim that new worries can always be raised, and that there is no a priori assurance that they can be laid to rest—except to say

---

1. For a discussion of Wittgenstein's (problematic) Jewishness and homosexuality, as well as for an excellent general discussion of the relation of his life to his work, see Monk (1990).

"yes, and just what did you have in mind? What have we ignored; whose voices have not been heard; what further, specific objections can you raise?" This process is neither absolutely grounded nor capricious: it can be engaged in conscientiously or dishonestly, democratically or autocratically; we do or do not have reason to trust it—but in any case there are things to say, ways to proceed, objections to raise and answers to give.

To say that at this point we are on the terrain not of reason but of politics is to invoke a distinction that does no work: if a particular discussion seems not to respect the facts or the formal relationships between the facts, that's something to say, something to argue; and if those arguments seem to be going nowhere, that may be reason to change the rules of the discussion. The point is that these are all things we do, things we know how to do, things we argue about the doing of; and there is nothing outside of what we do to determine whether or not we are doing it right, which is not to say that we cannot meaningfully be said to be doing it wrong, only that such a claim cannot rest on hand-waving. Anything we think might ground our practices—whether it be Reality or Reason—is just one more thing to argue about.

II PRIVILEGED MARGINALITY

As much as I am inclined to believe that the last couple of paragraphs are an appropriate response to the worries about grounding,[2] there is a problem with this response, signaled by my unmarked use of "we."

Feminists and others have urged caution about the uses of "we," as about the allegedly generic masculine or the reference to (generic) women.[3] Who is included, and who excluded, when, in particular, the relatively privileged use terms meant to include others in their scope? When I query the "we" of those paragraphs, it seems most centrally to refer to those who, marginal to the discussions in question, nonetheless have the standing to intervene in them, to make their voices heard, to articulate a critique simultaneously intelligible to those who "own" the discussion and adequate to the expression of dissatisfaction with it. The counsel of those paragraphs is likely to seem a cruel joke to those who stand little chance of being heard or who have to choose between saying what they mean and saying what those in power can understand.[4] From such a location what seems to make sense is, rather, either Scylla or Charybdis—either a deeply held conviction in the absolute wrongness of one's oppression and the faith that that conviction is warranted from some objective standpoint (for example, God's), or a determination to

---

2. They are analogous to the response Helen Longino (1990) gives to questions about objectivity, and she is concerned to address the analogous sorts of concerns with it.

3. For a very illuminating summary and critical discussion of these concerns, see Spelman (1988).

4. See Jordan (1985) for a discussion of this question in relation to Black English.

acquire the power to overthrow the structures of one's subordination, to acquire the might to make right.

The social location of the "we" of those paragraphs can, I think, best be understood as one of "privileged marginality." Privilege and marginality are central concepts in recent feminist and other liberatory theorizing, in which they are generally taken to be opposed to each other: Privilege resides at the center of whatever system is being analyzed, and marginality is the condition of being removed from that center, having an identity peripheral to the structures of privilege, being "different." But there are certain social locations that are at once privileged and marginal, complex amalgams that are of particular relevance for an understanding of the nature of philosophy and of theorizing.[5]

In particular, in societies such as ours, the position of the academic, and of the philosopher within the academy, are positions of privileged marginality. In each case—in society as a whole or in the academy—to the extent that power is centered anywhere, it is centered elsewhere than with the (non-technology- or policy-oriented)[6] academic or the philosopher, both of whom have identities regarded by most people as, literally, eccentric: philosophers are seen within the academy much as most academics are seen outside of it—as amusingly out of touch with what is regarded as the "real world." But in both cases a certain form of privilege attends the marginality, both the privilege of class that attaches to academic employment, along with the more specific privileges of tenure and academic freedom, and, again most strikingly in the case of philosophers, the privilege of being intellectually deferred to, even if not concerning anything regarded as of practical importance. The privilege and the marginality are not just two features of this social location; they are inextricably bound together. Philosophers and academics are privileged *as marginal:* their social location on the margin is itself a location of privilege.[7]

Privileged marginality is a location from which the felt need for the generic standpoint is peculiarly both poignant and problematic, a combination present throughout Wittgenstein's writings and enacted especially in the interchanges with the interlocutor in the *Investigations* and other later work. It is, consequently, a social location from which a radical break from epistemology can be called for, even as it is the location from which epistemology emerges and is pursued. (This doubleness is connected to

5. Some of the most useful attempts to complicate the margins are in the work of Patricia Hill Collins, bell hooks, and Patricia Williams, all of whom write from the complex social location of Black women in the academy. See, especially, Patricia Hill Collins (1990), bell hooks (1990), and Patricia Williams (1991).

6. Thanks to Sandra Harding for pointing out to me that the picture I had of academics was fed by a limited diet of examples, and ignored the burgeoning ranks of professors quite central to the exercise of political and economic power.

7. I discuss privileged marginality in relation to Jewish identity in Chapter 4.

Wittgenstein's characterization of philosophy as both the disease and the cure, as well as to the ways that for him the ills of philosophy both are and are not contained in our ordinary uses of language, as though the virus of being led astray both by and from those uses were one that infected everyone but made only some actually ill.)

It is, however, only the explicit politicizing of that location, along with the explicit politicizing of epistemology generally, that can take us beyond the diagnosis of the pull toward the generic—the pull, that is, away from diversity—to a clearer sense of how more responsibly to live in the forms of life we—variously—inhabit. Such a perspective provides a gloss on Wittgenstein's remark that "Not empiricism and yet realism in philosophy, that is the hardest thing" (*RFM* VI–23).[8] Empiricism is an epistemology of parsimony: the problem for knowledge is taken to be the problem of partiality in the sense of bias: what we need is to strip away the influence of everything that might lead to doxastic idiosyncrasy. The hallmark of reality, however, is that it looks different to those differently placed in it; consequently realism requires an epistemology of largesse: the problem for knowledge is the problem of partiality not in the sense of bias but in the sense of incompleteness.[9]

Not only do we have to learn from diversely located subjects, but we have to recognize when our own locations are distinctively limiting, when what we say is especially problematically partial. Central to this contention is the idea that, while it cannot be the task of philosophy to change the homes to which words need to be brought back, such changes are, in many areas of our lives, urgently called for, and that Wittgenstein is best read as recognizing that fact, however unsuited he took himself to be to engage in the—nonphilosophical—work that it entails.

III "GRIEF DESCRIBES A PATTERN . . . IN THE WEAVE OF OUR LIFE"

There is a scene in the film of Harvey Fierstein's *Torch Song Trilogy* (1988) in which Arnold, the gay protagonist, and his mother are at the cemetery where Arnold's father and his lover are both buried. His mother comes over from her husband's grave to Arnold at his lover's, furious at what she (correctly) perceives as his sense of commonality in their losses. It is obscene to her that he might take himself to feel anything like the grief she feels, to be deeply mourning his lover's death, to have shared with

8. See Cora Diamond's discussion (1991*d*), to which I am, however quixotically, indebted.
9. For the epistemic importance of partiality in the latter sense, see Haraway (1998).

Alan love in the same sense as the love between husband and wife. Significantly, the commonality in their actions is called into question along with the commonality of emotion. Arnold's mother demands to know what he thinks he's doing (he has taken a slip of paper from his pocket and is reading from it the Jewish prayer for the dead); when he replies that he's doing the same thing she's doing, she insists he's not: "I'm reciting Kaddish for my husband; you're blaspheming your religion."

What would it be to settle the dispute between them: is Arnold feeling what his mother is feeling, or is he not? One way of going about it would be to say that there is an objective fact of the matter, that our words "grief," "love," and the like refer to particular states that people can be in, states that we are not yet in a position to specify with any clarity, but when science has sufficiently progressed and we can do that, we will know the answer, and until then we can gather evidence that would point in one direction or the other.

Wittgenstein's remark that "'grief' describes a pattern which recurs, with different variations, in the weave of our life" (*PI* p. 174), is telling here. On a Wittgensteinian account the answer to the question of whether or not Arnold and his mother are feeling the same thing is not to be found above or below the details of what they say and do, but in those details and, importantly, in what those details mean in the contexts of their lives. Arnold and his mother disagree on whether or not the pattern of his feelings, in the context of his life with Alan, was a variation on the same pattern of feelings she felt, in the context of her life with her husband. The "facts" (both those we have and any we might acquire) tell us that there are similarities in their situations and that there are differences. The question is what those similarities and differences mean, how to weigh them, and we can answer that question only against the background of our beliefs and attitudes about, for example, homosexuality.

It is the background, the history, the context—and what we make of them—that make whatever is currently in Arnold's mind or heart (or head or molecules) *grief*, just as it is the background, the history, the context, that make the speaking of certain words reciting Kaddish. We need, that is, to see in Arnold's life and in his world a pattern that we will take as relevantly similar to the pattern in his mother's life and world. We need not only to know more about Arnold, but to situate what we know in what Jonathan Lear refers to as the "perceptions of salience, routes of interest, feelings of naturalness in following a rule that constitute being part of a form of life" (Lear 1984, p. 229).

Thinking about this scene, and about the film itself, especially about its ambitions with respect to the beliefs and attitudes of heterosexual audiences, can lead us to ask about diversity in locations within and relationships to a form of life. This is a slightly but crucially different way of framing such a question than the more usual one, the one Lear discusses, namely what to make of diversity—actual or imagined—among forms of life.[10] The question arises for Lear, as it does for most readers of Wittgenstein, as a way of placing Wittgenstein on the terrain of realism and idealism and, relatedly, of objectivism and relativism. For Lear, Wittgenstein's position in the *Philosophical Investigations* is a form of transcendental idealism, where empirical realism is secured by the "we are so-minded," which, on Lear's interpretation, accompanies all our judgments, as "I think" accompanies them for Kant, and by the lack of any empirical contrast to the "we." If we entertain the concrete empirical possibility of being differently minded, Lear argues, if we "make the 'we' vivid, then Wittgenstein's philosophy collapses into philosophical sociology, studying how one tribe among others goes on" (Lear 1984, p.238).

In some important sense, that is, the "we" disappears. But Lear is also concerned to allow that there is a place, although an odd and problematic one, on Wittgenstein's view for what Lear calls "reflective understanding." Although we are in need of "therapy" to treat the "neurosis" of "philosophical perplexity," the neurosis is neither silly nor peculiar to philosophers, and, crucially, "post-neurotic consciousness is fundamentally more complex than a healthy consciousness that has never suffered disease or cure" (Lear 1984, p.240). It is also possible to become aware of the fact "that our form of life is not some fixed, frozen entity existing totally independently of us" (Lear 1984, p.242). Lear notes the spatially metaphorical nature of his attempt to give an account of our reflective relationship to our form of life—we cannot, for example, "look down upon" it; we can be aware of it only "from the inside." But he does not consider the nature of the space within, of the epistemic resources of its internal differentiations, of its having, for example, margins.[11]

The issue is related to Barry Stroud's critique of Lear's paper. Stroud finds reason to resist Lear's Kantian reading of Wittgenstein in part because of what he takes to be the necessity, on such a reading, of taking another, highly problematic, step, one that would take us from the *necessity* of "we are so-minded" to its *objective validity*, a step corresponding to Kant's arguments for the categories as securing empirical realism.[12] For Stroud, we ought rather to resist the urge to start down that, or any other, metaphysical road in our reading of the

---

10. The possibility of such diversity is significantly much more obvious in a strikingly similar quote from Cavell (1969a): "That on the whole we do (make and understand the same projections) is a matter of our sharing routes of interest and feeling, modes of response, senses of humor and of significance and of fulfillment, of what is outrageous, of what is similar to what else, what a rebuke, what forgiveness, of when an utterance is an assertion, when an appeal, when an explanation—all the whirl of organism Wittgenstein calls 'forms of life.'" Both the nature of Cavell's list and his use of the plural ("*forms* of life") make it less likely that we will feel the temptation to transcendentalize that Lear's formulation produces.

11. Lear (1982) acknowledges both the changeableness of our forms of life and philosophy's role in bringing us to see that change is possible, but he locates Wittgenstein's lessons to us mainly at the point at which we run out of justifying things to say. I'm interested in giving a Wittgensteinian account of what goes on when we do have things to say, things that do not fit the usual accounts of what justification is. Cf. Diamond (1991a, 1991e).

12. In addition to his reply to Lear (Stroud, 1984), see Stroud (1983).

Investigations. While Lear downplays the importance to Wittgenstein's (or Kant's) aims of providing an answer to the skeptic, Stroud sees answering the skeptic's challenge as central—but he doesn't think that the answer is in the form of an argument that demonstrates, for example, that the skeptic is self-refuting.

The answer, Stroud argues, is not so much an argument to the conclusion that what the skeptic wants us to think might be so could not in fact be (coherently thought to be) so as it is an invitation to actually try to carry through the demands that the skeptic makes, with the aim of showing that what are taken to be impediments to an immediate, unquestionable epistemic relationship to reality, or at best mere pieces of stage-setting, are in fact crucial to anything we can mean by the questions we ask or by anything we would take as an answer. What we take to be either part of the problem or an irrelevant distraction is where we need to look, not for an answer to the questions we'd posed—there are no answers to the questions we'd posed; there is no "refuting" the skeptic—but for a less vexed relation to what we do, an attentive respect for the resources in our language and practices.

What I want to suggest is that part of what we can learn is that internal diversity in forms of life—the fact that we do not all stand in the same relationship to what "we" say and do—is part of what gives what we say and do a claim to legitimacy. If we take Wittgenstein as Lear does, then there being empirical, criticizable content to a form of life becomes a problem for anything that would count as realism; we seem to need, that is, to transcendentalize the idealism by disappearing the "we." But we needn't start down that path. The sort of awareness from within that Lear says we can in fact have of our form of life is frequently not nearly as evanescent and empirically contentless as he makes it out to be: it can be as concrete and as critical as what Arnold brings his mother—and the film aims to bring its heterosexual audience—to see about the forms of life they share but in which they occupy very different places.

Pattern perception—what is involved in deciding whether or not what Arnold feels is, like what his mother feels, grief—is sensitive to perceivers' locations, both as a matter of what can be seen and what is occluded, and as a matter of how what is seen is interpreted. We also have standards, sometimes explicitly moral standards, about what gets to count as the same. People who have lost pets, for example, often find others reluctant to take their feelings of loss as real grief. We are not all similarly minded about such things: we find, depending on our individual and cultural histories, different degrees of similarity and difference in the feelings some people have toward animals and the feelings people (are supposed to) have toward other people. Sometimes we just "agree to disagree," recognizing the limits to our shared practices (hence, to the objectivity of our judgments).[13] But there are occasions on which it can be important

---

13. Cf. the discussion of "fun" in Lovibond (1983, p. 66).

not to accept that we differ, but to argue about which set of attitudes is in some way better or more appropriate.[14]

With Arnold and his mother in the cemetery, the film clearly intends us to see the similarities as more salient than the differences. The burden of the film in relation to a heterosexual audience is to bring that audience to a recognition of shared humanity, of shared emotions, needs, and desires, with gay men, including those who, like Arnold, who works as a female impersonator, are not attempting to be in all respects but one indistinguishable from those who are normatively straight.

For Arnold's mother the form of life in which love and grief and the reciting of Kaddish have their home is the world of heterosexual marriage and family, a world in which Arnold is the "outsider within."[15] He knows that form of life, but he knows it from the margins—not from some disjoint elsewhere, but not simply from within. He wants marriage and family, and he knows what's needed to live them, but, unlike his mother, he doesn't see there being one man and one woman as a necessary part of the picture. As with love, grief, and the reciting of Kaddish, he parses the patterns of marriage and family differently, and, in so doing, sees the same.

The politics of the film are, I suspect, dated. It wants on the one hand to insist on Arnold's difference—gayness is his life, not, as his mother wishes he would keep it, simply a matter of what he does in the bedroom. At the same time it stresses a fundamental commitment to humanism: underneath our differences we are basically all the same. For many reasons, the AIDS crisis among them, the simultaneous foregrounding of similarity and difference has become less possible. The frightening rise in respectable homophobia has led many, in pressing for civil rights, to minimize the difference that homosexuality makes, to argue that in all the ways that society has any reason to care about, gay men and lesbians are just like straight people. Others, through the politics of queerness, have responded to the pandemics of AIDS and hatred with a principled refusal of the implicit bargain of conformity for compassion, refusing, in particular, to acknowledge the authority of what has been named "heteronormativity." Rather than simply asserting and celebrating queer difference, the politics of queerness challenges straight "sameness": "We are not like *you*, but *you* are a lot more like *us* than you like to think" (see Warner

---

14. Cf. the discussion of attitudes toward animals in Diamond (1991*b*, 1991*c*). See also feminist discussions about the relevance of similarities and differences among rape, pornography, and "normal" heterosexual activity. The classic statements of the view that salience lies in the similarities, that neither in representation nor in practice can the sexual be separated from the paradigms of dominance/subordination, can be found in the writing of Catharine MacKinnon and Andrea Dworkin. (Dworkin more than MacKinnon seems to think that the difference marked by lesbianism is capable of creating an alternative range of meanings; MacKinnon takes dominance/subordination to characterize the sexual *tout court*.) See, in particular, MacKinnon (1987) and Dworkin (1987).

15. I owe the term to Patricia Hill Collins. See, especially, Collins (1986).

1993, especially the Introduction). In this fracturing of responses to a politics of hate, into an attempt, on the one hand, to broaden the norms of sameness and, on the other, to reject their authority, we seem to have lost the space in which *Torch Song Trilogy* takes place, a space that does not require the minimizing of difference as the price for the recognition of commonality.

It is arguable that such a space was always only an illusion, that some differences (similar arguments have been made concerning, especially, race and gender) have always had to be denied or downplayed if those who are defined by them are to be enfranchised in liberal terms. Various separatisms and nationalisms are grounded precisely in the rejection of the terms of this liberal demand. Part of why *Torch Song Trilogy* works, I think, is that it can eloquently evoke nostalgia even in those for whom its politics were always an illusion and a trap. In the space of the film, liberal humanism provides a home to which worlds like 'grief' and 'love' could be brought. There was, the film is telling us, something we meant by those words, along with a hopeful, generous sense of who "we" were, something the homophobe, that is, could be brought to see—and it is this that we seem to have lost (as we seem, nostalgically, once to have had it, or at least the hope of it).

In the terms of the film, disputes such as those between Arnold and his mother about what we should say can be settled, but clearly not by noting what we do say. That is, contra many readers of Wittgenstein, the correctness of our judgments is not simply a matter of community agreement, which is surely in any event an odd way of thinking about the practices of creatures whose forms of life are so many of them character- ized by fractiousness and, in particular, fractiousness that makes sense only on the supposition that there is something to be arguing about, that one's antagonists are *wrong*. Arnold doesn't just want his mother to see things some other way—nor does the film want that of its audience: she and we are asked to get beyond prejudices that keep us from seeing the *truth*—that Arnold deeply loved Alan and is grieving his death.

But the matter is not so simple. Unlike the position of those like Arnold's mother, who would say that what Arnold claims is just *false*, those espousing a queer politics are more likely to recognize the element of choice that can, with the proper contextualization, be seen to underlie all our ascriptions. What they urge is not that the liberal invitation be shown to be somehow mistaken (sent, as it were, to the wrong address), but that it be *declined*. If one takes this response to be intelligible (whether or not one takes it to be politically advisable), a natural conclusion to draw is that it shows that all along, even when things seemed as they do in the movie, it really was (just) a matter of choice. Not only was there no fact of the matter above or below what Arnold and his mother said and felt and did in the contexts they were in, but there was no fact of the matter at all: it's just a (philosophical) mistake to talk about right or wrong, true or false.

Such a conclusion, I want to argue, is not one Wittgenstein would have us draw, nor is it one forced on us once we recognize the possibility that what holds our judgments in place, makes some claims true and others false, can be put into question (as, for example, by queer theory and politics). We are not, that is, forced into an uncritical relativism. To the extent that one believes in the possibility of objective knowledge about some range of phenomena (say, human emotions), one will be hopeful about the possibilities of reaching a sufficiently complex account of them to be adequate to the fullest possible range of diverse perspectives on them. One way of putting this point is that one will be a realist about those phenomena, meaning that one takes them to be the sort of things one can view from a range of different perspectives, learning different things about them in the process. Importantly, what goes on is not simply additive: different perspectives exist in critical relation to each other; we argue with as much as we supplement each other's views, and none of our perspectives would be rendered more reliable for being stripped of the interests and values that make it distinctive (See Haraway 1991).

Our not all going on in the same way about many things we all care about is part of the background against which our judgments get to be true or false about the world. The agreement in judgments Wittgenstein refers to (*PI* §242) does the work it does in part because we cannot take it for granted: we find it in some places and not in others. That is, in those cases where we can't quite imagine not finding it (the examples of counting and such), it's not that we *can't* question how we go on (as though someone or something were *stopping us):* rather, we can't quite make sense of the question; we don't feel the need to ask it. All that would be needed to make the question intelligible—and to give us a way of going about answering it—would be the real need to ask it. The questions that seem to lack answers are just the ones we have no need to ask.

Often, however, we do not find agreement where it seems important to us that we do, where consensus, at least among some group to which we (do or want to) belong, seems important and is lacking. In such cases, we have lots of resources to turn to (in any case, they might or might not be adequate)—resources that range from logical argument to an appeal to agreed-on facts to well-chosen images or metaphors to novels, poems, plays, movies.[16]

It is, on the other hand, also part of what "we" do to find ourselves needing to disrupt what others take to be settled consensus, to reopen what is taken to be closed.[17] Very often the "we" who do this are marginal to the practices in which consensus was reached; our voices hadn't been attended to; perhaps we had not yet found them. Justification is

---

16. On the prejudice involved in stigmatizing these latter sorts of things as not arguments and, hence, of no or lesser value when it comes to persuading those who are rational, see Diamond (1991a).

17. An emphasis on practices such as these as shaping an interpretation of Wittgenstein as a moral realist is at the heart of the argument in Lovibond (1983).

no less real for the continuing possibility that still others will someday find *their* voices: on the contrary, it is precisely acknowledging this possibility that gives our collective attempts at knowledge a claim to objectivity.[18]

As rich and diverse as are our ways of resolving disagreements, and as important as it is to note that those resources do frequently accomplish that aim and that when they do we are in the best position we can coherently want to be in to say that our claims are really true, nonetheless, it doesn't always work. And sometimes, speaking from the margins, what we want to do is not to make it work—not, that is, to accept the apparatus and shift the angle of vision. Rather than arguing, or showing, that as our words are used there is just no good reason (only, for example, reasons that spring from what we would call prejudice) not to go on with them as we would urge (not to include Arnold's experiences as ones of grief), we want to argue, or show, that the whole apparatus *is* an apparatus, and that it's one we do not have to accept, although the cost of rejecting it may well be unintelligibility, even, perhaps, to ourselves. We want to disrupt the prevailing sense that there is something we would all say about some situation not in favor of another, slightly or significantly different one, but to unsettle the sense that there *is* a "we," that we do share a from of life, that there is a home to which our words can be brought.[19] How can we make intelligible that depth and extent of dissatisfaction with the rough ground of our forms of life without invoking transcendent standards?

IV   TOWARD A DIASPORIC CONCEPTION OF HOME

Wittgenstein was concerned, throughout his work, with questions of where and how the self stands in relation to the world. Are we, as Descartes would have it, essentially separate from (the rest of) the world, though somehow in a position reliably to know it; or is the world, as Kant would have it, in some deep sense our world, one we constitute by our placement in it? Wittgenstein's response in the *Tractatus* is clearly on the Kantian side of this divide. His later work appears so as well, but, more deeply, it challenges the idea that one can, as both Kant and the earlier Wittgenstein would have us believe, prove the Cartesian skeptic wrong, using philosophy to demonstrate that the world is ours.[20]

18. Such a view of objectivity in science is worked out in Longino (1990).

19. For an understanding of queerness in this way—as naming not a given identity but a shifting positionality in resistance to heteronormativity—see Halperin (1995).

20. The (neo)Kantian character of Wittgenstein's work has, of course, been remarked, and much debated. See, in particular, Hacker (1972) along with the extensive rethinking of the relationship between Kant and Wittgenstein in the (much revised) second edition Hacker (1986), and Lear (1984). Intriguingly, Kant—in particular, the *Critique of Judgment*—has been used by some authors to ends similar to those to which I am using Wittgenstein, namely the articulation of the moral and political significance

In the *Tractatus* Wittgenstein provided, as had Kant, a "minimal metaphysics" to establish the mutually defining relation of the self to the knowable world, thereby delimiting the scope of properly philosophical inquiry. The very move that guaranteed to the self the knowability of the world made any more substantive metaphysical inquiry nonsensical precisely by putting such inquiry outside the bounds of the knowable (or sayable). To argue that the phenomenal world is constituted in part by the categories of the understanding, or that the limits of language are the limits of the world, simultaneously guarantees both the possibility of science and the impossibility of metaphysics: there is no place to stand from which we can meaningfully query, let alone describe, our relationship to the world we know.

Wittgenstein's later work, notably the private language argument in the *Investigations*, is in many ways still Kantian in spirit. The private language argument can be read on one level as a restatement of Kant's Refutation of Idealism. Both arguments have the form of rendering incoherent the purported stance of a knowing subject agnostic about the existence of anything outside the self, and they both do so by demonstrating the dependence of such a self's internal coherence—the possibility of an autobiography, however fragmentary—on the structures that ground the possibility of knowledge of an external world. Thus, for Kant, the self cannot be an object of experience, nor, as the empiricists would have it, store up impressions from which to infer the existence of an external world—without always already placing itself in a world of real external objects. For Wittgenstein, on this reading, the meaningful attribution to oneself of experiences, such as the having of sensations, is impossible without the criteria in terms of which such experiences can be ascribed to others or by others to oneself. As idealism is impossible for the Kantian self, solipsism is impossible for the later Wittgensteinian self.

But on this reading the unquestionable link of self to world that led to the embracing of an indescribable solipsism in the *Tractatus* remains, only now the "self" has been broadened to include all the others who with me make up the indescribable "we." Just as the earlier solipsism is indistinguishable from realism (since "my" or "from here" drop out: there is nothing they can mean, no contrast they can mark, no world that is "yours" or "hers" or "from there"), so the "we" of Lear's "we are so-minded" contrastlessly marks the limits of *our* world. The agreement in judgments that constitutes a "we" is what makes any language at all possible: what is incoherent is the picture, inherited in modern terms most explicitly from Locke, but implicit in even most twentieth-century theorizing about reference, that language rests at bottom on an immediate

---

of attending to diverse perspectives in a way that promotes, rather than undercuts, the achievement of rational consensus. See, for example, O'Neill (1986) and Disch (1993).

The point about the relationship of Wittgenstein's later work to skepticism is one I have learned from Stanley Cavell. See, in particular, Cavell (1979, 1990).

connection, in each individual speaker's mind or brain, between word and idea.

We cannot, however, take as *given* the conditions of agreement in judgments, of attunement in forms of life, that would shut the skeptic out of intelligibility. (I take it that something like this idea is central to Cavell's reading of the *Investigations* and of the private language argument in particular.)[21] To say that the loss of my knowing my way around a world I share with others carries with it the loss of my knowing my way around myself, is not to say that I cannot be so lost, nor that the threat or fear that I might become so or might even be so now, unknowingly, is an unreal one.

The philosophical demand for proof that the world is my world, that it makes sense to me, that I make sense in it, that I inhabit it with others who are intelligible to me and to whom I am intelligible leads words away from our uses of them not capriciously, but because those uses are seen as misleading, as not giving what we think we need of our words, be that definiteness of sense or assurance of reference. The illusion of philosophy is that we can get such definiteness, such assurance, by bringing words to what we take to be their true homes, whether that be in direct unmediated relation to ideas in each of our minds, in a Platonically ordered realm of concepts, or at the ends of scientifically respectable causal chains. Philosophy of language, on such views, becomes in part a matter of tracing how it can be that, getting their significance from their placement in such a realm, words can manage to work in the humdrum hodgepodge of our varied uses of them.

My characterization of the philosophers' move as one of bringing words to what (they take to be) their true homes is, of course, a deliberate echo of Wittgenstein's so describing his own task, where the homes to which he would bring our words are precisely the messy places from which the philosophers thought they needed to be extricated. Stanley Cavell writes in this context about the exile of words, and about the need to bring them home, "shepherding" them (Cavell 1989). He goes on to say that it is not just our words, but our "lives themselves [that] have to return," that they and we are lost, that the ordinariness of our words in the forms of our ordinary lives is neither immediately evident nor easily returned to.

I have in the past frequently responded to Cavell's writing out of an uneasy discrepancy I felt between the subject position in which the text placed me as a philosopher and my sense of myself as a woman. In the present instance I was struck by what seemed to me the same sort of discrepancy, but the identity in terms of which I felt it was that of a Diasporic Jew.[22] Cavell links his writing about Wittgenstein on exile and

21. See, for example, Cavell (1979) part four, "Skepticism and the Problem of Others." See also Lovibond (1983, pp. 109–10).

22. Cavell has himself explored the relevance of this identity, which is, of course, his as it is mine, in Cavell (1994).

home to Kierkegaard on faith, to the idea of being lost as perdition: "Spiritually and religiously understood, perdition consists in journeying into a foreign land, in being 'out' [i.e., 'never at home']."[23] What left me uneasy is the idea that to be where one ought to be, to be in the place in which one's words and one's actions are intelligible,[24] responsible, is to be at home, since I take it to be the task of Diasporic Jews, as it is of others who live diasporically, to find oneself properly in the world precisely not "at home."

I want to suggest that we can think about our words as diasporically linked to home, building on a view of diasporic identity brilliantly articulated by Daniel Boyarin and Jonathan Boyarin (1993), in which home is neither any presently existing location nor some place of transcendence. Rather, it presents itself to us as an ethical and political imperative to create forms of life that would place our words and us in right relation. To succeed in thus bringing our words home (or even to be sufficiently hopefully engaged in the struggle) would not demonstrate the falseness or unintelligibility of the skeptic's challenges, but would make us less desperately susceptible to them. On such a view it would be a mistake to bring our words prematurely home, to claim that the set of practices we now have for them are all right as they are. There are no other homes for our words than the ones we create in and through our practices, nor any predetermined ways of specifying what it is to have gotten those practices right, but that does not mean that there is no sense to the idea that we might not be going on as we should be.

V CONCLUSION

At the end of The Wizard of Oz Dorothy and the others appear before the Wizard to ask for what they take themselves to lack: a heart, a brain, courage, and the way home. Were the wizard a real one, he would grant those wishes. Being not a wizard but a balloonist from the Midwest, he cannot grant their wishes as expressed, but he can lead them to see that what they really wanted was not some magically granted "something," but rather qualities of character that they in fact already possessed, and that home, like heart, brain, and courage, was there for the asking, that the fearful journey away from it had been launched by a yearning for some place both obscurely grander and more in keeping with a dimly perceived sense of a "true self" inexpressible in Kansas, and that the journey could be reversed by a simple acknowledgment of the desire to return. All very well and good, but what about those of us who cannot quite bring

23. Cavell (1989, p. 39) is quoting Kierkegaard's The Book of Adler, or A Cycle of Ethico-Religious Essays.
24. I am indebted in how I think about intelligibility to Sarah Lucia Hoagland (1988), and to an unpublished paper by Janet Binder, as well as to Lovibond (1983).

ourselves to click our ruby slippers and intone "there's no place like home"? We may see through the illusions of Oz, give up on wizards, and still not be able to return to Kansas.

One way of making sense of the appeal of objectivist epistemologies and realist metaphysics to those who are oppressed is that such epistemologies and metaphysics are likely to seem the only alternative to an unacceptable acceptance of the status quo (see chapter 1). I have been arguing that we can find in Wittgenstein's later writing a way of rejecting that choice, by attending to those aspects of our practices that are critical and transformative, that are, as much as the unreflective following of a rule, part of what "we do." We can find, in our practices, many alternatives to simply staying in Kansas, accepting it as it is, and taking off for Oz. Objectivity becomes, on such a view, as Lovibond argues, less an epistemic than a social and political achievement (Lovibond 1983, pp. 210–19).

I mean the link between diasporic identity and a diasporic view of words to be more than metaphorical. If we are to reject both the idea that words have true, Platonic, homes and the idea that the homes afforded by current practice are in order just as they are, we need to confront the question of how such critiques can be made intelligible—by whom and to whom. Those who are wholly strangers to the form of life in which our words now find themselves may regard such forms of life as abhorrent, but are unlikely to bring to their abhorrence sufficient insight to give it any standing. Those who are wholly native to those practices are, on the other hand, unlikely to find them anything other than unquestionably natural: "we do what we do."

But there are others, people who are neither stranger nor native, who for the widest range of reasons, within and beyond their own choosing, live somewhere other than at the centers of the forms of life they inhabit. And the views from all those various "there"s can tell us a great deal about those forms of life and provide critical perspectives on them. The alternatives, that is, are not only two: the transcendentalizing of our lives or the claim to be viewing them from some mythical outside that is nowhere at all. It is, I would argue, an important part of the health at least of large, modern societies, that they have within them members who are not truly at home there, who see with the eyes of the "outsider within," and that such members are in positions to be listened to and to be intelligible.

Diasporic identity is one form the outsider within can take, and it is crucial to it that it's not a matter of just passing through, not having any real connection to the place where one finds oneself, caring deeply and responsibly only for home, wherever and whenever that may be. Rather, those who live diasporically can and often do bring resources of moral intelligence, conviction, and courage to the places in which they sojourn. On the rabbinical view articulated in Boyarin and Boyarin, one reason for this is clear—it's only by engaging in and ultimately succeeding at the work of world repair that we'll ever be able to go home. In Lovibond's account, one motivation is the overcoming of alienation, the creation of a world in which one will be able to speak one's words nonironically, without the inverted commas that mark an unwillingness to accept the commitments that would make one's words meaningful *en pleine voix* (Lovibond 1983, pp. 159–65).[25]

Rather than struggling concretely with and against this alienation, we can succumb to philosophy's promises of transcendence by, as Cora Diamond puts it, the "laying down of requirements" (Diamond 1991*e*). What we happen to do cannot, we think, possibly be the sort of thing that could tell us what we ought to do, what it would be right to do. But if what we ought to do is something quite different from what we *do* do, the question arises of how we can be persuaded that it is the right thing to do, whether morally or epistemically: Where do these requirements come from? (The problem has been most discussed under the heading of moral motivation, but the issues are the same in epistemology.) Probably the most common and compelling answer to that question within the philosophical tradition has been some variant of "they come from us, from our truest natures." We only find them alien, so the story goes, because we have been in some way led astray.

Again we have the image of home, but like the Platonic picture of the true, unearthly home for our words, this home is not anywhere that anyone actually lives. Those who would be at home in such places are not any actual ones of us, but the idea that those are our true homes feeds the sort of scapegoating that projects onto certain designated others the features of human existence that are taken to be the cause and the symptoms of our being led astray. The litany is a familiar one: all the messy business of being born and dying, along with the various dependencies that afflict us along the way, the vicissitudes of attachment and desire, and the need for physical labor to keep body and soul together.[26]

To finally resist those temptations would be to come to terms with the unseemly contingencies of being human, not to accept everything as we find it, but to give up on the fantasy of being saved from the human condition or of being, in our truest natures, not really defined by it. If we ask what makes our words refer, our sentences true or false, our moral injunctions truly binding, the answer is that nothing does, because nothing could. Only we can do such things for ourselves, and, if, as many of us

---

25. Richard Eldridge has suggested to me that I miss the depth, and the persuasiveness, of Wittgenstein's distrust of political solutions to the fantasy of the true home. His concern, which I think is right, is that we need not to lose the tension between this distrust and a serious political conviction that the world and the practices that shape it can and should be significantly better than they are. He is also right to note in my writing a tendency toward the political utopian and toward dismissing Wittgenstein's distrust as *simply* a matter of his own inability to acknowledge his politicized identities. My hope is that a view of diaspora that places home always beyond a receding horizon goes some way toward keeping that tension alive. For an interesting discussion of a similar tension, between commitment and irony, see Lovibond (1994).

26. Lovibond argues that for Wittgenstein "the sickness which philosophy sets out to treat . . . has its origins . . . in the incomplete acceptance of our embodied condition" (Lovibond 1983, p. 206).

think about many of our words, sentences, and injunctions, we have not yet succeeded at these tasks, it falls to us to do better, to create homes to which our words can be brought, words that would, as Sabina Lovibond puts it, "represent deeds I can perform without shame" (Lovibond 1983, p. 123).

ACKNOWLEDGMENTS

I read earlier versions of this paper at the University of South Florida, Cornell, and New York University, and I appreciate the comments I received, especially from Linda McAlister and Richard Boyd, as well as from the lesbian and gay faculty study group at NYU and from Michael Root. The Cornell Society for the Humanities has been a wonderful place in which to write, and I'm very grateful for the critical comments of my fellow fellows, especially David Halperin, Lauren Berlant, and Michael Warner, who helped me understand queer theory and its relevance to this project, and the friendly assistance of the staff, especially of Linda Allen, who rescued me when, in the final stages, my software crashed. My greatest thanks go to David Stem, who helped me to situate my essay in the context of Wittgenstein scholarship, and to him and Hans Sluga for extensive comments on earlier drafts.

Chapter 9

The Trustworthiness of Research: The Paradigm of Community-Based Research

Catherine Jordan, Susan Gust, and Naomi Scheman

Questions about trust and trustworthiness are very much in the air these days, from evaluating the evidence presented as reasons for going to war to weighing the claims made about global warming, genetically modified plants and animals, and the nutritional benefits and harms of various diets. Research universities, especially public ones, which are dependent on state funding and have special responsibilities to the citizens of the state, have important roles to play in ensuring the trustworthiness of much of the information on which we all rely. While much of the fiscal crisis currently facing public universities is the result of more general economic woes, there has been, even when the economy was booming, a steadily declining commitment to support for higher education on the part of most states.

We suggest that one explanation for this decline is a growing climate of cynicism about authority in general, and research-based expertise in particular. We will argue that the mistrust of researchers, their claims, and their institutions stems from the ethos (the characteristic and distinguishing elements) of the conventional practice of the scientific method itself. As a response to the current cynical climate we argue for a fundamental shift in the academic research culture, a shift that takes the ethos of community-based participatory research (CBPR)[1] as the preferred approach to instilling trust in the research enterprise. We do not, of

---

1. In the original article, we used 'CBR' with the following rationale: "Terminology in this area is diverse and contested, and our use of the broadest term, 'community-based research,' is in some ways better captured by the more explicit terms used by some researchers, such as 'Community-Based Participatory Research' or 'action research.' Those terms, however, generally refer to social scientific and directly policy-oriented research, while our argument will be that the practices and norms we discuss are not at all limited in scope and can be equally applicable to basic scientific research." Subsequent developments in the field, however, argue for using 'CBPR' to emphasize the collaborative roles of academic researchers and community partners. Increasingly, 'CBR' is used to refer to research that is merely located in a community and has few or none of the distinctive features we are addressing in this chapter. Accordingly, I have replaced occurrences of 'CBR' in this chapter with 'CBPR.' (Note added in 2010).

course, want to suggest that all research ought to be community-based, not even in the most expansive of the many ways one can interpret the term. Rather, we argue that the core CBPR value of trust should serve as a criterion by which research more generally is conceptualized, practiced, and evaluated, much as the norms and practices of laboratory science have implicitly or explicitly played that role.

Despite the sense of many members of the university faculty that they have little or nothing in common with their colleagues in different colleges, there are ways in which it is important to think about the university as a whole. For one thing, that is how researchers are most often thought about by the public with which they interact: when one research group approaches a community, the spirit in which they are received will have a lot to do with the actions and attitudes of others who preceded them. And, as administrators are coming more and more to recognize (largely as a result of well-publicized lapses in research integrity), the role that universities play in lending credibility to the claims made by academic researchers carries with it an obligation to cultivate and sustain a research climate of social and ethical responsibility.

Several years ago the University of Minnesota was required, as a condition of clearing its "exceptional status" with the NIH (imposed as a consequence of a transplant surgeon's marketing of an antirejection drug without FDA approval), to initiate training in the "Responsible Conduct of Research" for all members of the University community involved in any way in research activities. Subsequently, a similar requirement has been imposed nationwide. This creates an opportunity for a serious exploration of just what, beyond regulatory compliance, might be meant by "responsible conduct of research." It is far from clear that this opportunity is being seized, and this essay, and the initiative out of which it springs, are an attempt to open up this conversation. We feel that this conversation is one that must take place at all levels of the academy. In fact, we believe that the manner in which this question is answered will be of critical importance in determining the role that universities and university affiliated researchers will play in the twenty-first century, and we have taken on the task of convincing our colleagues of this.

We approach this project from three distinct perspectives: One of us (Gust) is a longtime community activist and organizer in the Phillips Community of Minneapolis.[2] Another (Jordan) is a research and clinical pediatric neuropsychologist whose research has focused on neurotoxicology and development. The third (Scheman) is a philosopher and former administrator working in feminist and other liberatory epistemology, whose intellectual skills lie mainly in integrating ideas and articulating them for others who may make use of them. Our conviction about the broadly transformative possibilities of the ethos of CBPR is rooted in the

---

2. The Phillips Community is one of eleven communities defined by the City of Minneapolis and is also a State Planning District.

work of two reflective practitioners (Gust and Jordan), with at least one foot apiece firmly grounded in the needs and values of the community and of science, respectively, whose reflections became entwined with those of a philosopher (Scheman), who was using trustworthiness to provide a conception of scientific objectivity that would work in a diverse democracy (see chapter 11).

Together we have arrived at what we feel is a critical axiom: *The value of research is a direct and primary consequence of its "trustworthiness."* Trustworthiness is what makes it rational for people to accept research findings—to build future research upon them, to utilize them to inform public policy, and to use them to guide individual choice and community action. The standard explanation for why lay people ought to believe what experts tell them rests on the paradigm of laboratory science. This paradigm is considered the research methodology that best controls for the subjective biases, confounding variables, and other sources of "noise" that are said to undermine the objectivity of research. However, this control is meant to reduce or nullify the effect of much of what we care about if we take social, ethical, or political trustworthiness seriously. That laboratory science serves as a paradigm can be seen in the premium placed on the researcher's ability to separate both the object under investigation and the investigator from the contexts in which they naturally occur. The former is extracted, purified, placed in a sterile environment, and otherwise isolated from confounding variables; the latter is decontaminated, white-coated, rubber-gloved, stripped of conflicts of interest, and, in reports of the research, masked behind impersonal prose.

That these norms of detachment, call them the *Standard Norms*, are seen as definitive of objectivity creates problems for research on human beings in general, but especially for CBPR. In fact CBPR, rather than acknowledging the norms and attempting to apply them as strictly as possible, blatantly flouts them. Instead of attempting to retreat to disinterested disconnection, the ethos of CBPR calls on researchers to move toward *responsible connection*. Objectivity understood as trustworthiness requires of researchers not detachment but, far more rigorously, responsible engagement; not the pretense of being a disinterested observer but the commitment to listening to and learning from a diverse group of individuals and communities who have a stake in the research product. Far from shrinking from this unorthodox rejection of the traditional paradigm, we propose that if we view trustworthiness as fundamental to the concept of objectivity, CBPR is a *better* way to realize objectivity than research that attempts to emulate the Standard Norms.

Although trust is at the heart of CBPR, it is neither easily come by nor easily sustained in the face of challenges to it from all sides, most important from the grassroots communities it needs to engage and from the scientific communities it needs to persuade. Through the lenses of our experiences at the University of Minnesota and in a Minneapolis neighborhood, we want to articulate the issues of trust surrounding traditional approaches to research and CBPR and to explain how a particular university-community research collaboration engendered trust, created sound scientific data, and made real social change. We then want to outline the principles and some of the projects of an initiative we have undertaken to use what we have learned about trust building to promote trustworthiness as a core virtue of research, researchers, and our research institution. We want to note that our perspectives are rooted in our commitments to economically disadvantaged, racially and culturally diverse, inner-city community activism; traditional, empirical scientific method; and public, land-grant research university administration. We will not attempt to generalize to different contexts (rural communities; qualitative, survey, or humanistic research methods; or private universities, for example), though we do hope that our discussion will be useful for those who work at such sites.

THE CONTEXT: THE PHILLIPS NEIGHBORHOOD HEALTHY HOUSING COLLABORATIVE

Two of the authors (Jordan and Gust) have been working together for nearly eleven years in a community-university collaboration, the Phillips Neighborhood Healthy Housing Collaborative. The Collaborative was initiated in 1993 by community leaders who invited the University of Minnesota, local businesses, community-based organizations, a foundation, and eventually, local and state health department personnel to join forces to address Phillips Community lead poisoning concerns. The Collaborative has sponsored two federally funded CBPR projects. The DREAMS Project (funded by the Maternal and Child Health Bureau) studied the developmental effects of lead poisoning in Phillips children eight to forty-eight months old. The Phillips Lead Poisoning Prevention Project (funded by the Maternal and Child Health Bureau and the Centers for Disease Control and Prevention) studied the efficacy of an intensive culture-specific peer education program in maintaining low blood lead levels in Phillips children from birth to age three.

In forming the Collaborative, the community did not initially set out to use research as a tool for achieving its environmental health goals. The academics convinced the neighborhood activists that essential data were needed before any credible campaign could be mounted by the neighborhood to effect change in public policy and enlist politicians and health care professionals in an effort to effectively deal with the problem of lead poisoning. The necessity of a well-conceived research project (including a control group) was not initially well received by the residents and activists in this newly formed collaboration. It took several years to come to agreement regarding the design of the research project because of mistrust and a host of barriers, including cultural differences, feelings of "less than," prejudices on both sides, varying norms and practices surrounding the concept of volunteerism, different problem-solving styles, and varying approaches to dealing with conflict.

Yet it was the very practice of working through the issues that seemed to separate us that allowed us to build not only a sustainable collaboration but also two grant-funded CBPR projects that spanned five years of data collection and four years of dissemination (e.g., Hughes, Jordan, Roche, and Shapiro, 2003; Jordan, 2001; Jordan, Hughes, Roche, and Shapiro, 2004; Jordan, Hughes, and Shapiro, 2003; Jordan, Lee, Hampton, and Pirie, 2004; Jordan, Lee, and Shapiro, 2000; Jordan, Yust, Robison, Hannan, and Deinard, 2003; Phillips Neighborhood Healthy Housing Collaborative, 2000; Robison, Jordan, Hughes, Zelinsky-Goldman, and Shapiro, 2003). Phillips Community, a large, economically disadvantaged, and ethnically diverse urban community, has served as the incubator for the thoughts discussed in the sections that follow, by Gust and Jordan in their own voices, as a community organizer and as an academic scientist, respectively.. Out of their experiences in Phillips came an understanding of the widespread mistrust of research by communities and the skepticism directed toward CBPR by researchers trained in the Standard Norms. Gust and Jordan also developed passionate beliefs about the benefits of CBPR both to communities and to the research enterprise.

TRUSTWORTHINESS AND CBPR: THE VIEW FROM THE COMMUNITY

As individuals within communities, we all intuitively know that we are affected by research, but we do not often contemplate this fact. We mostly let research happen and either reap the benefits through, for example, more and improved choices, treatments, policies, and technology or, on the negative side, complain about inadequate designs, unfair policies, or high costs. As in the political process, we do not fully use our rights and expertise as citizens to participate in the research process or in the forming of research-based policies; that this is a possibility may not even occur to many of us. Yet, while we may abdicate our responsibility out of apathy or ignorance, we are left at some level with the awareness that we are truly excluded, do not know how to get involved, do not believe our opinion would be appreciated, and do not even know ourselves if we truly have valuable expertise. Yet, just as in the political process, the research process would undoubtedly be better at meeting our basic human needs or improving the overall health of our communities if more of us knew how to be thoughtfully involved and respected in the process.

The consequence of this "research disenfranchisement" is that traditional research, like "politics as usual," has come to be mistrusted. The reasons for this mistrust include the following:

- Traditional researchers are perceived as undertaking a project primarily for their own personal, professional, or institutional gain. The fact that they might actually care about how their work contributes to the common good or that they may care about the community is hidden from the view of the community and of the research "subjects" through the practice of detachment.
- Being a cooperative subject in a traditionally designed study requires one to be subordinate to the researcher. In communities of color, economically disadvantaged geographic communities, or communities of specific concerns, this feeling of subordination is compounded by other feelings of being "less than" in areas such as education levels, economic class, employable skills, disease or impairment, and so on. Why should one choose to associate with another individual or institution when that association contributes to a feeling of decreased self-worth?
- Traditional researchers do not often share their findings with research participants in a way that would allow participants to use the information. The perceived and sometimes stated reason for this neglect is that the research is too technical or too preliminary for consumption beyond the scientific literature. In addition, researchers sometimes simply get too busy to follow up on promises to provide summaries of findings to participants. The community gets the message that we are not to be considered as equals or peers; that we are not smart enough to understand the research, let alone put it to good use; and that research, however popular in scope, is really for the advancement of the individuals and the institutions that conduct research, who apparently don't have the time or interest to communicate results to those who made the research possible.
- As we see it, the primary issue is power: who has it and who gets to use it. In a democracy, power is shared; we all have it and have the right to use it. But in traditional research, the thinking seems to be that the research will be more sound, more valid, more "objective" if one entity, the researcher, has disproportionate power over another, the research "subject." Why should communities become involved with researchers or institutions that appear to be acting primarily in their own self-interest, that reinforce participants' awareness of their relative powerlessness, and that take no action to share the franchise and privilege that the researchers clearly possess?

Consequently, although we acknowledge that research shapes our lives, from the design of the cars we drive to the methods available to us for birthing our children, it seems reasonable—even rational—from a community perspective, to mistrust researchers, their methods, and their findings. We strongly believe that CBPR, when done well, holds the key to overcoming the mistrust left in the wake of years of traditional research and to achieving the dramatic, positive change that is possible when everyday citizens act in partnership with progressive researchers using rigorous scientific methods.

By definition, CBPR is good for communities. Its goal is to address issues that communities have defined or recognized, in a manner that allows them to act on the resulting information. Through CBPR, communities are empowered both because their resources and assets are recognized and strengthened and because the expertise of researchers and the resources and power of a university are brought alongside their own political will. The capacity of the community is increased, through skill building and economic security, because its members are employed whenever possible to conduct the research. In the Phillips Community projects, the CBPR model benefited the community in the following ways:

- Resident leaders learned and taught specific skills and transferable techniques to level the playing field between residents and nonresidents. For example, we used no titles, only first and last names; we celebrated each other's life events; we socialized with each other's families during annual picnics; and we paid residents a stipend for attending Collaborative meetings to acknowledge that they were offering their expertise and experience, just as the researchers were offering theirs.
- Community residents were as valued as the researchers because we were teachers as well as learners, just as the researchers were. This reciprocity helped residents value their nontraditional skills, intuitive knowledge, and learned experiences and to see them as equal in importance to the more formally acquired knowledge and skills of the researchers. Some residents experienced considerable boosts in self-esteem and were able to make improvements in other areas of their personal and professional lives.
- Generally, compared to faculty participants, residents were collectively more accepting of conflict and able to express anger because conflict is part of our daily, community life. Since conflict is often a necessary component of change, residents' comfort level with conflict meant that we could sometimes make changes more openly and swiftly than the researchers. This capacity was valued by the researchers, and some researchers made concerted efforts to improve their own ability to deal openly with conflict.
- Residents were also more easily accepting of our own and each other's intuitive knowledge and the use of emotional expression as a way of forming and sustaining the collaboration. Therefore, we often were able to take leadership in designing and sustaining the collaborative model. Researchers and other nonresidents were able to learn ways of integrating their personal and professional lives through these collaborative relationships while still maintaining the boundaries essential for a research project.

- Community residents increased their knowledge about lead poisoning and about the value of the scientific method because the researchers taught and modeled the principles of scientific integrity and rigor. This information increased residents' ability to protect our children's health and to evaluate and use scientific data in order to make individual choices.
- The majority of the staff positions on the two research projects were filled by community residents. These residents, representing the ethnically and culturally diverse demographics of the community, received comprehensive training, were paid living wages, and received health benefits. Numerous resident employees were able to transfer the skills and experience acquired to subsequent positions that advanced their vocational goals.
- Parents who received lead poisoning prevention education through the lead prevention project commented that their positive relationship with their peer teacher and the project as a whole helped them to feel valued and to complete the three-year participation commitment, as well as to make the behavior changes necessary to maintain a lead-safe environment for their child.
- In the dissemination phase of this project, the community as a whole was valued by presenting the resulting data within the community before disseminating the information to academic journals. Community residents and researchers have partnered in presenting data both to journals and to the community media.
- The credibility gained by the community through successfully completing two multimillion-dollar research projects and sustaining an ongoing collaboration with the University of Minnesota, despite many cultural differences and systemic barriers, has facilitated the community residents' ability to change local public policy around environmental health issues. The city of Minneapolis now has a comprehensive, interagency, public-private partnership to address the childhood lead poisoning problem and other childhood environmental health issues.

BUT IS CBPR GOOD SCIENCE?

There is a perception that CBPR is a methodology in and of itself, and that it is more qualitative or "soft" than traditional research. Although CBPR has been used more extensively in the social sciences, any discipline can employ a CBPR approach. It is important to state that CBPR is an approach to a research process that does not dictate the methodology. Methodology is called for by the research question; basic or bench science could be part of a CBPR initiative. The practitioners of CBPR understand it to benefit the research at all stages, including conceptualization, design, implementation, dissemination, and application, and thereby to strengthen the validity and utility of the results. However, CBPR is sometimes criticized by professional colleagues, administrators, grant reviewers, and journal editors as inferior to approaches employing the Standard Norms, in which researchers control and conduct all phases of the project, and researchers, participants, and the issues studied are distanced from each other as much as possible.

This mistrust of CBPR likely stems from the cultural rift between academics and lay communities. Academics, and particularly scientific researchers, are socialized to view themselves as the experts and are trained to view issues narrowly, with precision, and in a reductionistic manner. Communities value the larger picture, the context, the relevancy and applicability of information, and the manner in which they themselves are treated in the process of research. The criticisms that result focus in part on the belief that CBPR's requirement to share power and decision-making authority with nonresearchers and to address the sometimes competing demands of the community will compromise the rigor of the research. A second set of criticisms focuses on the potential for bias, because the research participants or others in the community close to the research issue have input into design, implementation, and data interpretation. Finally, CBPR is sometimes viewed as locally limited and not generalizable to a broader population or to other locales.

The first two criticisms do not apply when CBPR is done appropriately. As part of the sharing of expertise within the collaborative relationship, researchers must communicate why the scientific method or particular research process will produce findings that will be valuable to the community and why this approach will increase their power to make change. If it's true that the research will be better when, for example, the researchers are detached from the interests that lie behind the research situation, they ought to be able to make that case, and they are obliged to do so. If they can't—if they insist on a model of scientific practice that they can't explain and justify—then there ought to be serious questions about the rationality of placing trust in them. Attention to scientific method, elements of research design, threats to validity, sources of bias, and risks of going beyond the data when interpreting findings is vital because it is rational to place greater trust in research and researchers that attend to these matters than in those that don't. Especially when coupled with researchers' demonstrated respect for communities and concern for the consequences of their research, we have found that community members come to recognize the need to be guided by the researchers when necessary on matters of research integrity. This process of education and justification is likely to be time-consuming and frequently contentious, but the reward is that academic and community collaborators can become coinvestigators committed to creating a well-designed project, to preserving the rigor of the research design, and to accurately interpreting data.

The third criticism, concerning the alleged lack of generalizability of research findings, can apply to CBPR, just as it can to any form of research, depending on the topic and research design. But there is nothing about CBPR that makes its results necessarily less generalizable. For example, in the lead poisoning work in the Phillips Community, findings regarding peer education efficacy and developmental effects of lead poisoning are certainly generalizable to other diverse, urban populations, which happen to be just the populations most relevant to the topic. Moreover, the richness and texture of local data can provide insights into the complexities of the phenomena under investigation that traditional approaches to research could only attribute to noise or random error. (This point will be discussed further below.)

It must be acknowledged that conducting CBPR surely does require more work than traditional approaches in order to control for threats to validity and rigor and for potential bias. That work is often in the form of building trust—of the community's expertise; of the researchers' intentions, knowledge and training; and of the scientific method. Though not directly applicable to all sorts of research, the respectful engagement that characterizes CBPR provides a paradigm of what trustworthy research looks like. This engagement occurs at all stages of the research. Advantages of the CBPR model at each phase of the research process are presented below, using illustrations from the Phillips Community experience, with the aim of demonstrating why the extra investment required by CBPR is worth it and why colleagues, grantors, public policy makers, and editors should trust the information produced via CBPR approaches.

Conceptualization

Conceptualization is the process of framing the right research question. Research questions can be designed in a way that increases meaningful understanding of a phenomenon or provides only partial, superficial, or narrow understanding; appropriately handles confounding variables or ignores their presence; and increases applicability of findings or restricts it. The conceptualization stage is one of the most important determinants of whether research findings will have relevance and impact. For increasing the depth of understanding contributing to the conceptualization process, CBPR is an ideal approach.

There are many research questions that tolerate, or even require, use of the Standard Norms. However, when you apply the Standard Norms to research with people and communities, particularly research that will inform public and social policy, you risk drawing incomplete and narrow conclusions. A Standard Norms approach to research creates artificial constriction of the scope of investigation in that it deliberately controls for the influence of some of the factors that may be most important in understanding how the complex human world works, and it eliminates valuable sources of expertise readily at hand that can be obtained by including nonacademic stakeholders in all stages of the research.

The process of coconceptualizing a research question with community collaborators possessing their own expertise greatly increases the likelihood that the research question will be framed in a manner that considers the many complexities and interrelationships involved, provides information that informs the scientific knowledge base, and delivers information the community can utilize to understand itself and can take action on. Community members have considerable "local knowledge" to share with researchers concerning how a phenomenon might work in their community and often have their own hypotheses about the root causes underlying issues to be studied. A collaborative research approach means that researchers will have greater trusted access to community-held information and knowledge. This information allows researchers to understand the topic more deeply, to identify more potentially confounding variables, to generate more alternative hypotheses, and to try out research hypotheses against a wider range of critical perspectives.

In the Phillips collaboration, neighborhood residents assisted researchers in conceptualizing lead poisoning and its effects as one set of variables within a complex web of factors and issues related to substandard housing, environmental discrimination, eviction, fear of homelessness, poverty, social justice, inadequate education, health care access and quality, and so on. As a result, the questions asked and the data gathered, particularly in relation to the developmental effects of lead poisoning, address multiple biological, demographic, environmental, home, parental, and community variables. Collection of detailed data on variables that may be involved in such complex interactions is allowing for sophisticated modeling of predictors of children's developmental outcome.

Design

Design is the process of creating ways of testing the research question so that it can be answered definitively and in its entirety. This is the stage when plans are made for how to recruit participants and sustain their participation, how to reliably deliver an intervention if the study is an experimental one, how to measure variables of interest in a standardized and controlled way, how to analyze data, and how to protect the project from situations that would compromise the ability to draw accurate conclusions. The expertise of community members can be invaluable in these efforts. Community members know how they would want to be approached to participate in a project, what would allow them to trust the intentions of the research, and what incentives would motivate them to join and continue participating in the study. They can anticipate when questions, measures, or procedures would be offensive, threatening, or culturally insensitive. And they may be able to predict when situations in their community might pose a threat to the validity of the project.

For example, Phillips Community residents informed researchers of the city's policy to make birth records public only for children of married couples. Had we implemented birth record searches as a primary recruiting mechanism, we would have introduced significant selection bias.

Implementation

Implementation is the process of setting the design into motion. It is the actual recruitment of participants, application of an intervention if called for, collection of data, and analysis of data. Community partners can provide information that facilitates implementation and avoids situations that would threaten the feasibility of the study. For example, Phillips Community residents informed researchers of the city's policy to condemn homes contaminated by lead, forcing families to move, sometimes to shelters or the streets. We were thus able to predict that our project might result in increased condemnations because of our frequent monitoring of blood lead levels and that this might deter participation. We were able to take preventive steps, including working with Collaborative residents to (1) change the city's policy and (2) create a "safety net" providing lead-safe transitional housing and advocacy for families affected by high lead levels.

Typically, CBPR projects hire individuals from within the community to conduct much of the research during the implementation stage. The project benefits through improved recruitment rates, lower attrition, increased compliance, improved accuracy of reported information, and fewer cultural and language barriers. These all strengthen the validity of the data. In the Phillips lead poisoning projects, program evaluation focus group participants stated that they might not have joined the project if they had been approached by a researcher, social worker, or nurse, because these professions are mistrusted by residents who have found them to be judgmental in the past (Jordan, Lee, Hampton, and Pirie, 2004). Community staff were not suspected of having an ulterior motive (such as career advancement), and their personal experience as a community member or as a parent (or specifically as a parent with a lead-exposed child) added to their credibility. Researchers observed that community staff were able to establish warm relationships with participants because they shared similar experiences, culture, and language. The connection with a peer seemed to maintain participants' involvement and compliance. The sharing of more personal information than would have been the case had participants been interviewed by academic researchers was vital to the collection of accurate data on confounding variables. Community staff established trust and rapport with participants and were therefore able to project confidence in the researchers' intentions and the appropriateness of the project's goals and ethics.

Interpretation

Interpretation is the process of constructing a story to explain the results. It is the process of making meaning out of information, often numbers, that seem disconnected and abstract. This stage requires the ability to integrate various pieces of information, generate possible explanations for how they work together, and anticipate the implications of various explanations. Because individuals tend to view such information through their own lens, whether that lens be formed by research training, disciplinary expertise, or lived community experience, this stage is vulnerable to tunnel vision and personal investment. This is as true of the researchers as of the nonresearchers. The participation of all collaborators in this process provides a system of checking the accuracy and rationality of interpretations against each other. Rather than create subjectivity, this part of the CBPR process tends to create a balance between various "takes" on the data, and therefore, greater objectivity. Consideration of multiple and sometimes diverse interpretations of the data can lead to appreciation of the complexities inherent in the object of investigation and can prevent oversimplification of the model constructed to explain the phenomenon.

Gust, the primary community research collaborator, participated in discussions with researchers regarding the interpretation of the data from the lead education project. Her expertise in commercial and residential construction and remodeling as well as her knowledge of the history of housing practices in her neighborhood allowed us to more effectively understand the sources of lead contamination within the homes of our participants. In addition, she, far more effectively than the researchers, was able to understand the implications of the results of the project for policy change recommendations.

Dissemination

Dissemination is telling the story to an audience. In traditional models of research, findings are reported in the scientific literature as the primary (or sole) method of dissemination. Sometimes the media may pick up on research data or investigators may seek out the media, resulting in broader dissemination. However, for the most part, traditional researchers tend to target their research reports to their peers. The result is that the translation of research data into public knowledge or practical application is very slow and nondeliberate and is typically out of the control of both academic researchers and community members. In CBPR, the results of research projects reach a wide and diverse audience because many people have become stakeholders in the data, possibly including community members, policy makers, and organizations, as well as scientists. As stakeholders, these groups and individuals are not only interested in receiving the information resulting from the study, but likely to participate in further dissemination of information within their own circles.

After the completion of the lead prevention education project in Phillips, community members and researchers collaborated in writing an insert for the neighborhood's newspaper. This twelve-page document featured articles by researchers concerning the findings of the study and also included articles by community residents addressing their personal experiences as participants in the project and the importance of the CBPR model in reducing lead poisoning in the neighborhood, thereby creating accessible information for the community, increasing the skill base and leadership potential within the community, and empowering the community to take action on the information provided via the research. The insert was published prior to any scientific journal articles in order to communicate respect for the community as the primary stakeholder in the resulting information. Years later, we continue to receive calls from readers seeking to utilize this information in their own professional work or personal decision-making.

Application

Application is using the data to guide decisions and to make changes. In traditional models of research, there is little focus on how research findings will be put into practice by others. In fact, the research process typically ends after dissemination, except when the researcher or other investigators utilize research findings to inform the generation of additional research questions. A fundamental tenet of CBPR is that information resulting from a research project is used to make change, such as in social programming, environmental regulation, medical practice, public health policy, or law enforcement. Having results applied within such arenas provides feedback about the data's ecological validity and can raise additional questions for the community to investigate that ultimately lead to a more complete understanding of the topic of study.

Information accumulated throughout the Phillips lead prevention project and through data analysis has been utilized by Department of Health programs and nonprofit agencies to design a comprehensive, inter-agency, public-private lead poisoning prevention program that combines educational and environmental approaches to prevention of lead poisoning.

In summary, the public has come to mistrust traditional research paradigms in which research "subjects" are placed in relatively weak positions of power that parallel societal power structures, and in which participants or communities rarely hear back from researchers, much less directly benefit from the research process or its findings. In the eyes of community members CBPR holds much promise because it equalizes power, addresses a need the community identifies as important in a manner the community defines as acceptable, directly benefits the community by addressing the need and supporting the economic, skill, and leadership development of the community, and increases the capacity of the community to utilize resulting information to take action. Yet CBPR is often mistrusted within academia and the systems that support it, mainly granting agencies and journals. It is argued above that the CBPR approach benefits the research at every stage of the research process and that typical criticisms of decreased rigor, bias, and lack of generalizability are not warranted. Heightened understanding within academic communities of the benefits of the CBPR approach to the research itself, as well as the increased impact of the research on society's problems, should result in increased trust of CBPR. With greater trust we may see a willingness to apply the ethos of the CBPR process to more traditional research methodologies and a shift in the research cultures within academia, granting agencies, and journals.

CBPR AS A MODEL FOR INSTITUTIONAL CHANGE: GRASS ROUTES

In 2000, Scheman, a philosopher and feminist epistemologist, was introduced to Gust and Jordan because of her interest in the importance of trust to the mission of research universities, and in the part played by demonstrated commitments to social responsibility and social justice in grounding trustworthiness. At the time the three began working together, Scheman was about to become an associate dean in the Graduate School. University administration provided her, through work with Gust, Jordan, and other faculty, administrators, and community members, with a unique laboratory in which to practice "applied epistemology" by exploring issues of trust and trustworthiness and ways of overcoming increasingly prevalent mistrust on the part of diverse publics. She has argued that such mistrust stands in the way of the creation of truly objective knowledge and that this (very traditional) goal will come into reach only when diverse communities become full collaborators in research as well as respected critics of it (see chapter 11).

The three authors first worked together on a conference, "Designing Research for Change," held at the University of Minnesota in February 2001, as part of the University president's series of events in recognition of the university's sesquicentennial. The conference brought together university researchers, community members, policy makers, and funders to map the barriers they perceived to genuinely collaborative research and to begin to strategize ways of overcoming them. The participants identified barriers to CBPR and, specifically, the challenges to forming the respectful, trusting community-university partnerships that are essential for this work to successfully occur. The work of the conference participants laid the ground for the authors' subsequent development of GRASS

Routes (Grass Roots Activism, Sciences, and Scholarship), an initiative to support preparation for and facilitation of CBPR at the University of Minnesota, and to help extend the ethos of CBPR as intrinsic to the University's research mission.

The development of GRASS Routes has coincided with the work of the University's Council on Public Engagement, which helped to raise the profile of and to better prepare the ground for CBPR as one among many ways the University, in its teaching, research, and service missions, can more fully engage with diverse communities. It has been gratifying to discover just how timely the ideas from the conference and GRASS Routes are, not only locally but nationally, as many people and institutions grapple with the changing face of the public research university and its relationships with the publics that are called on to support it and that it is intended to serve.

In response to the energy and enthusiasm of the participants in the "Designing Research for Change" conference, and their rich ideas regarding barriers to CBPR, Jordan, Gust, and Scheman developed GRASS Routes with the aims of bringing together and making accessible the forms of knowledge that reside in diverse locales—from community to laboratory—in the conviction that those who hold that knowledge will together show the way from research need or idea through to the dissemination and use of research findings. This initiative has been financially supported by the University's Academic Health Center, Graduate School, and central administration. The activities of GRASS Routes focus on four major areas of need identified by conference participants.[3]

First is the need for education of faculty, graduate students, and community members in methods and skills of collaborative research. Second is the locating of intersections, the matches of interests and abilities between community groups and university researchers. Third is the need for mentorship of collaborations to ensure sustainability. And fourth is the dissemination of research findings, within the community and more broadly, thereby making those findings available where they will do many sorts of good: empowering the community for change, informing and influencing public policy, and raising the profile of collaborative research within the University and in academic journals.

Several sets of activities have been conducted or planned to address each area of need. For example, a faculty development seminar series was aimed at providing practical skills; teaching principles of CBPR and its parallels, community-based education (CBE) or service learning;

---

3. GRASS Routes is no longer active, and the initiatives discussed below are not on-going. Partly as a result of their work with GRASS Routes, Jordan and Gust have taken up positions that have continued their commitments to CBPR. Since 2004 Jordan has been the Director of the University of Minnesota's Children, Youth, and Family Consortium and is the founding editor of www.CES4Health.info, a mechanism for the rigorous peer review and online publication of products of community-engaged scholarship.; and Gust has become a member, and is currently Chair, of the Board of Directors of Community-Campus Partnerships for Health. (note added in 2010)

preparing faculty for typical hurdles; assisting faculty in solving problems in their community-based work; and more generally, increasing the appreciation of trust, power, and privilege as the fundamental issues to address within partnerships. As a result of this faculty development series, it is expected that faculty will increase their community-based work and will serve as ambassadors, promoting the ethos of CBPR within their own disciplines and academic units, integrating concepts into their teaching and mentoring, and recruiting additional faculty and students into this work. In addition, GRASS Routes is developing a series of Responsible Conduct of Research forums on the ethics of CBPR.

A network of university and community members are being recruited to serve as guides, available to meet with community members in their own locales, to help navigate the enormous complexity that makes up the University's research capacity. These guides will help communities frame their ideas and questions; search for faculty with relevant expertise, time, and interest; and facilitate introductions of community leaders to these potential research partners at the University.

All collaborations run into problems along the way, and short-term assistance from others who have witnessed or weathered such storms can help to deal with miscommunication, mismatched expectations, conflicts of personality or style, and inevitable stretches of frustration and explosions of anger. GRASS Routes has provided mentorship to an interdisciplinary faculty-student initiative within the Academic Health Center as they designed a community learning experience within a local community clinic. In addition, networks of experienced university faculty and community members will be recruited to serve as mentors to collaborations wanting assistance forming trusting relationships or resolving problems.

Finally, funds will be raised for a small grants program that will be called the PUBLICation Fund. Grants will be given to CBPR partnerships seeking to disseminate research findings to immediate stakeholders (community residents, community-based organizations, policymakers, etc.) via nonacademic vehicles. For example, if it is important for high school students to receive information resulting from a CBPR project on sexual health, the PUBLICation Fund might grant money for the production of an interactive theater piece to be performed at high schools.

CONCLUSION

Alongside the forces that push today's public research university toward corporate funding, entrepreneurial profit making, and conservative ways of evaluating research, there is another, at least potentially opposing, trend in higher education. Colleges and universities are increasingly including what is usually called "service-learning" in their undergraduate curricula, and some are launching broader initiatives, like the University of Minnesota's Council on Public Engagement (established by Robert

Bruininks, then executive vice-president and provost and later president). While traditional service-learning fits comfortably under the mantle of "compassionate conservatism," instilling the value of charitable good works on the part of the privileged, many of the broader initiatives are fueled by a deeply alternative vision, which includes among a university's mission ideals of community empowerment, reinvigorated democratic engagement, and social justice. In the terms of such an alternative vision, "service-learning" is renamed "civic-learning," and the transformative experiences are aimed at graduate students and faculty as much as undergraduates.

We want to argue that public universities cannot afford to give up on a claim to broad-based public support, and that in order to earn such support, it is necessary to embrace the ideals articulated in that alternative vision. Though CBPR is not the only way research universities can realize those ideals, it is both a clear expression of them and a way to build the sort of good will and spirit of civic engagement that will make other projects more feasible. Especially when embraced by the university as something to be especially proud of and to vigorously support, CBPR projects can do a great deal to change the image of an aloof and arrogant institution and provide grounds for those outside it to trust what goes on within. And the core ethos of cultivating mutual trustworthiness is one that can serve as a guide even for research quite distant in approach from CBPR, much as the ethos of laboratory science has served as a paradigm of objectivity in a wide range of fields even outside the sciences.

Trust, especially trust in academic research, is among the most important resources that research universities need to draw on. Most fundamentally, untrusted research is worthless. Even the most basic, nonapplied forms of research are meant to be taken up by other research-ers and to become part of larger, shared bodies of knowledge and theory. Despite the expectation of replicability of research findings, there is no getting away from dependence on webs of trust in the work of con-temporary and earlier researchers.

Beyond being taken up by other researchers, most research directly or indirectly, sooner or later, enters into a broader public context in which the trust of nonscientists is relevant, and that trust is all too often lacking. Public mistrust of academic research is a frequent occasion for faculty and administrative lament. It is intrinsically frustrating to have something one regards as valuable and useful scorned, especially by those for whom one intended it to be useful. More practically, trust in the research done at a public university contributes to the willingness of the state's citizens to support the university with their tax money (as well as to want their children to be educated there). The erosion of that trust is arguably a significant contributor to the national mood of pulling back on such support.

Universities and those who run them also ought to be, and frequently are, concerned about how well or badly, rationally or irrationally, ordinary people form beliefs. One of the principle tasks of universities, especially in democracies, is to help to raise the general level of informed, critical discussion, debate, and belief-formation, both directly by educating some people and indirectly by educating the parents, teachers, and others who help to shape us. It seems abundantly clear that there has been massive failure somewhere along the line: most people tend to be either credulous, cynical, or some odd combination of both when it comes to most of the questions that are vital to our individual and collective well-being, whether in the realm of food safety or national security, history or economics. The blame can be spread around widely, but it's important for universities to take responsibility for their failure to consider the possibility that it might not be *rational* for members of diverse publics to trust academic research.

Especially public universities, out of a concern for the recognized social value of the research done there, need to attend to what typically are regarded as peripheral issues of social justice. Differences that mark inequities of power and privilege, such as race or ethnicity, class, gender, or sexual identity, affect not only the psychological likelihood of trust but also its rationality. It is not rational to trust those whom you perceive to have a track record of disrespectfully treating members of a community you identify with, or whose publicly reported views about your community seem to be either lies or stupid mistakes, or who appear to take no interest in what members of your community have to say to them or in the effects that their views about your community have on the people in it. Given the depth and pervasiveness of social, political, and economic inequality in the United States today, it needn't take malevolence or malfeasance for researchers to act in ways that give rise to such perceptions. Ordinary, orthodox scientific method frequently provides sufficient grounds for mistrust, given the gulf that already exists especially between poor, immigrant, and/or racially stigmatized communities and "institutions of higher learning," which, whatever else they do, serve to train and educate the ruling and managerial elites and to produce knowledge useful to them.

Ironically, part of the problem lies in the norms that are designed precisely to underwrite trustworthiness, as understood from within the university: the Standard Norms of disinterest and dispassionate, disengaged objectivity; the cultivation of an impersonal style of writing and argument; the replacement of experience as a ground of belief with observation (measured, controlled, stripped of subjectivity or idiosyncrasy). These signs of trustworthiness, typically demanded by disciplinary training, can hardly function in the same way from the vantage point of those who see very clearly the complicity of universities in the structures of their subordination. From such a vantage point what seems to be going on is an elaborate shell game, where the interests being served may never actually be visible, but are nonetheless guiding the enterprise.

Universities have increasingly taken on, or been given, the task of certifying that research meets certain ethical standards through, for example, Institutional Review Boards for research involving human participants and, more recently by federal mandate, of educating researchers in the Responsible Conduct of Research. The scope of such certification and education does not, however, generally include social responsibility, let alone social justice, among the norms of responsible research. Rather, a commitment to truth as the goal of research and protection of the individual participant is taken to be sufficient, with questions of the social consequences of research left to others (including, on the haberdashery theory of scientific responsibility, to researchers with their citizen hats on).

But this separation doesn't work. Those outside of the university who are taken to be objects of knowledge rather than knowing subjects, and are researched only by people who do not also listen to and learn from them, will, insofar as they are rational, be mistrustful of university-based research. The absence of their voices will seriously compromise the dissemination and acceptance of the research and, even more seriously, its very objectivity and validity.

The methodology of CBPR is grounded in the conviction that a pluralistic democratic conception of knowers enriches, rather than undermines, empirical scientific research. When those whose lives and communities are being researched are empowered as knowers, alongside and in collaboration with academic researchers, the knowledge that results is more complex, better supported by a wider range of evidence, less subject to unexamined bias, and far more likely to be taken up and put to use.

ACKNOWLEDGMENTS

We appreciate the thoughtful critique of our ideas and manuscript by Dr. Steven Hughes. Special thanks to the families of the Phillips Community who care so deeply about the futures of their children and generously gave their time, sometimes for several years, in support of the data collection phase of the projects described in this essay. The University of Minnesota investigators participating in this project will forever do our work differently thanks to the thoughtful and tenacious teachings and leadership of the current resident members of the Phillips Neighborhood Healthy Housing Collaborative (PNHHC): James Big Bear, Jody Deloria, Susan Gust, Mary Johnson, Shannon Moon, Michelle Nickaboine, and Sheila Shavers, as well as past members: Erin Bluejacket, Wendy Boppert, Lilly Bresina, Kay and Rene Cabrera, Rep. Karen Clark, Charles (Doc) Davis, Nicole Diaz Romero, Marc Flores, Teresa Ford, Star Grigsby, Keith Johnson, Beth Hart, Gwendolyn Hill, Mary Ellen Kaluza, Leah La Chapelle, Donna Morgan, Darin Packard, Mary Parkhurst, Cathy Strobel, Deb Terwillger, Deb Whitefeather, and Cathy Winter. We also express our tremendous gratitude to the community staff members, many of whom also served on the PNHHC, for their excellent work and dedication to the research. The work of the PNHHC and its contributions to the research could not have been accomplished without the tireless efforts of its staff over the years: Carol Flavin, Kim Kelker, Ed Petsche, Kim Rowe, and Jermaine Toney.

Chapter 10

Narrative, Complexity, and Context: Autonomy as an Epistemic Value

> Those masterful images because complete
> Grew in pure mind, but out of what began?
> A mound of refuse or the sweepings of a street,
> Old kettles, old bottles, and a broken can,
> Old iron, old bones, old rags, that raving slut
> Who keeps the till. Now that my ladder's gone,
> I must lie down where all the ladders start
> In the foul rag and bone shop of the heart.
>
> W. B. Yeats, "The Circus Animals' Desertion"

> Human beings are not at the pinnacle of intelligence, smarter than other animals, far smarter than plants, farther still from rocks and other non-living things. It is, in fact, the other way around: the rocks, being oldest, know the most, followed by plants and by animals older than we are. As the youngest, the most recent inhabitants of this place, we humans are the most ignorant and have the most to learn from our elders.
>
> Paraphrased from Paul Schultz, elder,
White Earth band of Ojibwe

In Margaret Drabble's novel *The Sea Lady*, a man and a woman in late middle age travel toward a small city on the English coast, near where they met as children, to receive honorary doctorates and—as it turns out, not coincidentally—to meet for the first time in thirty years. They had parted after a brief and disastrous marriage following a love affair that, in its intensity of both passion and happiness, shadowed the rest of their lives. The book ends shortly after their reunion, leaving open what will occur between them.

Humphrey is a distinguished marine biologist, renowned as a perceptive observer of the complexity and interdependency of aquatic life. His career and reputation have, however, been overtaken by the disciplinary shift away from the study of animals in the sea toward the study of cells and molecules in the laboratory. Ailsa is a pioneering feminist critic of art, literature, culture, and everyday life. A desultory scholar, she has been an energetic thinker and a charismatic *provocateuse*, brilliantly bringing together eclectic mixes of theory and subject matter that helped to shape the spirit of a time—radical, restless, and rhyzomatic (rooted not in the stability of depth, but in a network of surface entanglements).

I want to explore a possibility suggested by Humphrey and Ailsa's tentative reconciliation at the end of the novel. Seeing that reconciliation in terms of the coming together of C. P. Snow's "two cultures"—the careful scientist and the allusive aesthete—is thwarted by Humphrey's current status as an outsider to the culture of science. His scientific discipline has, to his dismay and disapproval, embraced the mereology that has characterized modern laboratory science. From a mereological perspective, the properties and behavior of objects are the consequence of the properties and behavior of their parts. Objects of study need to be abstracted from their surroundings in order to discover how they are the (kinds of) things they are in virtue of the constitution of their parts. Humphrey's complexly contextualized knowledge of the sea creatures he studies seems at least as distant from this conception of science as from Ailsa's richly suggestive, but unsystematic, musings. Both he and she see knowledge of the world in terms of relationships—of contiguity as much as of similarity—and knowledge of things as inseparable from the contexts in which those things take shape. Those affinities were camouflaged by the very different positions in which they stood in relation to the authoritative culture of science—Humphrey as an obsolete remnant of an earlier, premodern, age, and Alisa as the seductive siren of avant-garde, postmodern critique. The authoritative culture of serious knowledge has not only dismissed them both, but has done so in terms that disguised their affinities and held apart their potential for collaboration—in fashioning either a personal life together or a way of seeing the world that married his attentiveness to detail to her flashes of analogical insight.

How might the ethical and epistemological norms that underlie modern science—including both biomedical research and a great deal of, especially evidence-based, medical practice—differ if Humphrey and Ailsa were together to help to shape them? What, in particular, would research and clinical ethics, specifically as protecting the autonomy of human subjects and patients, look like if knowers and the objects of their knowledge were not abstracted from their relationships with each other and with the worlds in which they live, and if those relationships were themselves conceived of as epistemic resources? Standing as the "before" and "after" to scientific modernity, Humphrey and Ailsa set in relief its distinctive ways of knowing: as different as they are from each other, they share a passionate commitment to what modern science downplays—context, connection, contingency, and particularity.

WHY DOES AUTONOMY MATTER?

Respect for the autonomy of one's (human) subjects is a core concept in the ethics of research, but autonomy is typically characterized individualistically, as something that persons simply have and that others are called on to respect by not violating. Furthermore, respect for autonomy is conceptualized as arising from considerations extrinsic to the distinctively epistemic aims of science. I want to argue, rather, that scientists need to recognize and act on a specifically *epistemic* interest in the autonomy of their research subjects (if any) as well as in the autonomy of others who stand to be affected by their research or who are in a position to know and care about the objects of that research. Furthermore, acting appropriately on this epistemic interest requires a conception of autonomy as relational and contextual, as manifested in particular interpersonal situations, through mutual engagement. Such a conception is also ethically preferable in that it reveals the connections between autonomy and other aspects of human flourishing, making it clearer why it matters, both to the person whose autonomy is in question and to others.

Ethical rules concerning the use of human subjects in research are typically regarded as putting the brakes on the unacceptable behavior in which scientists might engage, were they guided solely by narrowly scientific norms. Such a characterization has its roots in the two emblematic scenarios out of which such rules arose: Nazi experimentation on prisoners in concentration camps and the Tuskegee study of the unchecked progress of syphilis in poor, Black men. These two cases, along with less notorious others, merged with the cultural image of the "mad scientist," whose madness constituted, rather than undermined, his (male pronoun intended) scientific genius. As the dark side of the scientific and technological progress of modernity, epistemic lust was regarded as needing to be held in check by something external to the search for truth.

Not all ethical norms for science share this epistemologically extrinsic quality. In particular, those that serve to protect the scientific enterprise itself seem directly related to the search for truth. Thus, prohibitions on falsifying data, or even on stealing the work of others or misusing research funds, are seen as intrinsically, even if not immediately, related to the aims of scientific discovery. The mediating link is the need for scientists to trust each other and to trust the workings of the institutions (from laboratories to universities to journals) that make their work and its dissemination possible. The trust of wider publics is not, however, seen as similarly intrinsic to the enterprise: even when bemoaning public ignorance or irrational credulity, scientists don't usually regard that lamentable situation as affecting the quality of the science they do—except in the indirect ways of leading to reductions in public funding or the enactment of restrictive legislation. This distinction—between the scientifically intrinsic nature of trust among scientists and the scientific irrelevance or merely instrumental relevance of public trust—marks a substantive difference in how scientists (are supposed to) think about respecting those toward whom they have ethical responsibilities.

In the case of fellow scientists, respect is rooted in participation in a shared enterprise and the need for each other's intelligence and perspectives: the trust engendered by respect (or endangered by disrespect) is intrinsic to the relationships that constitute a necessarily collective enterprise. In the case of research subjects or of the public more broadly, both respect and the trust it engenders are either epistemically irrelevant or merely instrumental: members of the public, unlike other scientists, are not collaborators in a collective activity, but merely objects (i.e., research "subjects"), supporters, victims, or beneficiaries of the activities of scientists. This difference—between treating others respectfully because one recognizes the need for their active engagement in and with one's work and treating them respectfully because to do otherwise would be either morally wrong or instrumentally troublesome—is the difference between having and not having a specifically *epistemic* interest in others' autonomy. I want to suggest that the picture in terms of which scientists do *not* have such an interest in the autonomy either of their subjects or of others variously related to their objects of research is mistaken. Rather, the requirement of respect for the autonomy of human subjects ought to reflect a broader, epistemic interest in the autonomy of diverse (human and, as my paraphrase from Paul Schultz suggests, nonhuman) others.

Underlying the view of human subjects as needing to be protected from, rather than as collaborating in, scientific research is a conception of knowers and the objects of their knowledge (human or not) as fundamentally and normatively separate. Blurring the boundaries between them is thought to pose not only an ethical but, more fundamentally, an epistemic threat. The disciplining of the researcher and the isolation and abstraction of the object of knowledge are meant to prepare them for an encounter that will not fundamentally change either of them but rather allow them both to be most essentially themselves. The researcher, as generically rational and disciplined, is able to reveal the nature of the object, abstracted from the confounding variables of its life outside the laboratory. Recent work in science studies has argued for a deeply different way of thinking about the encounter between subjects and objects of knowledge, according to which the material-discursive context of that encounter helps to constitute the objects being studied.[1] Much as the

---

1. As I was doing the final revisions of this essay, I received two books that articulate such a conception of the epistemology and ontology of science. One, Karen Barad's *Meeting the Universe Halfway: Quantum Physics and the Entanglement of Matter and Meaning* (2007), develops her theory of *agential realism*, which she draws from Niels Bohr's physics and philosophy; the book is brilliant and, hopefully, germinal in its revolutionary conception of a metaphysics that is relational and—hence, she argues—ethical all the way down. The second, *Pluripotent Circulations: Putting Actor-Network Theory to Work on Stem Cells in the USA, Prior to 2001*, a doctoral dissertation by Morten Sager (2006) (in History of Ideas and Theory of Science, Gothenburg University), develops and applies a version of actor-network theory (ANT), drawing primarily on the work of Bruno Latour and Michel Callon, to argue similarly for the emergence of objects of study—reality—in and through material-discursive practice. Strikingly—and

normative "view from nowhere" has been criticized as neither possible nor, even as an ideal, conducive to actual objectivity (Haraway 1988), so the laboratory has been argued to be a quite particular place, the site of quite particular relationships, which shape all the participants in the construction of knowledge that occurs there. (See, for example, Latour 1979, Pickering 1995, Rouse 2002, and Traweek 1988.)

Since that knowledge is meant to apply to, and to be applicable in, the world outside the laboratory, it's important to ask what the knowledge is knowledge *of*. Real problems arise about the applicability of research findings beyond the research setting, and one way of framing those problems is in terms of whether, and to what extent, the objects of the research are relevantly different from the objects in the wider world they are taken to exemplify. Given the conceptual (and frequently material) abstraction of objects of research, as well as their subsequent reinscription within the specific parameters of the research context, the applicability of research depends on tracing relationships between objects of research and the objects to which the research is meant to apply, whether those objects be people or rocks or the genomes of plants.

I want to argue for an epistemology and ethics of research that draw attention to the contexts in which objects (and subjects) of knowledge exist both in the laboratory and "in the wild," into which discoveries will eventually move, as drugs are administered to patients, seeds are planted in fields, public policies are enacted in communities. It can take at least as much material and conceptual labor to successfully integrate scientific knowledge into the world as it took to extract the objects of that knowledge from it. The tools for this labor will not, however, generally reside in scientists' toolboxes. Some of the tools will be found in the engaged praxis and situated knowledge of those who are enmeshed in the world out of which the objects of knowledge were extracted and refined, and others will need to be collaboratively custom-crafted. A central aim of this essay will be to say something useful about the nature of those tools and about the work to which they need to be put. I want to suggest that Hilde Lindemann's work on the role of narrative in "holding another in personhood" (Nelson 2001, Lindemann 2008) can be generalized to account for the ontological continuity between the contexts of research and of application (whether theoretical or practical: my concern is not just with research applications in the usual sense, but with the more basic notion of "aboutness"—our being able to say that research actually tells us something about our lives and about the world around us). I want to extend Lindemann's use of narrative to consider nonhumans, as well as humans, as both the objects of narrative and as narrators; and it will be as narrators that research subjects (and other objects of research, as well

this is not an aspect of their work with which I was familiar—both Barad and Sager (and other ANT theorists) articulate and employ a conception of agency that is not confined to the human or even the animate or organic.

as other people and things related to those objects) will be normatively autonomous.

NARRATIVE AND ONTOLOGY

> If they are not machines, then what are organisms? A metaphor far more to my liking is this. Imagine a child playing in a woodland stream, poking a stick into an eddy in the flowing current, thereby disrupting it. But the eddy quickly reforms. The child disperses it again. Again it reforms, and the fascinating game goes on. There you have it! Organisms are resilient patterns in a turbulent flow—patterns in an energy flow.
>
> Carl R. Woese, "A New Biology for a New Century"[2]

In returning to the "rag and bone shop of the heart," Yeats's poet speaks to all those—scientists included—who are tempted by the clarity, cleanliness, and uplift of grand and pure ideas. And the return is for real—he does not just root around for inspiration, or data: he casts his lot with the refuse, the old, the broken, the "foul." Yeats means to draw himself, and us, back to where those grand and pure ideas start, and to where we must return, lest those ideas take on the appearance of a life of their own, a life we are at risk of being seduced into regarding as realer or more important than the messy ones we're living.

This (re)turn of attention to the ordinary is a naturalizing move, seeking norms that emerge from the details of practice, rather than originating in some privileged elsewhere. Our attention is also drawn to narrative, to details as meaningfully connected in a particular context. In its most basic manifestation, narrative is simply *space and time made salient*: here and now; then and there; once upon a time, long long ago and far far away. Stories are organized from a point of view; salience is perspectival, a matter of how the world appears from here, to the narrator now, in the light of her, his, or its own particular interests, needs, desires, and capacities. Narrative is also intrinsically connected to autonomy, in particular to "perceptual autonomy," the ability to recognize, articulate, and effectively communicate how the world appears from one's particular location in it. Those in subordinated, marginalized, or closeted social locations typically learn—in order to be taken seriously—the skill of periscopic vision: refracting their line of sight to correspond to the privileged "view from nowhere."[3] Autonomous narration thus requires

---

2. I came upon this quote in Dyson (2007).

3. See Haraway (1988), and Williams (1991), especially the latter's account of two parents (she says they must be lawyers, but they could as well be philosophers) trying to persuade their terrified toddler that the "slavering wolfhound" drooling over him is essentially no different from the laughably harmless

that the narrator be situationally capable of and credited with a legitimate, nonperiscopic point of view.

Narrative begins in the ways in which aspects of the world are differently salient for and to different things—as geological formations bear the traces of volcanoes and the rise and recession of rivers and glaciers, while perhaps remaining indifferent to the dry or rainy summers, warmer or colder winters that leave their traces in the rings of trees, or to the presence of flora and fauna that shape each other through the coevolution of predator and prey. At its most fundamental, narrative and narrative saliency constitute the ontology of complex objects as more than the sum of their parts. As I've argued elsewhere about the self, any object can be thought of as a *locus of idiosyncrasy* (Scheman 1993*a*), as fundamentally adverbial, a way of being in the world, a nexus of causes and effects, distinctively salient to its surroundings, as they are distinctively salient to it. What makes something a *thing* (an organism, but even an ordinary-sized physical object, like a stone) is its *integrity*, its propensity to continue in existence as the particular (sort of) thing that it is, along with its entering as an organized whole into relationships of cause and effect. (What I mean by 'integrity' is, I believe, related to what Spinoza meant by '*conatus*'.) Its integrity (its separateness and distinctness) is thus essentially bound up with its relationships with other things in its environment: it and they reciprocally define each other's boundaries, capabilities, susceptibilities, and identities.

It was reflections such as these that led me to appreciate the inverted "smartness" pyramid I learned from Paul Schultz, which I initially had difficulty understanding with any degree of literalness. Think, for example, about ordinary cases of (human) embodied knowledge, such as knowing how to perform activities that we would clumsily fail at if we tried consciously to enunciate each step of what we were doing. In almost as ordinary a way, we speak of our bodies as remembering previous experiences: think of vaccinations and allergic reactions. Our bodies, as complex entities, bear the traces of earlier experiences and act in the present in ways informed by those experiences.[4] Similarly, as a locus of idiosyncratic saliencies, a cliff side or a tree or a species bears a story about the times it has lived through and that have made it what it is. Our learning that story requires our respecting the perspectival autonomy of that thing, listening and attending specifically to its integrity, its being what it is, in this place, over time. It is what it is because of what it has witnessed, and the specificities of its witnessing were shaped by its being the sort of thing that it is. We need to attend as well to our own relationships to the things we are learning from, to how we come to be where we

Pekinese he towers over: Dogs are dogs, at least from the parents' perspective, informed not only by height but by science.

4. The immune system is an especially interesting site for reflection on bodily constitution of identity. See, for example, Haraway (1999).

are, to what we want of these things and how what we want relates to the histories and the relationships that predate our arrival.[5]

This sort of attention helps to bridge the gap between the laboratory and the wider world. In her discussions about those who cannot, or can no longer, narrate their own lives, hence hold their own personhood, Lindemann describes a special case of what (she also argues) is generally true: we are not the sole narrators of our own lives, the sole arbiters of our ontological structure and boundaries (Lindemann 2008). Nor do the relationships that help to constitute us as the particular beings we are remain within the specific contexts in which they most centrally arise: they accompany us, to greater or lesser extents, more or less tenaciously, as we move from place to place. What is true of us is true quite generally, and tracing the relationships and the narratives that cling to and continue to help to constitute objects of research plays an important role in the applicability of that research. As Lindemann's narrator accompanies her unconscious friend through the decisions about his care, by embodying and voicing the story of who he is, so too do the voices of those who are narratively entwined, in the wider world, with the people or objects in research settings need to be heard in those settings, in order to maintain the ontological continuity needed for the applicability of research.

As the doctors treating Lindemann's unconscious patient risk treating not *him* but the congeries of symptoms that reveal themselves to their diagnostic tools and modes of perception, so similarly researchers risk learning about an object constrained and defined by their tools and methods in ways that are discontinuous with the lives of the objects in the contexts from which they were abstracted. As in Lindemann's story, what we need to aim for is not the irrelevance of the expert's tools and perspective, but rather a larger story into which the story they reveal can be inserted; we need accompanying narratives to preserve the "aboutness" of the expert's knowledge. Respecting the autonomy both of the objects of study (including, but not limited to, human subjects) as well as of those things and persons with which they are enmeshed in "real life" is thus not an ethical demand superimposed on epistemic norms, but rather constitutive of those norms. And the autonomy in need of respect is, as feminist theorists have argued, relational, not to be understood in terms of separateness or of the primacy of already bounded individuals (Keller 1985, Mackenzie and Stoljar 2000, and—specifically in the context if medical ethics—Kukla 2005).

---

5. It is, of course, true that we no more have direct, unmediated access to narratives than we do to anything else. Anything we say about the narratives of geological formations or anything else will be our story about its story. Such iterative narrativity complicates matters in practice, but my fundamental point remains: we need to practice the respectfully interactive telling of non-humans' stories, just as we need to practice the respectfully interactive telling of the stories of persons whose capacity for autonomous narration has been problematically denied. My attributing the role of narrator to non-humans is part of the shift in conceptions of agency also characteristic of theories and methods such as Actor-Network Theory and agential realism. See footnote 1.

Though there is little to say in general terms about what such respect would actually look like, it is clear that its demands will be frequently in conflict with established scientific practice. Think, for example, of the controversies surrounding archeology's collection and study of ceremonial objects. There is a tension between the meaning such objects have for descendants of their original users and the means employed by archeologists to study them—starting with removing them from the sites at which the archeologists found them. This relocation engenders mistrust on the part of those whose relationships with the objects are the last links in the narrative chain that constitutes the objects' sacredness. The severing of those relationships—or their inaccessibility to researchers—means that however the objects come to be known, they will, in important ways, not be known as the particular sorts of things that they were. Similarly, the scientific study of plants that have ceremonial or healing roles in various traditional societies raises questions about the identity of what is being studied: to what extent do the "purified" samples and isolated "active ingredients" correspond to the plants as they are used indigenously? To what extent can the healing properties of the plants be abstracted from the practices that surround their indigenous use? Taking such questions seriously entails engaging with those whose lives and practices have been entwined with the plants, those entrusted with the stories of the plants' powers; and the possibility for such engagement is undermined when those people, practices, and stories are treated as irrelevant to the search for the presumptive essence of the plants.[6]

CLINICAL EPISTEMOLOGY

A recurring theme in doctors' stories of becoming patients is discovering that, as patients, they are not presumed to know anything about the illness or injury they are currently suffering and for which they are being treated. Being the patient, that is, does not put one in a socially recognized position to contribute distinctively to efforts to understand either the problem or the effects of attempted solutions. The fact that it is doctors' own bodies that are ill and injured and their bodies that are experiencing the effects of the treatments, far from especially qualifying them to speak about how things are going, marks them as epistemically compromised.

This epistemic disenfranchisement is similar to that experienced by other social groups—notably children, women, homosexuals, and the disabled—who are taken, by their membership in the group (defined

6. In addition to Paul Schultz, I am especially indebted in thinking about these issues to Maggie Adamek, Jill Doerfler, Craig Hassel, Karl Lorenz, and George Spengler, especially in connection with the conflicts between the University of Minnesota and the White Earth Reservation concerning University research on wild rice (Manoomin), a grain sacred to the Ojibwe.

and named by others), to be in no position to have reliable beliefs about their own lives. In the case of children (and people with severe cognitive disabilities), there is a degree of justification for this view: young children, or those with the cognitive abilities of a young child, are typically unable to comprehend the more complex aspects of their own lives and well-being. But even in such cases, as children's rights and, especially, disability rights activists have argued, this dismissal is carried farther than is either necessary or justifiable, as well as being extended to people with disabilities that in no way hinder their understanding of their own lives.

As feminist, queer, and disability theorists have argued, in the cases of women and of variously queer and disabled people, the presumption of epistemic incompetence, concerning especially one's own life, is a cornerstone of sexist, heterosexist, and ableist ideology. Being the scrutinized object of the gaze of the epistemically privileged, presumptively unable to return that gaze or, specifically, to regard oneself with any authority, is at the heart of the discursive practices that create homosexuals, transsexuals, the disabled, and perhaps even women as such—as particular sorts of people, rather than people who just happen to have certain sorts of sexual desires and proclivities or to have bodies or minds that differ in certain ways from what is considered "normal."

But it is hardly necessary to "extend" such an account to cover patients (or, as will be discussed below, research subjects). Rather, what in the cases of women, homosexuals, transsexuals, and the disabled requires argument and engenders controversy is—in the case of people being treated for illness or injury—lying incontrovertibly there on the surface. Such people are *patients*, something you cannot be—no matter how gravely ill or grievously injured—unless you are under the care of someone taken to be in a position to diagnose your condition and prescribe and administer remedies for it. Your place in the relationship that constitutes your patienthood (specifically and especially within Western, science-based medicine) defines you as subject to an expert gaze presumed capable—as you are presumed incapable—of naming what is wrong with you and directing the course of your treatment.

One might object that patients are continually being asked how they feel, whether it hurts when the doctor presses there, where their pain is on a scale of one to ten, and whether it is worse in the morning or the evening. True enough; but like the things that "native informants" tell anthropologists, the answers to such questions are taken as mere raw material for authorized knowers to interpret in the light of their own observations and using their theoretical tools. As I have argued elsewhere—following Uma Narayan and other postcolonial theorists—indigenous knowledge is treated as though it were a bodily secretion that "natives" give off, that they cannot help but know and deserve no credit (not even a personal footnote) for knowing (Narayan 1997, chapter 7 here). Nor does this knowledge, for example of the healing properties of plants, give them power: rather, taken by the expert outsider and spun into something else, it becomes part of a toolkit for the outsiders to use in subordinating and exploiting the "natives." From the perspective of the outsider expert, the indigenous people don't really know what they're doing, nor do they know what they have. It takes the expert's science to turn folk practices into real knowledge, as it takes that science to turn raw material into standardized pharmaceuticals; and it is the added value of scientific expertise that is taken to be the real—commercial, patentable—value of the healing substances. Similarly, patients' reports of their perceptions and sensations are informative without counting as knowledge. They serve the same function as do measuring instruments (from thermometers to CT scans), with, however, the drawbacks of vagueness, nonstandardization, and idiosyncratic subjectivity. Doctors' reliance on what patients tell them is thus merely a necessary expedient, the best they can do until the invention of devices that will provide better, objective, and objectively comparable data.

How then should we characterize what patients know about themselves and their conditions if they are to count as legitimate contributors to the acquisition of knowledge about their own injuries and illnesses—if they are, that is, to be active participants in their own health care? If we move away from the philosophical picture of our having privileged access to what only we can know and we cannot help but know, it becomes clear that patients are in a position to make such contributions. (For a discussion of the problems with the notion of privileged access, see chapters 1 and 7.) They can detect regularities and patterns in how they feel, they can hazard hypotheses about where in their bodies sensations are originating, they can note correlations between how they feel and things that are going on in and around their bodies, and they can note apparent similarities between their experiences and the descriptions of symptoms of various disorders. In all of these cases, they might be wrong: they might misremember, or under- or overestimate the severity of their pains, or they might be succumbing to the hypochondria that has afflicted medical students when they first encounter descriptions of the symptoms of obscure diseases and that now afflicts everyone who turns to the internet to check out some new twinge, rash, or change in a bodily function. Paradoxically, being thought liable to mistake is a necessary, though not, of course, a sufficient condition of being taken as a participant in the conversation. What matters is that the judgment that the patient is wrong not be taken as an excuse for dismissing her, as one would dispose of a faulty thermometer, or at least send it back for repairs: one wouldn't *argue* with it.

It is precisely that engagement—the giving and taking of critique—that marks the sort of respect for autonomy that has epistemic value. It is when the doctor sees the patient as an active participant in coming to know what the problem is and what to do about it that the doctor is in a position to learn from what the patient knows and believes, not just from what the patient's body shows. In such a relationship the doctor is committed not just to respecting the patient's autonomy, in the sense of not violating bounds of selfhood the patient is presumed to have independently of the clinical relationship, but rather to valuing the patient's autonomy as interpersonal and emergent, and as valuable *to the doctor* because of the contextual, relational, and idiosyncratic knowledge the patient comes to have.

Patients' knowledge is not only thoughtful and fallible; it is narrative. Its value lies precisely in its being not an unmediated report of a bare sensation, but rather a contextualized counterweight to the scientific knowledge that the clinician brings, hence an aid to the clinician committed to bridging the gap between generalized knowledge and the particularities of this patient's situation. Such considerations can be extended to the setting of biomedical research and the relationship between researchers and their subjects. If patients have a difficult time making their voices heard, research subjects face the same obstacles plus an additional one: unlike patients, they are not in general presumed to have any direct interest in what is going on.[7]

The active engagement of research subjects can inform research, even when the researchers think they know what they are looking for and active collaboration is not required for them to obtain it. The frequency of unexpected side effects and, more happily, of serendipitous discoveries argues for fostering relationships within which subjects can reflect on and discuss their sensations and perceptions beyond those they are specifically asked to attend to. Such discussions do in fact take place, especially when research is conducted in a hospital setting but, rather than occurring between doctors and other "experts," they typically occur between patients/subjects and nurses, in which case it may be as much the nurse as it is the patient who is being discredited. As Joan Liaschenko and Debra DeBruin have argued (2003), the less structured and less bounded interactions that nurses typically have with patients/subjects are the locus of an ethically problematic blurring of the distinction between treatment and research, but also the site for the cultivation of the patient's perceptual competence and autonomy and the emergence of potentially useful information.

COMMUNITY-BASED PARTICIPATORY RESEARCH

The meanings of our lives and experiences, including of those experiences connected with whatever it is that researchers are seeking to learn about us, are not ours alone, as individuals, but are embedded in the

---

7. The question of subjects' stake in research is, in fact, typically addressed in the context of clinical trials, when the concern is ensuring that subjects have no expectation that the experimental treatment will benefit them.

communities to which we belong. And it is not primarily in relation with researchers that we develop a voice and the ability to articulate the world from our own particular perspective. One principal value of community-based participatory research is the ability to tap into communities of meaning, thus increasing the likelihood both that the data obtained will be as complete and accurate as possible and that the integration of research findings into people's lives will go as smoothly as possible.

From the definition of a researchable problem to the recruitment and retention of subjects, to their compliance with research protocols and the honesty and richness of their responses, and to the analysis of findings and translation into interventions, the trusting, active engagement of community members, with the confidence and the power to make a difference, can be invaluable (see chapter 9). In this sense, any research involving human subjects, and much that does not, can be to at least some extent community-based and participatory: all that is required is that others than the designated researchers have relationships with the objects of knowledge and hence be in positions to know something about those objects and their relationships with other things in the world, and that the relationships among researchers and community members be genuinely reciprocal and respectful.

From such a perspective we can raise questions about communities' standing in relation to the potential promises of benefits and risks of harm from research that do not immediately founder (as such questions now tend to do) on the issue of whether anyone is authorized to sign the informed consent form. Just as the requirement of researchers' respect for the autonomy of their subjects neither starts nor ends with informed consent, so the requirement of respect for concerned communities demands sustained engagement and real relationship and promises not just ethical acceptability but epistemic advantage. Communities are the repositories of the narratives in terms of which the researchers' findings will, for better or worse, be—or fail to be—integrated into the wild; and the multiplicity and contradictoriness of those narratives are reason for, not against, engaging with them. Unlike the logic of the laboratory, based on abstraction and generalization, community-based knowledge is based on logics of salience and connection, of particularity and idiosyncrasy, on narratives of space and time, on history and hope.

The cultivation of relationships of trust between researchers and the communities within which they work may, as critics of community-based research charge, pose temptations to tell people what they would like to hear, but it can more seriously provide solid ground on which difficult truths can be articulated, listened to, and heeded. When the process of research itself is empowering to a community, such truths have a context in which to be understood and taken on, rather than just being dropped from on high. Communities can frame more useful, in part because more truthful, stories about themselves, rather than leaving that framing in the hands of researchers or more socially, economically, and politically powerful others.

Scientists need to respect communities for the same, intrinsic reasons they respect other scientists, as active participants in making meaning and as contributors to discovery. Cultivating such respect requires guarding both against scientists' arrogance and against communities' diffidence and deference on the one hand and mistrust on the other. It requires cooperative work to create discursive space for "subjugated knowledges," importantly including space for mutually critical engagement, rather than the sort of uncritical appropriation described above. This discursive space needs to be commodious enough to hold diverse perspectives and ways of making sense—while being sufficiently structured by shared understandings to reveal points of disagreement needing resolution.

ACROSS THE DISCIPLINING DEMANDS OF MODERNITY

To return to Humphrey and Ailsa: Their affair took place in the romantic realm outside of normal time and space—the "green world" of Shakespearean comedy, a magical retreat from normality, after which the characters return to the everyday world, that is, to marriage (Cavell 1981). For Humphrey and Ailsa, that return was disastrous: there was no way for them to be together in the same version of a real world. What separated them was modernity, and the ways neither of them fit into it. Humphrey's way of being a scientist was distinctively premodern, while Ailsa's cultural *bricolage* was distinctively postmodern. Their shared discomfort with the disciplining of modernity may have initially brought them together, but it failed to provide them with any other (sufficiently real) place to be. I want to connect Humphrey and Alisa's problem to a problematic linking of the pre- and the postmodern that periodically surfaces in feminist and other liberatory theorizing. The linking comes up in discussions about individualism and related aspects of modern ontology that reveal similarities between feminist accounts (e.g., of personhood) and analogous accounts in premodern Europe (often tinged by anachronistic nostalgia) or in various indigenous societies (often romanticized). Feminists can end up defending themselves against charges on the one hand of making common cause with reactionaries or on the other of appropriative exoticizing. While both worries need, in particular situations, to be taken seriously, it can be instructive to focus instead on what is peculiarly distinctive about modernity, rather than allowing it to be the unquestioned background against which the similarities among premodern Europe, various indigenous societies, and present-day feminist theorizing can seem both striking and problematic.

Those apparent similarities can, rather, throw into relief the particularity of atomism and individualism, as pictures within which Eurocentric modernity is trapped (in Wittgenstein's image, like the fly in the fly bottle, with its limits being the limits of language, of intelligibility, of the world). The manifestation of individualism I want to focus on concerns not subjectivity and personhood (the usual focus of discussion) but rather the ontology of science, in particular the typically unarticulated and un-argued-for presumptions of atomism, the demand that the properties and behavior of large objects be, at least in theory, accounted for in terms of the properties and behavior of smaller objects that make them up. Causality, on such a view, is "from the bottom up," that is, from the smaller and simpler to the larger and more complex. Atomism so under-stood is a hallmark of scientific modernity, and in this sense biology became modern through the shift of emphasis—from organisms in their environment to cells and molecules in the laboratory—that Humphrey deplored and that left him behind. Biology came so late to modernity, in fact, that physics, the presumptive authority on the ultimate constituents of reality, had already abandoned the atomistic commitment that had arguably largely accounted for that authority. (For a similar observation, see Woese 2004.)

It would be ironic indeed if biology's challenge to the epistemically paradigmatic status of physics were to rest on its embrace of a discredited atomism, rather than on its having a leg up on physics precisely because of the more obvious irreducibility of its objects of study to the workings of their constituent parts. Physics discovered belatedly what biology often seems determined to forget, that middle-sized complex objects follow laws quite different from those that apply to the very much smaller things of which they are comprised. As I suggested above, in my discussion of the "thing-ness" (*conatus*) of complex objects, not only organisms, but even such things as rocks enter into relationships of cause and effect as particu-lar, complex things-in-relation, not just as the sums of their parts.

It ought not to seem surprising that historically disparate ways of thinking—pre-, post-, and nonmodern—converge on such an ontology, since it is strongly suggested by ordinary interactions and denied only by the historically distinctive, even if currently globally hegemonic, dis-course of scientific modernity. One need only think about how small particles—dust, seeds, germs, and the like—get transported across vast distances by getting caught up in such macro-phenomena as avalanches, tornadoes, ship ballast, birds, and international travelers. And, as every union organizer knows, structured organizations acquire causal powers that are greater than the sum of the individuals that make them up, in part because they are perceived and responded to by relevant parts of their environments as particular sorts of things—unions, but also political parties, religions, states—with distinctive capabilities and susceptibilities. (This ontological point is also evident to those campaigning for same-sex marriage.) And the geological formations, tree trunks, and predator and prey species of my earlier discussion are what they are because of their complex structures, the complex structures of the things with which they share a stretch of space and time, and the complex interactions among them. It takes a particular, powerful and decidedly peculiar, picture of the world to think that all of that is epiphenomenal.

Neither Humphrey nor Ailsa is comfortable with the discourse of scientific modernity. But while Humphrey seems trapped in the past, Ailsa is sailing into a brand new future. The question on which the end of the novel leaves them—and us—hanging is whether they—or we— have the resources to reach across the disciplining demands of modernity to find other ways to live. We will need to draw on a very mixed bag of humanly available resources, while recognizing that "humanly available" is far too abstract. We risk tripping over the cultural divides imposed in large measure by the very different relationships in which the specific manifestations of those resources stand to hegemonic modernity. If it is difficult for Humphrey and Ailsa to help themselves to each other's strengths—Humphrey's disciplined attentiveness to detail, Ailsa's asso- ciative imagination—how much harder is it to imagine, for example, postmodern metropolitan feminists helping ourselves to the insights of present-day traditionally grounded indigenous peoples, even—or espe- cially—when we inhabit their ancestral homes.

If we are to imagine such a thing, it will need to be piecemeal, as particular ones of us, in particular relationships, care across various differ- ences about particular problems, specific to those who share a place and a time and enough of a story about what matters there and then. Scientific researchers, even those most comfortable in laboratories, have important roles to play, but they can play those roles well—even by epistemic standards—only insofar as they think of themselves and the knowledge they create as framed by, and responsible to, the relationships in which, whether they recognize it or not, they are enmeshed.

ACKNOWLEDGMENTS

In addition to those acknowledged in note 6, my thinking in this essay owes a great deal to others in Minnesota: especially my GRASS Routes colleagues, Susan Gust and Cathy Jordan, Nick Jordan, and members of the Bioethics Center. I greatly benefited from discussions with the editors and the other authors of the section of the volume in which this chapter appeared at a working meeting in Groningen in the fall of 2006, and from detailed criticism on an earlier draft from Hilde Lindemann and, especially, Michael Root. Hilde's faith and encouragement have been invaluable.

Chapter 11

Epistemology Resuscitated: Objectivity as Trustworthiness

INTRODUCTION: WITH FRIENDS LIKE THESE, WHO NEEDS ENEMIES?

A growing chorus of scientists, historians, and philosophers, many of whom self-identify as on the left of the political spectrum, would have us add objectivity, along with truth and rationality, to the endangered species list, with feminist epistemologists and philosophers of science among those responsible for the cultural environmental degradation that poses the threat.[1] As with efforts to protect endangered animals and plants, however, it is not always obvious just which forces endanger and which protect, or even how to characterize what it is we should be trying to preserve. Much as environmental preservationist projects need to be grounded in an understanding of the value of biodiversity, so objectivity preservationist projects need to ask just what it is about objectivity that makes its preservation so important. I want to argue that feminist epistemologists and philosophers of science are not the enemies of objectivity they are made out to be by the critics (as I will follow Elizabeth Lloyd in calling those who charge feminist epistemology, along with science studies and postmodern critical theories, with endangering objectivity). What the critics misidentify as a threat is better understood as an attempt to save objectivity by understanding why it matters and why and how it is truly threatened.

Objectivity, along with reason, truth, and rationality, is a normative concept with which we evaluate our own and each other's assertions and beliefs. Central to what we do when we call an argument, conclusion, or

---

1. For a recent collection of papers making the case against science studies, see Koertge 1998. It is also noteworthy that all three of the Presidential Addresses to the APA in 1997–98 addressed issues around objectivity. See Fine 1998, Nozick 1998, and Kitcher 1998. Only Fine's address discussed feminist work in this area; the omission is especially striking in Nozick's case. Alison Wylie (2000) points out that Nozick's "third way" between the relativism supposed to follow from the acknowledgment of the role of contextual values in science and an objectivism that denies (the importance of) such a role has been long at the center of, in particular, feminist philosophy of science and science studies—and precisely in the way Nozick claimed in his spoken address, namely in the argument that the interplay of contextual values in science, far from undermining objectivity, serves to secure it. Oddly, the published version drops the discussion of values.

decision "objective" is to recommend it to others, and, importantly, to suggest that they *ought* to accept it, that they would be doxastically irresponsible to reject it without giving reasons that made similar claims to universal acceptability. Objective claims, that is, are always disputable, but they are not, without dispute, rejectable—as one can, without disputing a film critic's judgment, reject their recommendation of a particular movie simply on the grounds that one doesn't share their taste. Although some feminists and others have argued, on a wide range of grounds, against the value of objectivity as a norm, the disputes I want to focus on are not between objectivity's self-declared enemies and its self-declared friends but between self-declared friends who charge each other with being enemies in friends' clothing.[2] I'm concerned, that is, not with feminist arguments *against* objectivity, but rather with those feminist arguments that explicitly take their aims to be the articulation and defense of alternative conceptions of objectivity, and with the critics who insist that these feminists cannot possibly mean what they say.

In order to break up the logjam of disputes over who the "real enemies" of objectivity are, I am suggesting that we start by asking what it is about objectivity that makes a sustainable claim to being a real friend so valuable, why it is that objectivity and its similarly endangered relatives *matter*. Although I agree with Lorraine Code that the ground rules for legitimate philosophical argument have problematically framed these issues in ways that foreclose discussion by setting up relativism as a dismissably irrational position (Code 1995*b*), my approach is somewhat different from hers: Rather than defending relativism (or some other alternative to objectivity as an ideal), I want to start with the fact that we (diversely) do often want or need knowledge claims to be acceptable by broader constituencies, or criticizable by those constituencies. I take it to be an open question, not to be answered in advance or in general, how broad such a constituency can, or should, be—that is, how broad a consensus we ought to seek or can plausibly expect for particular sorts of knowledge claims: when, for example, we might want not to exempt ourselves from what we take to be a problematically broad assertion but rather *contest* it. I will focus on the case that can be made for the objectivity (the universal acceptability) of the paradigm cases—namely, the claims of the sciences. Stated more broadly, the issue is: When, and insofar as, it actually matters that knowledge claims be acceptable to—or criticizable by—a broader constituency, what do we actually have to *do*, and what counts as doing it right? I take this project to be complementary

---

2. For a distillation of these arguments, see Lloyd (1996) and Gross (1998). Objectivity does have self-declared enemies, some feminist theorists among them, but the disputes I want to focus on are those between self-declared friends. In particular, I want to ask why antifeminist "friends" are so convinced (wrongly, I will argue) that feminist pro-objectivity claims must be either insincere or inconsistent, and, conversely, why feminist "friends" take themselves (correctly, I will argue) to be better, truer friends than those with whom objectivity has usually hung out.

to Code's defense of relativism, in particular in the attention that I will argue we need to pay to the particularities and, especially, social locations of the subjects, objects, and (passive or active) audiences of knowledge claims.

In the disputes over who are the real friends and who the real enemies of objectivity one point of agreement is that other things that we care about depend on it and are imperiled by its actual or perceived enfeeblement or demise (whether as a consequence of the head-on attacks of its alleged enemies or as a side-effect of various social and cultural developments). What are these other things, and why might their well-being depend on the well-being of objectivity? According to Paul Gross and Norman Levitt, "What is threatened [by, *inter alia*, feminist science studies, which, they allege, attack or repudiate objectivity] is the capability of the larger culture, which embraces the mass media as well as the more serious processes of education, to interact fruitfully with the sciences, to draw insight from scientific advances, and, above all, to evaluate science intelligently" (Gross and Levitt 1994, p. 9, quoted in Lloyd 1996, p. 220; and Gross 1998, p. 102). The underlying assumptions here are that the sciences produce something of value ("advances"), and ("above all") that "science" ought not to be accepted uncritically but ought to be subject to intelligent evaluation by "the larger culture." While the details of this formulation will turn out to be contentious—What are the consequences of acknowledging the nonhomogeneity of "the larger culture"? What makes some processes of education "more serious"? How do we identify scientific "advances"? What makes an evaluation of science "intelligent"? What are the relevant objects of evaluation: scientific results, scientific practice, or both?—the general formulation and the assumptions behind it would, I think, be acceptable to the feminist epistemologists and philosophers of science who are cited as objectivity's alleged enemies.

How does objectivity figure in this story such that its real or perceived enfeeblement or a widespread loss of belief in its possibility or desirability would pose such a threat? Rather than defining what objectivity *is*, I want to propose an answer to a different question, one about what objectivity *does* (what it's good for). The proposal is this: A sustainable attribution of objectivity serves to underwrite a significant degree of—objectively refutable—authority, and it does so by rationally grounding trust. When we characterize something (an epistemic practice or product) as objective, we commend it or its results to others than those who engaged in or produced it, including to those whose perspectives and interests might differ.[3] It gets its importance from the extent that we are epistemically

---

3. My point here is related to Carl Ginet's distinction between interested and disinterested justification. Beliefs, Ginet argues, can reasonably be counted as justified even if their justification is tied to the subject's desire that the belief be true; but *disinterested* justification, which is required for knowledge—that is, belief that anyone at all has reason to accept—cannot so depend. See Ginet 1975, pp. 28–31.

dependent on others who are in a range of ways—spatially, temporally, culturally, attitudinally, cognitively—distant from us. Given the extraordinary and increasing degree of both interconnectedness and technological complexity of the contemporary world, the need for objectivity cannot be overstated: We are all downwind of the activities of the sciences and other culturally authoritative sites of knowledge production, dependent on them both for much that we need and desire and for much that we cannot avoid. If objective judgments are judgments we can rationally trust, we need them more than ever; and the "we"s that need them are, especially, the "we"s least in a position either to identify with or to independently check out the judgments produced by socially recognized authorities. Furthermore, and perhaps even more importantly, we (diversely located "we"s) need to be able to enter into dialogue with authoritative knowledge producers, to become and be recognized as credible even if nonexpert critics—to, in Gross and Levitt's terms, "evaluate science intelligently"—and to have our perspectives recognized as potentially contributing to fuller, more adequate accounts.

If something like this is what objectivity is good for, what can we say about the disputes over who its real friends and enemies are? The antifeminist friends of objectivity are, I want to argue, the sorts of friends alleged to render enemies superfluous. Like snake oil salesmen, they purvey a quack remedy for a real problem. And like most quack remedies, this one is worse than useless: worse, because in purporting to be the real thing, it effectively diverts us from pursuing an effective remedy for what actually ails us.[4] By contrast, feminist epistemologists and philosophers of science such as Donna Haraway, Sandra Harding, Evelyn Fox Keller, and Helen Longino (to cite just those most widely targeted by the antifeminists),[5] along with others engaged in related projects of what can be called "liberatory epistemology," are developing accounts of objectivity that take seriously our need for it: If objectivity is an instrumental good, then it has actually to function so as to produce the good it promises; what we label "objective" has actually to be worthy of our trust and the trust of a diverse range of others.

In the tradition of analytic philosophers' giving acronyms to the theses they argue for, I want to suggest "CPR" as an acronym (sort of) for the projects of liberatory epistemology. As befits a loose collection of projects, as opposed to a clearly specifiable thesis, the acronym doesn't stand for any one label, beyond that of marking the connection to the practice of cardio-pulmonary resuscitation—reviving by breathing life back into a moribund subject. Rather, oddly and for no particular reason that I can

---

4. For an account of the role of central philosophical theses as in this sense quack remedies, see chapter 1.

5. All have published extensively on these topics. Some representative and frequently cited works are: Haraway 1988; Harding 1986 and 1991; Keller 1985; and Longino 1990. Anthologies in feminist philosophy of science include Tuana 1987; Keller and Longino 1996; and Nelson and Nelson 1996.

think of, those letters jointly cover a large number of the central concepts that characterize epistemology resuscitated: critical, contextual (See Longino 1990), committed, "corresponsible" (See Heldke 1988), and commonable (see Code 1987); perspectival, pragmatic,[6] practical, political, participatory, pluralist,[7] and partial (see Haraway 1988); and radical, relational, and responsible (see Heldke and Kellert 1995)—all of which characterize revised notions of reason, rationality, and realism.[8]

I will not be surveying these feminist objectivity projects or addressing the sometimes contentious differences among them. Rather, my aim is to provide a framework within which to understand them and to argue that projects within such a framework give us the most *useful* ways of understanding and defending objectivity. Briefly, my argument will be that liberatory politics such as feminism are intrinsically related to objectivity in their commitment to struggling for social institutions that are worthy of trust on the part of all those whose lives are affected by them: A "bias" in favor of such struggles is a bias in favor of the conditions that would make objectivity a real possibility, rather than a merely theoretical gesture.[9] Ironically, as Stephen Kellert points out, "the imposition of Modern Western Scientific Knowledge and its applications on people without their involvement and consent" is a "barrier to the achievement of genuinely universal scientific knowledge," which requires "a kind of radical democracy" (Kellert 1999, p. 196). Whether, when, and why objectivity *is* a real possibility—and whether, when, why, and how various "we"s ought to struggle to make it so—are deep and divisive political questions, not avoidable by metaphysical or methodological fiat.

THE CASE FOR SCIENTIFIC OBJECTIVITY, TRADITIONALLY UNDERSTOOD

Objectivity's antifeminist defenders locate the threat to objectivity presumed to be posed by feminist epistemology, philosophy of science, and science studies primarily in the feminist analyses of the sciences as social practices, in the claims that as such science is typically problematically implicated in the inequities of the broader society, and in the conclusion that such implication undermines science's claims to objectivity. For the

6. See Heldke 1987 for connections between feminist epistemology and John Dewey's, and see Seigfried 1996 on the connections between feminist philosophy and pragmatism generally.

7. On the need to have pluralism from the beginning, in the structure of a theory—not as a footnote at the end—see Lugones 1991.

8. The intended scope of "CPR" is illustrated by what I take to be two exemplary texts: Collins 1990 and Dupré 1993. (I've characterized Dupré's position as "Committed Promiscuous Realism.")

9. Sabina Lovibond comes to a similar conclusion at the end of her *Realism and Imagination in Ethics*. Drawing on Gramsci, she argues that the "expressivist view of language" she has been arguing for, both positively and as a reading of Wittgenstein, "commits us . . . to interpreting the idea of an 'absolute conception of reality' not in transcendent, but in immanent terms—not as a conception of reality from which all traces of human perspective would be excluded, but as one in which the individual or local perspectives of all human beings would be able to find harmonious expression" (1983, p. 218).

critics of feminist science studies, science is the paradigm example of objectivity; hence such arguments are taken to be an attack on objectivity itself. There is, in fact, good reason for thinking of objectivity as the defining virtue of modern science—that is, as the guiding aim of scientific method and practice—but it doesn't follow from that connection that we cannot meaningfully ask about how it is that scientific practices achieve that aim to the extent that they do and why and how they might fall short of it, or even about whether the particular conceptions of objectivity embedded in scientific method as usually understood (especially by philosophers of science) might not be fundamentally flawed. By attending to the function of objectivity in rationally grounding the trust we are called on to have in what scientists do, we can get a handle on understanding both why and how scientific practices are objective and why and how they are not.

We can start by noting that objectivity has a history—one intimately and honorably bound up with the democratization of knowledge, the wresting of epistemic authority away from those with entrenched religious, political, or economic power—and a track record—comprising all of the successes of modern science. Defenders of scientific objectivity need not argue that the methods of science always work or even that they are not subject to systematic distortions, owing, in part, to their contamination by the injustices that characterize universities, primary and secondary educational systems, scientific funding establishments, and the society at large. There is no reason why those defenders have to argue that anything about the doing of science can entirely rule out any of those influences, nor even that good science could possibly thrive in a seriously unjust society. That there are external conditions that set the stage for the effective working of scientific methods is surely something that can be conceded by those who nonetheless maintain that it is adherence to those methods, whenever and whyever they are adhered to, that constitutes objectivity and gives us good reason to believe what scientists come up with.

Furthermore, the critics can grant that the plural ("scientific *methods*") is crucial: There is no one such method, nor is there even a codifiable range of them. Science is a complex set of social practices governed by a complex set of norms that share little more than the aim precisely of ensuring that the results of scientific investigation will be trustworthy, meaning that those results will be credible not only to the scientists who came up with them but also to others who may not share their particular experiences, biases, perspectives, interests, and the like. The norms of science work—when and to the extent that they *do* work—by factoring out of scientific knowledge claims the biasing effects of, among other things, the sorts of injustices that characterize the world in which science is done. When the rest of us trust what scientists come up with, what we are trusting them to do is to conform to the norms of good scientific practice; and we trust their results to the extent that we believe that they have done so and because we trust that conforming to those norms reliably tends to lead to the truth.

Certainly (the critics can concede), political considerations come into play around questions of research priorities, notably decisions about funding; and there is reason to argue for the greater involvement of a diverse range of scientists and nonscientists in these decisions, and for specific attention to the perspectives of those whose voices have been silenced, ignored, or distorted. But when it comes to the research itself, and to the evaluation of research results, it will be claimed that such diversity is idle. Certainly, it is a loss to science that some potentially productive researchers are undiscovered or unsuccessful for reasons having to do with discrimination and other social inequities, but there is no reason to believe that the loss is of some *distinctive* contribution—beyond, for example, that of bringing a particular passion to questions that have special relevance to their own lives and to the lives of those they identify with. If they bring anything *else* from the specificities of their lives into the doing of science, they are importing the same sort of bias that has led to sexist, racist, or homophobic science. The passion they bring ought to fuel a desire to discover the truth, whatever it might be, not to come up with answers that will accord with the political interests of a particular group, no matter how justified those interests might be.

I could go on, along what I take to be familiar lines, articulating the reasons for regarding science as an epistemically privileged means of revealing the truth (or an approximation to it) about a real world that exists independently of our needs, interests, and desires, as well as for thinking that especially those on the left—in solidarity with the subordinated and marginalized—have good reasons to believe in science so conceived.[10] For one, being less powerful, we have a need for the sort of neutral referee science promises to be, and, for another, we are (presumably) confident that the objective truth will, if it has political implications at all, support our judgments (that, for example, those who are White men are not intrinsically superior to those who are not).

The central point is this: According to the critics, feminists are claiming that trust in scientific method is misplaced, amounting to trust in those who wield unjust forms of privilege and who use that privilege—buttressed by the cultural capital of scientific expertise—to shield themselves from possibly legitimate forms of criticism. Rather, the critics claim, trust in scientific method is trust in a set of mechanisms and practices that are designed precisely to *rule out* these sorts of abuses. Expertise, on this model, is acquired and justified not through the possession of various forms of unjust privilege but through the necessary talent, time, and

---

10. This appeal to progressive, left politics (along with the citing of leftist credentials), frequently made by the critics of feminist theorists, is unavoidably reminiscent of the Phil Ochs song, "Love Me, I'm a Liberal"; but it also reflects a serious divide in left politics, going back at least to disputes about scientific/scientistic readings of Marx.

energy that go into becoming able to understand, hence to be both a contributor to and a credible critic of, a difficult and complex area of knowledge. Given the extraordinary difficulty and complexity of contemporary science, we have no choice but to delegate epistemic authority to those who understand what we never will and to trust that what they come up with is what we would come up with if we had the talent, time, and energy to acquire their expertise; and that their being different from us in a whole range of ways other than their being experts (their being, for example, at the present time overwhelmingly White, male, middle class, heterosexual, and relatively able-bodied) is morally and politically lamentable but epistemically irrelevant.

DEPENDENCY AND TRUST

Certainly these defenses of scientific objectivity are apt and the beginnings of serious arguments, the playing out of which has produced a voluminous literature. But rather than review those arguments, I want to focus on a central and (so far as I can tell) indisputable but oddly underacknowledged fact about the vast majority of what we know or believe; namely, the extent to which we are irremediably dependent on others. I want to argue that taking this fact seriously gives us good reason to be suspicious of what I will call "internalist" defenses of scientific objectivity, such as those of the critics of feminist science studies.

The fact of our epistemic dependency, and the implication that knowledge rests on trust as much as it rests on such epistemological staples as perception, reason, and memory, has only recently come to play a significant role in analytic epistemology and philosophy of science.[11] Even now that role is deeply disputed: The fact of epistemic dependency might not be contestable, but its centrality to epistemology is hardly universally acknowledged. Taking trust to be a central epistemological issue tends to mark one as belonging to a particular, still academically marginal, subfield—that of social epistemology.[12] It is, as usual, interesting to note what is and what is not linguistically marked: the contrast (unmarked epistemology proper) is presumably nonsocial, individualist, taking as its subject the generic knower-as-such—what Lorraine Code (1991) has dubbed "S knows that p" epistemology. The issue of epistemic dependency, when it arises in "unmarked" epistemology, is addressed as the specific and separable problem of "testimony"—whether and, if so, when

---

11. In addition to work in feminist epistemology and social epistemology, see Craig 1990.

12. On the failure of much, even explicitly social, epistemology to appreciate the importance of feminist perspectives, see Rooney 1998. Rooney notes the failure even of much of the work in naturalized, social philosophy of science to take feminist work seriously—that is, she argues, to take "naturalizing" or "socializing" seriously. My point is not that seeing knowledge in social and historical terms is sufficient for recognizing the relevance of feminist work, only that is it necessary.

and how and why and to what extent S (the generic knower) should believe some particular claim because someone else says it is so.[13]

What is masked by S's generic nature are not so much S's individual properties but rather the particularities of S's relationships to others as a fully social being, including the relationships that constitute S's gender, race, class, sexual identity, and so on. With respect to generic knowers, if "trust" is used at all, it is only as (roughly) a synonym for "believe," as in "I trust the train will be here any minute." And certainly some of my own uses of it thus far can be understood that way. But it is one of the central claims of this chapter that thinking about objectivity requires thinking about diversely situated subjects and about the possibilities for and barriers to trust between them. What is needed for that task is a much more full-blown notion of trust, involving an indefinite range of moral, political, and interpersonal factors that we can never fully spell out. Even when we do enumerate what we take to be the grounds for accepting what another tells us, that explicitness depends on webs of social connection that lie below the level of what we can check out. Such dependence, I want to argue, is ineliminable, but it can be more or less rational, and the trust that rests on it more or less justified. It is this "full-blown" notion of trust, and the dependency that necessitates it, that have been largely ignored in modern epistemology and that I want to argue need to be at the center of discussions of objectivity.[14]

The marginality of epistemic dependence within epistemology reflects the emergence of the field in its distinctively modern form in the seventeenth century, in the attempts to liberate the individual knower from dependence on various, particularly religious, forms of authority. The strongly individualist slant of the field reflects the religious, political, and economic individualism of early modernity; and the fact that on the most fundamental theoretical level individuals were and are taken to be generic reflects modernity's democratic egalitarianism. Difference is always relational: generic subjects are subjects who (for purposes of analysis) are understood as standing in no particular relation either to specific others or to social norms and institutions. The crises of trust out of which modern science arose—the need to find foundations for knowledge that would survive challenges to authority—were resolved by finding firm ground on which such individual generic knowers could stand and by articulating a notion of rational personhood that guaranteed that each

---

13. Michael Root, following Hume, has argued that, while testimony is epistemologically important, our reliance on it can and should be understood not in terms of trust but as straightforwardly evidential: We ought to believe, on Root's view, when and to the extent that we have good reason to take our informant to be both sincere and relevantly competent (1998). For an argument against a similar position, see Hardwig 1991.

14. This paragraph is a (probably unsuccessful) attempt to answer Michael Root's arguments (1998 and in conversation) that what justifies us in believing another is not such an amorphous sense of trust but, rather, sufficient evidence of the other's credibility, much as we need to check out the reliability of an instrument we are using to collect data.

such knower would come up with the same answers as any other, if only each followed a proper method. In the first instance (for example, in the founding texts of the field, Descartes's *Meditations* and *Discourse on Method*), this guarantee is meant to underwrite extreme epistemic autonomy: Each of us should pursue knowledge on our own, confident that if we follow the rules we will end up with the same results.

In practice, however, what the guarantee has underwritten is our dependence, oddly grounded in the denial of the relationships that make us different from each other. We are meant to trust each other epistemically only to the extent that we are assured that each of us is acting in ways uninflected by any of our actual relationships. My confidence in the generic nature of our arithmetic abilities, for example, allows me to ask you to count the candies and to divide them equally among the children at the party: I needn't worry that for you the correct answer would be different from what it would be for me.

Such dependence has not been, in practice, comfortable to acknowledge. Even if I can be confident that arithmetic is not different for you from what it is for me, I cannot be confident that you will not make a mistake, either inadvertently or in order to give some favored child more than a fair share of candies. I need to trust *you*, not just arithmetic-for-you, and no amount of nonrelativist absolutism about the truths of arithmetic can deal with the worries I might have about whether or not you are trustworthy. In theory, that is, your doing arithmetic is the same as my doing it; in practice I have all sorts of reasons to worry about the consequences of trusting you to do it. These worries are, in part, what motivated Descartes's emphasis on epistemic autonomy: Even if he can satisfactorily conclude that others are, like him, conscious, rational beings, he cannot so confidently rule out the possibility that they are careless or mendacious.

Such extreme epistemic autonomy is of a piece with Descartes's rationalism. Though observation had a place in his scientific method, that place was subsidiary to the workings of reason, which in his view were not in any essential way social.[15] Considerations of trust, specifically of those one took to be peers, were, by contrast, central to the development of experimental science, as Steven Shapin argues in *The Social History of Truth* (1994). As important as it was that experimental results be replicable, it was clearly impractical for every knower actually to replicate every experiment the results of which contributed to something he took himself to know. That, by and large, knowers were men was, in fact, one of the consequences of the need to provide socially salient signs of one's credibility, signs that rested on indications of competence and character that

---

15. Annette Baier argues against a disembodied, asocial reading of Descartes on the nature of the mind, but she notes that "our genuine theoretical need for a standard of excellence, or correctness, in thought, is met, on Descartes's account, not by fellow finite thinkers, but by that divine mind to which we have direct innate nonmediated access" (1985a, p. 77).

were, most explicitly, focused on class, with consequences for gender—notably, the economic independence of gentlemen, which was taken to be a necessary condition for intellectual independence, and the related importance for gentlemen of an honorable reputation, marked, for example, by a willingness to duel to defend that honor against suggestions of lying (Shapin 1994, chapters 2 and 3; on dueling, pp.107–14; on women, pp.87–91). By contrast, the significant number of women Cartesians can be seen as a consequence of the absence of any such demand in the case of knowledge conceived as Descartes did: If you can and think you should check anyone else's reasoning yourself, there is no need to rely on socially recognizable marks of integrity.[16]

No one thought, of course, that some experimental result was true *because* it was reported by a gentleman, still less that being so reported was what truth *was*. But we can say that a significant part of the justification for believing such a report was that it was made by a gentleman: In other words, its being so reported was a good reason for taking it to be (likely to be) true, and those who believed the report did so in part because it was so reported. Epistemologically, issues of honorable character and the ways of giving recognizable demonstrations of such character, were in practice ineliminable—as are the present-day ways of ensuring the integrity of scientific results: peer review of research and researchers, replication of experimental results, and the like. To argue for a distinctively feminist epistemology, therefore, is not to argue for some dubious claim about sex differences in individual cognitive capacities: Rather, it is to argue, far more plausibly, for the relevance of gender to the ways in which different people regard—and ought to regard—others as more or less worthy of trust.[17] And whatever one wants to say about the nature of truth claims, claims to credibility—what makes our beliefs justified—rest in large part on such socially grounded reasons for trusting.[18]

We can, of course, meaningfully ask if such trust is well or ill-placed: Was it in fact the case that the social and economic position of gentlemen made them better observers and more trustworthy informants, or that the present-day oversight mechanisms of peer-reviewed journals are effective in inhibiting and screening for fraud? Recent efforts in the United States

16. It is noteworthy in this regard that when (in the *Discourse on Method* Part VI) Descartes explicitly discusses the role of others in the development of scientific knowledge, he is speaking about the doing of experiments.

17. For a discussion of how to understand the projects of feminist epistemology, see chapter 2, and the critical response by Louise Antony that, along with my rejoinder, was published with it (Antony 1995).

18. See Root 1998 for an account of the role played by policing norms in science in underwriting the credibility of scientific reports, and reasons for thinking that such norms work far more effectively among scientists than they do between scientists and the lay public. See Fricker 1998 for an illuminating argument, using Shapin 1994 and Craig 1990, for the need to attend to the ways in which political factors are inevitably—albeit through political change, reparably—implicated in our conceptions of knowledge. Though the focus of my argument is somewhat different from Fricker's, I found her discussion deeply suggestive, including on the relevance of Shapin's study for these questions.

to deal with highly publicized cases of alleged scientific fraud are cases in point: It is an empirical question how effective various mechanisms are for guiding the justification of belief, and when we discover that some mechanism has been working badly, we can attempt to make it work better.[19] But our ability to check on particular means for giving evidence of trustworthiness does not mean that we can, even in theory, eliminate the need for trust altogether—as, for example, I could in the case of asking you to count the candies. In that case, whatever I might be relying on in taking you to be trustworthy (both arithmetically competent and honest) can be independently verified: All I have to do is count and divide the candies myself and see if I get the same result. I don't *have* to trust you, and I can, without trusting you or anyone else, determine whether, when I *did* trust you, I was justified. In this case, it appears, it is not just that there is an *ontological* difference between my being justified in trusting you and your answer's actually being correct, but there is an *epistemological* difference between the sort of justification I have from whatever grounds my trust in you and the (greater) justification I have from checking it out myself—a difference that makes it reasonable to say that my need for trust can, at least in theory, be eliminated. What are the epistemological consequences if the need for trust is not eliminable?

THE INELIMINABILITY OF TRUST

When Descartes urged extreme epistemic autonomy, he did not think that he was thereby narrowing the scope of what he might know. His ambition, to encompass all there was to know about the natural world (including, he thought, ethics) within the limits of his own ability to verify both evidence and reasoning, was not nearly as wild an idea in his time as it appears in ours. It is said that Leibniz was the last person who could have known all there was to know, and the conceptual distance between then and now is immense. That distance is strikingly illustrated in a paper by John Hardwig (1991), in which he draws on examples from physics and mathematics to argue for the epistemological ineliminability of trust in the moral character of others even among experts in a field, who need to rely on the results of collaborators whose work they cannot replicate or, even, in many cases, fully understand. It is not, Hardwig

19. A central point of Fricker 1998 and 2007 is that we rely on what she calls "working indicator properties," to pick out those to whom we accord credibility. But, insofar as those properties track such things as class, race, and gender, they are unreliable indicators of actual "rational authority"; namely, the "competence" and "trustworthiness" that in fact correlate with reliably having and reporting truths. See also Code 1995b for a discussion of what she calls "incredulity," the refusal to acknowledge another's utterances as credible. Code's principle focus is on how such refusals deny to the subordinated the ability to make (what will count as) truth claims, but she also discusses the use of incredulity (by the subordinated toward the claims of the privileged) as a strategy of resistance.

argues, just as lay persons or even as scientists in distant fields that we are required to take the results of science on trust.

What we can do is to put in place practices that we have good reason to believe are effective in certifying the trustworthiness—the competence and integrity—of those on whom we are dependent. Despite our having, even in theory, no independent way of checking on the effectiveness of those practices, we do have ways of playing some of them off against others, of building in redundancies, of constructing overlapping ropes of trust that make our dependency reasonable, not abject. But, as Hardwig points out (1991), such trust-grounding practices are just that: actual practices, engaged in by actual people, and subject to all the vagaries that affect other forms of social interaction. Hardwig's analysis, however, focuses on the importance of individual character and on the role to be played by the teaching of ethics to researchers. He doesn't address my central concern here, namely, the systematically trust-eroding effects of various forms of social, political, and economic injustice. Who, for a start, are the "we" who put in place the mechanisms meant to ensure the integrity of scientific results?

One way of framing the dispute between feminist objectivity theorists and their critics is with the question of whether we ought to understand objectivity (as exemplified by science) in terms of the norms and methods of scientific practice (an internalist account), or whether we can and should go beneath or beyond those norms and methods and the practices that embody them to find critical ground (an externalist account).[20] (To put the dispute in more normative, less naturalized, terms: the question is whether the norms that are meant to yield objectivity are narrowly epistemic or also broadly moral and political.) When the critics take the first, internalist, option, it is in part because the methods and practices of science are supposed to give us reason to believe that the answer to the question, "Who are 'we'?" is, in *theory*, all of us, for whom scientists stand in appropriate proxy. Going beneath or beyond the precincts of science is seen as leaving the domain of objectivity, allowing in to the conversation just the sorts of differences in interest and perspective that are seen as damaging to the trustworthiness of science's knowledge claims. Those of us on the outside of science are urged to trust what goes on within its domains not despite but precisely because of our not participating in its

20. It might seem that, by framing the discussion around the question of the instrumental value of objectivity I am, if not begging the question, at least stacking the deck in favor of the externalists. I do think that such a frame does, if one takes it seriously, support the externalist position, but the frame itself is suggested strongly by the tenor of the critics' attacks on feminist objectivity theories, as well as by their defense of internalism: They emphasize repeatedly that the acceptance of scientific method as the best guarantor of objectivity is something we all benefit from and would suffer from attacks on.

innermost practices (as we are, for example, meant to trust the judiciary precisely because of the insulation of judges from public opinion).[21]

Much of the appeal of the internalist account has to do with its rootedness in the democratic egalitarianism of modernity (it is not supposed to matter that some of us discover truths for the rest of us to take on trust, because we are all supposed, in all relevant respects, to be interchangeable); and it suffers fatally from the flaws and limits of that egalitarianism. As Shapin's study shows, the actual practices of demonstrating scientific credibility have always been shaped—how could they not be?—by more general practices of judging people as worthy of trust, practices that have not been—how could they be?—immune from the practices that structure and maintain various forms of privilege.[22] It is quite likely that those whose economic exploitation grounded the economic "independence" of gentlemen would not have found a gentlemanly readiness to duel a sign of trustworthiness, or, if they did, it is hard not to see that trust as misplaced. It may well have been reasonable for anyone to conclude that a readiness to duel reliably signified some form of honorable behavior among those to whom it applied, but there would have been no good reason for those excluded from that system to think that those guarantees should carry any weight for them. For all they were in a position to conclude (assuming, as seems reasonable, that they were unable independently to verify the claims of gentlemen, hence to form their own judgment about the reliability of those trust-ensuring practices), the whole code of honor might underwrite an attempt to buttress a set of falsehoods supporting the upper-class privileges shared by the gentlemen who gave each other signs of mutual trustworthiness.[23]

I'm not denying (at this point in the argument) that even socially unjust codes of trustworthiness might actually be reliable as "trackers of truth": That's a different question from whether or not someone in particular has good reason to think that they are. And to the extent that such codes are articulated and enforced by, accessible to, and understood by an unjustly privileged elite, those excluded from those privileges have, in fact, little reason to trust them. It does not help to be told that you are included in the "we" in whose name those norms are set and enforced—that you are,

21. See Kellert 1999 for a "situated defense of universalism," an argument specifically from the perspective of Jewish intellectuals for a conception of knowledge that abstracts from the social location of knowers. Building on recent rethinkings of the historical development of logical positivism, Kellert argues that such abstracting—and the articulation of conceptions of knowing and knowers that rendered social location irrelevant—was a politically impassioned counter to the rise of Nazism, and that there are good, situated reasons for valorizing rootless "cosmopolitanism" in the face of calls for the primacy of the pure and the native.

22. For a thoughtful discussion of the resulting "epistemic injustice," see Fricker 1998 and 2007.

23. Bernard Porter (1999), reviewing David Vincent's *The Culture of Secrecy in Britain 1832–1998*, discusses the "gentlemanly" traits of character and mind, specifically as cultivated by the upper-middle classes, that underlay the extraordinary secrecy of the British secret services. Far from underwriting trust on the part of the British public outside those circles, the class-based exclusiveness of gentlemanly codes of honor fed the mistrust that welled up after grammar-school graduate "outsiders within" blew the whistle.

in all important respects, the same as those who actually do the setting and enforcing—when what you know is that the chances are minuscule that someone like you (however you understand that) might actually participate in that "we," and, furthermore, that the structures that keep you from participation are the same ones that provide the participants with the means of recognizing each other's trustworthiness. Though scientists no longer have to be gentlemen, there are many people in the world today who are effectively excluded from the ranks of those who set and enforce scientific norms, people for whom identifying with the "we" that does so would be an act of bad faith, hence for whom the only alternative to abject dependency with respect to the claims of science is cynical rejection, an attitude that in fact, to the dismay of scientists, seems increasingly to characterize much of public opinion.[24]

The central problem with the internalist account is thus that it fails to seriously confront the problem of justification as it actually arises. Epistemic dependency means that justification requires rationally grounded trust, and trust needs to be convincingly demonstrated—not just abstractly demonstrable. The world of contemporary science is large and impersonal, and the practices that ground and demonstrate trust are embedded in the workings of institutions such as universities, corporate research departments, government agencies, and academic journals. The trustworthiness of scientific methods derives, in practice, from the effective working of those institutional structures; and justified belief in that trustworthiness derives from the justified belief that those institutions do in practice what they are supposed to do in theory: ground knowledge claims that are acceptable to all of us, not just to those of us with certain forms of privilege, who see the world through certain lenses, from certain biased perspectives. If you believe (as presumably those on the political left *do* believe) that the institutions in question are problematically complicit in society's racism, sexism, classism, heterosexism, and so on, then you ought to be suspicious of the ability of those institutions to ground the trustworthiness of scientific knowledge—even if it seems to you clear that such complicity has no discernible effect on the specific trust-ensuring practices themselves. The important terms there are "seems *to you*" and "discernible" (*by you*): What can you say, and why do you think you should be believed, when those whose experience of those

24. I am writing as though cynicism about the results of science were confined to those who have good reason to feel alienated from mainstream institutions. Clearly, it is not: Many of those in whose interests those institutions work are dismissive of science, especially when—as, of course, happens frequently—particular scientific results do not support their views of the world. My primary interest in this chapter, however, is to explore how "the science question" divides those who are otherwise allied, or might expect to be—why, that is, there is antagonism on the part of many who situate themselves on the political left toward what they characterize as "the academic left." See, for example, Gross and Levitt 1994.

institutions is one of oppression, marginalization, or exclusion ask you why *they* should trust what comes out of them?[25]

The situation is analogous to the one facing the criminal justice system, notably when it comes to seeking convictions for Black defendants.[26] The task of the prosecution is to convince a jury that the prosecution's case demonstrates the defendant's guilt beyond a reasonable doubt. Meeting that epistemic standard is in general impossible without the jury's having a great deal of trust in the competence and integrity of those who are presenting the state's case. To a certain extent what the state (in the person of police, forensic experts, and the prosecuting attorneys them-selves) presents can be backed up relatively independently of what those people say, but to a great extent the credibility of testimony rests on the credibility of the testifiers, and, crucially, of the institutions within which they work and that enforce the norms to which they are accountable. When, as arguably in the O. J. Simpson case, the jury is convinced that those institutions are corrupt—that they are, specifically, racist—there does not have to be a story to tell about just how that corruption could have tainted the specific evidence on which the case rests. Rather, all that is necessary for the standard of persuasion beyond a reasonable doubt to

25. As I was doing the final revisions on this chapter, I read Jeremy Waldron's review of John Rawls's *Collected Papers* (Waldron 1999) and was struck by the fact that I seem to be echoing Rawls's insistence that, to be considered just, a social order needs to be justifiable to those who are least well off. On the face of it, an epistemological analogue, such as requiring those with knowledge to justify their claims to those who know least, seems mad: holding expertise hostage to ignorance. But there is, I think, something to be made of pushing the analogy. We can no more simply presume that those who hold disproportionate shares of socially validated epistemic authority do so in ways that are to the benefit of all than we can make the same presumption about those who wield disproportionate shares of political or economic power. And while it is admittedly difficult to specify what it would mean to seriously democratize epistemic accountability, Waldron's discussion makes it clear how far we are from such understanding in the political and economic realms to which Rawls's theory of justice is meant to apply.

26. The parallel with the criminal justice system was noted by the prime minister of Iceland, David Oddsson, in discussing the controversial plan to allow a scientist, Kari Stefansson, the founder of Decode Genetics, to compile and sell a database of genetic and epidemiological information about Icelanders, a uniquely genetically isolated and well-documented population. Oddsson says about the controversy: "Obviously, this is all about trust. . . . In Iceland, trust is everything. I once saw a documentary about a famous defense attorney. He was asked, 'How do you choose a jury?' He said, 'First, I take out all people who wear bow ties—because they are not likely to be part of a team. Then I get rid of everyone of Northern European descent. They are too trusting and they all believe in authority. When the police testify, Northern Europeans and Scandinavians tend to believe they are telling the truth.' At first I was outraged and considered it a complete stereotype. But I sat there and thought about it for five minutes and I realized he was completely right. I happen to be proud of that quality and think it says something about why we are willing to put ourselves forward and make this database work." The scientific research done on the database is made possible by the trust of Icelanders not only in scientific authorities but in their own health-care providers as well as in the state, which guarantees health care to everyone, making, for example, the problem of the use of genetic information by insurers a nonissue. And all these webs of trust are, as Oddsson recognizes, interwoven in the wider webs of Scandinavian and Northern European attitudes toward authority. This trust is not, however, without its critics: After the authorizing bill passed, "critics compared the database project to the Nazi experiments with racial hygiene and the exploitation of poor blacks in the Tuskegee study" (Specter 1999, pp. 50–1). (Note added 2010: Icelanders' trust turned out to be horribly misplaced, as deCODE Genomics was an integral part of the wild speculation that led to the collapse of the country's economy. See Fortun 2008).

be unreachable is that the jury not find the institutions of the state trustworthy.[27]

Many of the discussions in the so-called science wars ignore, as many discussions of the O. J. Simpson case ignored, the specifically epistemological nature of the issues, in particular, the centrality of the notion of justification and the importance of attending to the background context that, for particular believers, either grounds or undermines the trust that is needed for any reasonable standard of justification to be met. The credibility of science suffers, and, importantly, *ought* to suffer—just as the credibility of the prosecution suffers and ought to suffer—when its claims to trustworthiness are grounded in the workings of institutions that are demonstrably unjust—even when those injustices cannot be shown to be responsible for particular lapses in evidence gathering or reasoning. Credibility will suffer especially when the scientists in question, or those to whom they are believed to be close or beholden, are thought to have a stake in what they are reporting, as, for example, in research on racial differences in IQ, on the safety of drugs or food additives, or on the reliability of nuclear reactors. Those who are concerned (as, for example, scientists should be) that the results of science be not just true but justifiably believed to be true by the lay public as well as by other scientists need to be concerned about the systematic complicities with unjust privilege that systematically undermine the trustworthiness of the institutions on which such justified belief depends.

Thus, for example, it ought to be a matter of concern to scientists, if not to internalist philosophers of science, that mainstream medical research on the causes and treatment of AIDS is widely mistrusted in African American communities. According to a survey of African Americans conducted in 1997, 18 percent said they believed HIV was "an engineered microbe" and nearly 10 percent said they believed AIDS was part of a plot to kill Black people. To lay such skepticism about science at the door of the "academic left" is to blame the messenger: Rather than blaming the academic theorists who attempt to understand this mistrust, it makes much more sense to blame the practices in and around science that engender it. The same survey reported that fully 74 percent of African Americans "believed they were very likely or somewhat likely to be used by doctors as guinea pigs without their consent." Surely such a belief has a lot to do with the fact that, to take the most notorious example, in the Tuskegee syphilis experiment African American men *were* so used, and surely such mistrust has a lot to do with the mistrust of what doctors and medical researchers report. As Dr. Alvin Poussaint puts it, "When people don't know science, and most people don't, it's not hard to convince them that something unsavory may be going on. And this becomes a conspiracy to get black people. That's how much they

---

27. For discussions of the epistemological issues raised by the Simpson case, see Morrison and Lacour 1997.

believe that doctors in the system want to kill them" (France 1998).[28] The problem isn't the theories of the academic left: The problem is racism. As Elizabeth Lloyd puts the point more generally:

> The spectacles of corruption and waste in the manufacture and design of our best military technology, lack of responsiveness within all parts of the health and medical technology professions during the first decade of the AIDS pandemic, and lying and cheating for money and prestige within the top universities and research institutes in the world, and even the waffling on dietary guidelines regarding cholesterol, eggs, and oat bran—all have produced a public mistrust of both the disinterestedness and competence of scientists in general, and thereby of science itself.

Lloyd suggests that the critics of science studies can be seen as "scapegoating" those who are "investigating the possibilities that such things are *built into* the social systems of the sciences as they stand: they might be structural, institutional, and predictable" (Lloyd 1996, p. 236). The critics' insistence that nonetheless internalist epistemological resources provide the only proper tools for identifying and remedying such trust-destroying activities looks less like the high-minded defense of objectivity than like the defensive warding off of an appropriately democratic demand for accountability.

BEYOND HEURISTICS: IF YOU WANT TRUTH, FIGHT FOR JUSTICE

One might object at this point that, while what I've said might well be true when it comes to the *credibility* of science, it doesn't affect the question of scientific *truth*, provided that science is working as it should, according to its own norms. One might, that is, concede that in the absence of better reasons than are now available for many members of the lay public to trust the institutions of science, their cynicism about what scientists say might well be more justified than their credulity would be. The problem (admittedly a large and important one) would be to find ways of convincing the lay public—especially those among them who are understandably alienated from the institutions of the epistemic establishment—that those institutions are worthy of their trust, or at least that they would be if they lived up to their own, internally justified norms. One could further agree that the solution cannot and should not be seen as a matter of image manipulation: Possibly the only effective but certainly the only proper way of producing such confidence would be to work to make the institutions in question—and, generally, the broader society within which they exist—more genuinely just, more truly worthy

---

28. The survey was conducted by the Institute of Minority Health Research at Emory University's Rollins School of Public Health.

of everyone's trust. One could concede all this and still argue that the results of scientific research, conducted according to internal norms, are in fact, objectively, true (or, more reasonably, leading toward the truth), and justifiably believed by anyone who is in a position—as the lay public lamentably is not—to see how it is that the practices of trust-grounding work, despite the injustices of the institutions in which they are housed.

But how *do* those practices work, and why should *anyone* trust them? Why, specifically, do *I* trust them?—because the fact is that, to a very great extent, I do. (To a very great extent, actually, most people do, when it comes to the more settled and well-established fields of science: we cross bridges, go up and down in elevators, use household appliances, fly in airplanes, believe in the solar system, viruses, and electrons, confidently expect eclipses, tides, and comets.) What I want to suggest is that an externalist focus on epistemic dependency and the epistemological centrality of trust enables both better prescriptive accounts of how justification ought to work and better descriptive accounts of how it actually does work, including when its working is apparently accounted for in internalist terms.

Two of the chapters in the volume in which this essay was originally published (Tuana & Morgen, 2001) provide instructive examples of the epistemic role of trust and of the epistemic consequences of its being undermined. Sue Campbell argues against the efforts of the False Memory Syndrome Foundation and its supporters to systematically undermine the confidence of those who experience what they take to be recovered memories of childhood sexual abuse. She compares such efforts to Descartes's evocation of the evil demon: In both cases we are urged to see ourselves as systematically defective, as unable to trust our own faculties, or those of others relevantly like us. As Campbell puts it:

> The FMSF, in effect, argues that the public should support a shift in project that excludes the woman with a troubled past from participating as an epistemic agent in an understanding of her past and in contributing to social knowledge of childhood sexual abuse. . . . Through charging bias and evoking scientific objectivity, the activities of the False Memory Syndrome Foundation instead attempt a skeptical destruction of one of the contexts that allows a woman to understand a troubled and abusive past. But her perspective is critical to any communal project of objective knowledge of sexual harm. (Campbell 2001, p. 157)

Specifically, Campbell points to the attempts of the FMSF to present the setting of feminist therapy, one in which the collaborative work of reconstructing a coherent life story goes on, as a systematically distorting one, one that ought not to be trusted. Campbell's point is not that false memories are impossible, or that feminist therapists are always trustworthy: Rather, she argues, the interpretative frame provided by the FMSF undercuts the trust without which even accurate memories cannot be retrieved. "We require," she concludes, "an account of objectivity that can endorse the contexts in which knowledge emerges only through relationships of trust, the influence of imagination, and protection from premature criticism. The cost of supporting these contexts may indeed often be uncertainty about whether our beliefs or commitments are fully justified; the cost of withdrawing our support from these contexts will be the silencing of these perspectives" (Campbell 2001, p. 169).

In Sarah Hoagland's chapter, she raises for feminist philosophers of science extremely challenging questions about the limits of trustworthiness: how ought we think about our commitment—in the name of objectivity—to broadening the critical context within which scientific claims are articulated and evaluated, when some of the women whose voices and perspectives we are bringing into the conversation have good reasons for not wanting their stories told to those whom they do not trust not to misuse them? (Hoagland 2001, pp.137–38) Are we, she asks, dangerously naive, in trusting the powerful to hear the stories of the powerless, and in trusting our own ability to tell those stories in ways that will enfranchise, rather than endanger, those who trusted us with them? Hoagland raises these worries in concrete form with the story of a rural Gambian woman, Kaddy Sisay, whose use of birth control was aimed not at reducing the number of children she bore but of maximizing her chances of a successful pregnancy, and of the Western woman anthropologist, Carolyn Bledsoe, who told Sisay's story in a conference setting, as an illustration of the value of attending to "anomalous data."

Hoagland quotes Bledsoe as arguing for the importance of understanding Sisay's use of Depo-Provera on the grounds that "[n]owhere is the need to understand the dynamics of high fertility more obvious than sub-Saharan Africa," to which Hoagland responds: "Why? Whose need? And why the need, exactly?" In a footnote she lists the sources of support for Bledsoe's research, including Gambian governmental agencies and U.S. and British academic institutions and foundations (Hoagland 2001, p. 145). Hoagland argues that the ethical obligations of those who would be Kaddy Sisay's trustworthy allies would preclude even inadvertently transmitting her story to those who would use it against her. She characterizes "the scientific move to 'objectivity' [as] an effort to exclude others from meaning-making, deauthorizing all voices it has not trained/tamed" (Hoagland 2001, p. 137), arguing that feminist projects to achieve greater objectivity by bringing into the conversation silenced or marginalized voices ignore the ways in which such voices get distorted by the reframing necessary to make them scientifically intelligible, and the ways in which, so distorted, those voices get used against those from whose mouths they come.

Part of Hoagland's point is that it is a mistake to think that dominant discourses have no use for what the nondominant might have to say: The roles of the "native informant" and the research "subject" (i.e., object) are well recognized. That's part of the problem: The voices of the subordinated are all too easy to slot into predetermined places, as producers of "data" the interpretation of which remains in the hands of the dominant. Such placement is facilitated when those voices are transmitted by people with the status of accredited insiders, including feminist philosophers of science—even if we happen to be, to use Patricia Hill Collins's term, "outsiders within" (Collins 1986). Exclusion from meaning-making has never meant that one's life, culture, and body were off limits for "incorporation" by epistemological omnivores, who have always acknowledged that objectivity requires extensive, wide-ranging data collection. In our uneasy (or not uneasy enough) placement *in* universities but not, we think, really *of* them, we (feminist scientists and philosophers of science) pose a real danger to women whose absence from the academy might be as much avoidance as exclusion.

Hoagland's separatism is grounded in her pessimism about the possibilities of trust between the dominant and those they dominate. Specifically *epistemological* separatism follows from her recognition of the epistemic importance of trust. If we accept, as I argue that we should, the conception of objectivity articulated by its feminist friends, then Hoagland poses a deep and serious challenge: We may be barred from pursuing more objective knowledge so long as the conditions of trust are lacking—so long, that is, as some pieces of the perspectival puzzle cannot be added to dominant accounts without betraying those whose perspectives they are.[29] Not only would adding those pieces to *this* puzzle distort them (they are not accurately translatable into dominant terms), but the attempt to do so, to communicate them to those who control the dominant discourse, is a betrayal, a telling of secrets to those who cannot be trusted with them. In the absence of good grounds for trust, the critical work of striving toward objectivity cannot (and *should not*) go on.

OBJECTIVITY, DEPENDENCY, AND INEQUALITY

Return to the democratic ideals that motivated and provided the theoretical underpinnings for the epistemology of modern science. According to those ideals, all knowers are ideally interchangeable, meaning both that individually arrived-at results should be the same for all reasoners and that we can effectively function as each other's surrogate knowers. Our epistemic dependency, that is, is either eliminable or benign. But that assumption—that we are dependent on only our peers, who can, as our peers, be trusted—is, in the real world, false, and not only because many

---

29. It should be clear that it is not just "add women and stir" projects that are threatened: Even the far more critical engagements of more theoretically sophisticated feminist scholars are subject to the same critique. It is dangerously naive, on Hoagland's view, for us to think that we control the terms of the discourse or even to think that the dominant *don't*. She asks: "If feminist scientists are going to study women, I want to know who, and who is the audience? To whose understanding are you attending as you write? In what frame of reference are you trying to make sense? Who are you trying to represent to whom and why?" (Hoagland 2001, p. 139).

of us have been expected to be irrationally dependent on those who have been our oppressors. The dependency of scientists on other scientists—of peers on peers within shared institutional settings—while less obviously irrational, needs also to be called into question in the light of what are widely acknowledged to be the problematic ways in which power and privilege shape the workings of the practices meant to ensure trustworthiness. But there is an additional, deeper problem than those involving the trustworthiness of scientists and of scientific practices. All along, those who have been the authorized knowers have been, in subtle and complex ways, dependent on those whom they would not have acknowledged, except, perhaps, in the most purely theoretical of terms, as their peers; and those forms of dependency have gone unacknowledged and unaccounted for in terms of assessing the trustworthiness of knowledge claims.

The norms of epistemic self-sufficiency and, failing that, dependency on trusted peers, were connected to the individualism of early modernity not just through the ideal of theoretical egalitarianism but also through the picture of persons as essentially competent adults—Hobbes's men sprung up like mushrooms, to take that picture's most striking evocation. If the sort of extreme dependency that characterizes infancy and childhood is acknowledged at all, it is to mark it as something that has, intellectually, to be superseded: The ground that we in fact traversed in our parents' arms has to be retraversed under our own power, in order to prove that the place where we have ended up is one we could and would have reached had we done the entire journey under the direction of our own adult intelligence.[30] Projects of rational reconstruction and the distinction between the realm of discovery and the realm of justification are versions of this project, which has as one of its aims the demonstration that a route to knowledge that in fact crossed over swamps and bogs and very shaky bridges could have been undertaken proceeding solely on firm ground; in other words, that any trusting of those whose trustworthiness cannot be independently verified can be shown to be dispensable.[31] Beyond parents and teachers (those Descartes, for example, charges with having filled his head with unverifiable beliefs before he reached the age of reason), there are those whose unrecognized labor goes into grounding the trustworthiness of scientific endeavors: the workers who make or clean laboratory equipment, for example, or set the type for scientific publications, or, for that matter, the informants who are presumed not to be making up funny stories to tell the various social scientists who pry into their lives.

30. Making a similar point, Code writes, "As Seyla Benhabib wryly notes, 'it is a strange world from which this picture of knowledge is derived: a world in which individuals are grown up before they have been born; in which boys are men before they have been children; a world where neither mother, nor sister, nor wife exist'" (1995b, p. 46).

31. Thanks to Jennifer Hornsby for reminding me of this point, that is, of how dependent the most presumptively independent of the early moderns in fact were.

Annette Baier has been working out the consequences, for moral and political philosophy as well as for epistemology, of starting theory with the universal experiences of infancy and childhood. Such a starting point provides a salutary contrast to the tendentious appeals to the alleged universality of some particular conception of reason that is the starting point of internalist accounts of scientific objectivity. It is, to say the least, odd that something we all do, non-tendentiously, have in common—we were born and remained for a considerable time wholly dependent on others not only for our physical survival but for our acquisition of what Baier calls "the essential arts of personhood" (Baier 1985*b*, p. 84)—should be seen, if it is seen at all, as an obstacle to the universality that objectivity aims for, as a site for the acquisition only of limiting, biasing forms of particularity from which we need, as autonomous adults, to wean ourselves. Baier's project has been to rethink adult epistemic, moral, and political competence as an achievement of maturation, involving neither an uncritical acceptance of the lessons and the ties of childhood, nor a fantasy of self-generation. Central to that achievement is the ability to trust when, and only when, it is appropriate to do so.[32]

Thus, to acknowledge the complex webs of dependencies—of lay persons on scientists, of scientists on other scientists, and of scientists on non-scientists—that undergird the workings of objectivity, is to acknowledge the necessity, throughout those webs, for trust to be both psychologically possible and rationally justifiable. If we cannot trust those on whom we are epistemically dependent, we will not believe when we should; and if we ought not to trust them, we risk believing when we should not. Much of what goes into both the psychological possibility and the rational justifiability of trust lies both below and outside of (as well as, in each of our lives, temporally prior to) the explicit norms of scientific practice; and without such grounding, we are powerless to effectively answer the skeptic, who speaks to us from a place of alienation from that ground—whether that alienation be a philosophical conceit or a material reality. As Baier puts it, "the secular equivalent of faith in God (which performs this anti-skeptical role, e.g., in Descartes's Third Meditation), which we need in morality as well as in science or knowledge acquisition, is faith in the human community and its evolving procedures—in the prospect for many-handed cognitive ambitions and moral hopes" (Baier 1980, p. 293).

It is the task of the projects I have collectively referred to as "CPR" to argue for the dependence of objectivity on the conditions of social justice that would justify this faith; for the claim that, in the absence of such conditions, objectivity is inevitably compromised; and for the necessity for those who would be objectivity's true friends to struggle for social justice. Such a view of objectivity differs from an internalist account

---

32. Lorraine Code has explored at length the specifically epistemological consequences of Baier's work on trust and on second-personhood. See, especially, Code 1991 and 1995*c*.

largely in being far more rigorous and demanding: Sandra Harding's term "strong objectivity" is not just a rhetorical ploy (Harding 1993, p. 69). The internalist provides an account of rational credibility that rests on the suitability of some people to serve as surrogate knowers for the rest of us, who are ineliminably dependent on their expertise, while denying the relevance of many of the questions we might be inclined to ask if we were to take seriously the issue of their trustworthiness. It is, in short, irrational to expect people to place their trust in the results of practices about which they know little and that emerge from institutions—universities, corporations, government agencies—which they know to be inequitable. Even those who are insiders to those institutions have reason to be skeptical about the adequacy of those practices to ensure objectivity, independent of and unchecked by critical scrutiny of the conditions within which they operate. There is, for anyone, little reason to trust that partiality can be adequately dealt with by ruling it out of order or that concrete issues of trust and dependency can be adequately dealt with by systems of rules that pride themselves on studied inattention to the world in which they operate.

Internalist defenses of scientific objectivity are collectivized versions of the methological solipsism that convinced Descartes that the most stringent criticisms of his arguments were those generated by a figment of his own imagination. Insofar as the practices of science do adequately ensure trustworthiness, it ought to be possible to make that case—actually make it, to actual people with actual reasons for being skeptical, importantly including reasons that have to do with the economic and social inequities that underlie the selection and training of experts.[33] Charges of irrationalism are oddly directed at those who point out—correctly, from their perspective—that they do not have good reason to believe what experts say. And it is simply arrogant to be certain that the effort genuinely to engage with those who have been excluded could be of only heuristic value, that all the worthwhile criticisms and advances are generated from within. Objectivity on an externalist account is not an all or nothing matter, settled by rules laid down in advance; it is, rather, a rolling horizon we move toward as we increasingly democratize our epistemic practices.

Hoagland's separatist epistemology is, therefore, a challenge to "CPR" theorists, who, I want to suggest, can be seen as arguing for a *diasporic* epistemology, one that is sufficiently hopeful about universalist liberatory politics to sustain, and even to encourage less privileged others to sustain, faith in a not-yet-existent human community. (See chap. 8) That we (feminist academics) might be fools is the least of our worries, Hoagland

---

33. Michael Root raises the question of whose skepticism needs to be taken seriously: Do evolutionary biologists need to persuade creationists in order for their accounts to be considered objective? There is, I would argue, no general, formal answer to such questions, nor can we expect answers in particular cases that are prior to or less contentious than the substantive issues under dispute. See footnote 27 and Scheman 1991 for thoughts about parallels between political and epistemic democratic accountability.

warns; if our faith is misplaced, we'll be guilty of betrayal. To be a friend of objectivity and simultaneously a friend to those who do not share one's relatively privileged social location is a moral and political risk. There will be times when we will judge such a risk to be worth taking, though I urge those of us who take it to also take Hoagland's warnings to heart. What I am certain of is that no defense of objectivity can be made on ground less politically contentious than this.

Those who hold on to internalist conceptions of scientific objectivity do so in part because they believe that a naturalized account of science as a social practice is a wholly different endeavor from a normative account of it as truth producing. Historical and sociological studies such as Shapin's (1994) do typically eschew what is taken to be the central epistemological question: how *ought* we to pursue knowledge? My contention in this chapter has been that it is precisely as a social practice, naturalistically understood, that science needs to be evaluated—especially if what we care about is its objectivity. The normativity that characterizes epistemology can be found not in ahistorical canons of rationality but in the normativity of politics.[34]

ACKNOWLEDGMENTS

Over the past few years, a number of graduate students at the University of Minnesota have been working on issues of trust and testimony. I have learned a lot from them: Nancy Nyquist Potter, Heidi Grasswick, Peg O'Connor, Lisa Bergin, Amanda Vizedom, and Jan Binder. I owe a special debt to students, colleagues, and friends in Gothenburg, Örebro, and Helsinki, where I taught short graduate courses in 1997 and 1998, in which I developed these ideas in dialogue; and to the Feminist Studies Department at the University of Gothenburg for a wonderfully congenial work environment. Thanks to Michael Root and Stephen Kellert for comments on earlier drafts.

34. Here and elsewhere, my indebtedness to Helen Longino will be evident to all who have read her work. To those who haven't: Do.

References

Alcoff, Linda. 1988. Cultural Feminism Versus Post-structuralism: The Identity Crisis in Feminist Theory. *Signs* 13(3): 405–36.

———and Elizabeth Potter, eds. 1993. *Feminist Epistemologies*. New York: Routledge.

Almog, Oz. 1997. *The Sabra: A Profile*. Tel Aviv: Am Oved.

Antony, Louise. 1995. Comment on Naomi Scheman. *Metaphilosophy* 26(3): 191–98.

———and Charlotte Witt, eds. 1992. *A Mind of One's Own: Feminist Essays on Reason and Objectivity*. Boulder, Colo.: Westview Press.

Anzaldúa, Gloria. 1987. *Borderlands/La Frontera: The New Mestiza*. San Francisco: Spinsters/Aunt Lute.

Appiah, Anthony. 1986. The Uncompleted Argument: Du Bois and the Illusion of Race. In *Race, Writing, and Difference*, ed. Henry Louis Gates, Jr. Chicago: University of Chicago Press.

Arendt, Hannah. 1973. *The Origins of Totalitarianism*. 2nd edn. New York: Harcourt, Brace, Jovanovich.

———. 1978. The Jew as Pariah: A Hidden Tradition (April 1944). In *The Jew as Pariah: Jewish Identity and Politics in the Modern Age*, ed. Ron H. Feldman. New York: Grove.

Austin, John Langshaw. 1962. *How to Do Things with Words*. Oxford: Clarendon.

Babbitt, Susan. 1992. "Feminists and Nature: A Defense of Essentialism." York University. Address to the Canadian Society of Women in Philosophy. Reprinted in Babbitt 1996.

———. 1996. *Impossible Dreams: Rationality, Integrity, and Moral Imagination*. Boulder, Colo.: Westview Press.

Baier, Annette. 1980. Secular Faith. *Canadian Journal of Philosophy* 10: 131–48. Reprinted in Baier 1985b.

———. 1985a. Cartesian Persons. In Baier 1985b.

———. 1985b. *Postures of the Mind: Essays on Mind and Morals*. Minneapolis: University of Minnesota Press.

Baker, Lynne Rudder. 2007. *The Metaphysics of Everyday Life: An Essay in Practical Realism*. Cambridge: Cambridge University Press.

Bar On, Bat-Ami. 1994. Meditations on National Identity and Friendship. *Hypatia* 9(2): 40–62.

Barad, Karen. 2007. *Meeting the Universe Halfway: Quantum Physics and the Entanglement of Matter and Meaning*. Durham, N.C.: Duke University Press.

Benhabib, Seyla, Judith Butler, Drucilla Cornell, and Nancy Fraser. 1995. *Feminist Contentions: A Philosophical Exchange*. New York: Routledge.

Berger, Maurice. 1999. *White Lies*. New York: Farrar, Strauss, and Giroux.

Biale, David. 1986. *Power and Powerlessness in Jewish History*. New York: Schocken.

Binder, Janet. 2000. *Journeys of Understanding: The Epistemic Value of Movement*. Ph.D. dissertation, University of Minnesota.

Bornstein, Kate. 1994. *Gender Outlaw: On Men, Women, and the Rest of Us*. New York: Routledge.

Boyarin, Daniel. 1994. *A Radical Jew: Paul and the Politics of Identity*. Berkeley: University of California Press.

———. 1995. Freud's Baby, Fliess's Maybe: Homophobia, Anti-Semitism, and the Invention of Oedipus. *GLQ: A Journal of Lesbian and Gay Studies* 2(1–2): 115–47.

———. 1997. *Unheroic Conduct: The Rise of Heterosexuality and the Invention of the Jewish Man*. Berkeley: University of California Press.

———and Jonathan Boyarin. 1993. Diaspora: Generation and the Ground of Jewish Identity. *Critical Inquiry* 19(4): 693–725.

Boyarin, Jonathan. 1995. Before the Law There Stands a Woman: *In Re Taylor v. Butler* (With Court-Appointed Yiddish Translator). *Cardozo Law Review* 16 (3–4): 1303–23.

Boyd, Richard. 1988. How to Be a Moral Realist. In *Essays on Moral Realism*, ed. Geoffrey Sayre-McCord. Ithaca, N.Y.: Cornell University Press.

———. 1991. On the Current Status of Scientific Realism. In *The Philosophy of Science*, ed. Richard Boyd, Philip Gasper, and J. D. Trout. Cambridge, Mass.: MIT Press.

Breines, Paul. 1990. *Tough Jews: Political Fantasies and the Moral Dilemma of American Jewry*. New York: Basic Books.

Butler, Judith. 1990. *Gender Trouble: Feminism and the Subversion of Identity*. New York: Routledge.

Campbell, Susan. 1993. *Interpreting the Personal: Expression and the Individuation of Feeling*. PhD dissertation. University of Toronto. Revised as Campbell 1998.

———. 1998. *Interpreting the Personal: Expression and the Formation of Feelings*. New York: Cornell University Press.

———. 2001. Memory, Suggestibility, and Social Skepticism. In Tuana and Morgen 2001.

Camper, Carol, ed. 1994. *Miscegenation Blues: Voices of Mixed-Race Women*. Toronto: Sister Vision.

Card, Claudia, ed. 1991. *Feminist Ethics*. Lawrence: University of Kansas Press.

Carnap, Rudolf. 1963. Intellectual Autobiography. In *The Philosophy of Rudolf Carnap*, ed. Paul Arthur Schillp. La Salle, Ill.: Open Court.

Cavell, Stanley. 1969a. The Availability of Wittgenstein's Later Philosophy. In Cavell 1969c.

———. 1969b. Knowing and Acknowledging. In Cavell 1969c.

———. 1969c. *Must We Mean What We Say?*. New York: Scribner's.

———. 1979. *The Claim of Reason: Wittgenstein, Skepticism, Morality, and Tragedy*. Oxford: Oxford University Press.

———. 1981. *Pursuits of Happiness; The Hollywood Comedy of Remarriage*. Cambridge, Mass.: Harvard University Press.

———. 1989. *This New Yet Unapproachable America: Lectures After Emerson After Wittgenstein*. Albuquerque: Living Batch Press.

———. 1990. The Argument of the Ordinary: Scenes of Instruction in Wittgenstein and in Kripke. In *Conditions Handsome and Unhandsome: The Constitution of Emersonian Perfectionism*. Chicago: University of Chicago Press.

————. 1994. *A Pitch of Philosophy: Autobiographical Exercises*. Cambridge, Mass.: Harvard University Press.

Code, Lorraine. 1987. *Epistemic Responsibility*. Hanover, N.H.: University Press of New England.

————. 1991. *What Can She Know?: Feminist Theory and the Construction of Knowledge*. Ithaca, N.Y.: Cornell University Press.

————. 1995a. Incredulity, Experientialism, and the Politics of Knowledge. In Code 1995c.

————. 1995b. Must a Feminist Be a Relativist After All? In Code 1995c.

————. 1995c. *Rhetorical Spaces: Essays on Gendered Location*. New York: Routledge.

————. 1995d. Taking Subjectivity into Account. In Code 1995c.

Collins, Patricia Hill. 1986. Learning from the Outsider Within: The Social Significance of Black Feminist Thought. *Social Problems* 33(8): 14–32. Reprinted in *Beyond Methodology: Feminist Scholarship as Lived Research*, ed. Mary Margaret Fonow and Judith A. Cook. Bloomington: Indiana University Press, 1991.

————. 1990. *Black Feminist Thought: Knowledge, Consciousness, and the Politics of Empowerment*. Boston: Unwin Hyman.

Craig, Edward. 1990. *Knowledge and the State of Nature: An Essay in Conceptual Synthesis*. Oxford: Clarendon.

Davidson, Donald. 1980. The Individuation of Events. In *Actions and Events*. Oxford: Oxford University Press.

Delgado, Richard, ed. 1995. *Critical Race Theory: The Cutting Edge*. Philadelphia: Temple University Press.

Diamond, Cora. 1991a. Anything but Argument. In Diamond 1991f.

————. 1991b. Eating Meat and Eating People. In Diamond 1991f.

————. 1991c. Experimenting on Animals: A Problem in Ethics. In Diamond 1991f.

————. 1991d. Realism and the Realistic Spirit. In Diamond 1991f.

————. 1991e. Introduction II: Wittgenstein and Metaphysics. In Diamond 1991f.

————. 1991f. *The Realistic Spirit: Wittgenstein, Philosophy, and the Mind*. Cambridge, Mass.: MIT Press.

————. 1993. Sahibs and Jews. In Goldberg and Krausz 1993.

Disch, Lisa J. 1993. More Truth than Fact: Storytelling as Critical Understanding in the Writings of Hannah Arendt. *Political Theory* 21: 665–94.

Drabble, Margaret. 2006. *The Sea Lady*. London: Penguin.

Du Bois, William Edward Burghardt. 1966. The Conservation of Races. In *Negro Social and Political Thought 1850–1920*, ed. Howard Brotz. New York: Basic Books.

Dupré, John. 1993. *The Disorder of Things: Metaphysical Foundations of the Disunity of Science*. Cambridge, Mass.: Harvard University Press.

Dworkin, Andrea. 1987. *Intercourse*. New York: Free Press.

Dyson, Freeman. 2007. Our Biotech Future. *New York Review* 54(12): 4–8.

Eagleton, Terry. 1993. *Wittgenstein: The Terry Eagleton Script/The Derek Jarman Film*. London: British Film Institute.

Ehrenreich, Barbara, and Janet McIntosh. 1997. The New Creationism: Biology under Attack. *Nation* (9 June): 11–16.

Epstein, Julia, and Kristina Straub, eds. 1991. *Body Guards: The Cultural Politics of Gender Ambiguity*. New York: Routledge.

Feinberg, Leslie. 1993. *Stone Butch Blues*. Ithaca, N.Y.: Firebrand Books.

———. 1999. Trans Liberation: Beyond Pink or Blue. Boston: Beacon Press.

Fine, Arthur. 1998. The Viewpoint of No One in Particular. *Proceedings and Addresses of the American Philosophical Association* 72(2): 9–20.

Fortun, Michael A. 2008. *Promising Genomics: Iceland and deCODE Genetics in a World of Speculation*. Berkeley: University of California Press.

France, David. 1998. Challenging the Conventional Stance on AIDS. *New York Times* (22 December): F6.

Fraser, Nancy. 1989. Struggle over Needs: Outline of a Socialist Feminist Theory of Late Capitalist Political Culture. In *Unruly Practices: Power, Discourse, and Gender in Contemporary Social Theory*. Oxford: Polity Press.

Fricker, Miranda. 1998. Rational Authority and Social Power: Towards a Truly Social Epistemology. *Proceedings of the Aristotelian Society* 98(2): 159–77.

———. 2007. *Epistemic Injustice: Power and the Ethics of Knowing*. Oxford: Oxford University Press.

———and Jennifer Hornsby, eds. 2000. *Cambridge Companion to Feminism in Philosophy*. Cambridge: Cambridge University Press.

Friedman, Marilyn. 1991. The Social Self and the Partiality Debates. In Card 1991.

Frost, Robert. 1914. Death of a Hired Man. In *North of Boston*. New York: Holt.

Frye, Marilyn. 1983a. In and Out of Harm's Way: Arrogance and Love. In Frye 1983b.

———. 1983b. A Note on Anger. In Frye 1983c.

———. 1983c. *The Politics of Reality*. Trumansburg, N.Y.: Crossing Press.

———. 1983d. To Be and Be Seen: The Politics of Reality. In Frye 1983b.

———. 2000. Ethnocentrism/Essentialism: The Failure of the Ontological Cure. In *Is Academic Feminism Dead?: Theory in Practice*, ed. Rose Brewer, Mary Lou Fellows, Shirley Nelson Garner, Amy Kaminsky, Jennifer Pierce, and Naomi Scheman. New York: New York University Press.

Gabriel, Davina Anne. 1995. Interview with the Transsexual Vampire: Sandy Stone's Dark Gift. *TransSisters: The Journal of Transsexual Feminism* 8: 14–27.

Gallop, Jane, ed. 1995. *Pedagogy: The Question of Impersonation*. Bloomington: Indiana University Press.

Gates, Henry Louis, Jr. 1988. *The Signifying Monkey: A Theory of African-American Literary Criticism*. New York: Oxford University Press.

Geller, Jay. 1993. A Paleontological View of Freud's Study of Religion: Unearthing the *Leitfossil* Circumcision. *Modern Judaism* 13: 49–70.

Gilman, Sander. 1991. *The Jew's Body*. New York: Routledge.

Ginet, Carl. 1975. *Knowledge, Perception, and Memory*. Dordrecht: Reidel.

Ginzberg, Ruth. 1989a. Feminism, Rationality, and Logic. *APA Newsletter on Feminism and Philosophy* 88: 34–39.

———. 1989b. Teaching Feminist Logic. *APA Newsletter on Feminism and Philosophy* 88: 58–62.

Goldberg, David Theo, and Michael Krausz, eds. 1993. *Jewish Identity*. Philadelphia: Temple University Press.

Goldfarb, Warren. 1983. I Want You to Bring Me a Slab: Remarks on the Opening Sections of the *Philosophical Investigations*. *Synthèse* 56: 265–82.

Goldstein, Leon J. 1993. Thoughts on Jewish Identity. In Goldberg and Krausz (1993).

Grahn, Judy. 1973. The Common Woman Poems, Stanza VII. In *Rising Tides: Twentieth Century American Women Poets*, ed. Laura Chester and Sharon Barba. New York: Pocket Books.

Grasswick, Heidi E. 2004. Individuals-in-Communities: The Search for a Feminist Model of Epistemic Subjects. *Hypatia* 19: 85–120.

Grimshaw, Jean. 1986. *Philosophy and Feminist Theory*. Minneapolis: University of Minnesota Press.

Gross, Paul R. 1998. Evidence-Free Forensics and Enemies of Objectivity. In Koertge 1998.

———and Norman Levitt. 1994. *Higher Superstition: The Academic Left and Its Quarrels with Science*. Baltimore: Johns Hopkins University Press.

Hacker, Peter Michael Stephan. 1972. *Insight and Illusion: Wittgenstein on Philosophy and the Metaphysics of Experience*. Oxford: Oxford University Press.

———. 1986. *Insight and Illusion: Themes in the Philosophy of Wittgenstein* (rev. 2nd edn. of Hacker 1972). Oxford: Oxford University Press.

Hacking, Ian. 1986. Making People Up. In *Reconstructing Individualism*, ed. Thomas C. Heller, Morton Sosna, and David E. Wellbery. Palo Alto: Stanford University Press.

———. 1992. World-Making by Kind-Making: Child Abuse for Example. In *How Classification Works: Nelson Goodman and the Social Sciences*, ed. Mary Douglas and David L. Hull. Edinburgh: Edinburgh University Press.

Hale, Jacob. 1995. Transgendered Strategies for Refusing Gender. Paper delivered at a meeting of the Pacific Division of the Society for Women in Philosophy, Los Angeles, 20 May.

———. 1996. Are Lesbians Women? *Hypatia* 11(2): 94–121.

Halperin, David. 1995. The Queer Politics of Michel Foucault. In *Saint Foucault: Two Essays in Gay Hagiography*. New York: Oxford University Press.

Haraway, Donna. 1988. Situated Knowledges: The Science Question in Feminism and the Privilege of Partial Perspective. *Feminist Studies* 14: 575–99. Reprinted in Haraway (1991) and in Keller and Longino (1996).

———. 1991. *Simians, Cyborgs, and Women: The Reinvention of Nature*. New York: Routledge.

———. 1999. The Biopolitics of Postmodern Bodies: Determinations of Self in Immune System Discourse. In *Feminist Theory and the Body: A Reader*, ed. Janet Price and Margrit Shildrick. New York: Routledge.

Harding, Sandra. 1986. *The Science Question in Feminism*. Ithaca, N.Y.: Cornell University Press.

———. 1991. *Whose Science? Whose Knowledge?: Thinking from Women's Lives*. Ithaca, N.Y.: Cornell University Press.

———. 1993. Rethinking Standpoint Epistemology. In Alcoff and Potter 1993.

Hardwig, John. 1991. The Role of Trust in Knowledge. *Journal of Philosophy* 88: 693–70.

Haugeland, John. 1982. Weak Supervenience. *American Philosophical Quarterly* 19: 93–103.

Heldke, Lisa. 1987. John Dewey and Evelyn Fox Keller: A Shared Epistemological Tradition. *Hypatia* 2: 129–40.

———. 1988. Recipes for Theory-Making. *Hypatia* 3: 15–30.

———and Stephen H. Kellert. 1995. Objectivity as Responsibility. *Metaphilosophy* 26(4): 360–78.

Hoagland, Sarah Lucia. 1988. *Lesbian Ethics: Toward New Value*. Palo Alto: Institute of Lesbian Studies.

———. 2001. Resisting Rationality. In Tuana and Morgen 2001.

———. 2002. Moving Toward Uncertainty. In Scheman and O'Connor 2002.

hooks, bell. 1990. *Yearnings: Race, Gender, and Cultural Politics*. Boston: South End Press.

Hornsby, Jennifer. 1997. *Simple Mindedness: In Defense of Naïve Naturalism in the Philosophy of Mind*. Cambridge, Mass.: Harvard University Press.

———. 2000. Personal and Sub-Personal: A Defense of Dennett's Original Distinction. In special issue, ed. J. Bermudez and M. Elton. *Philosophical Explanations* 3: 6–24.

Hughes, S., C. Jordan, B. Roche, and E. Shapiro. 2003. Two Factor Parent Model Predicts Development at 36 Months in At Risk Children. Poster presented at the annual meeting of the International Neuropsychological Society, Honolulu, February 5–8.

Hylton, Peter. 2007. *Quine*. New York: Routledge.

Jaggar, Alison M. 1989. Love and Knowledge: Emotion in Feminist Epistemology. *Inquiry: An Interdisciplinary Journal of Philosophy* 32: 151–76. Also in *Women, Knowledge, and Reality: Explorations in Feminist Epistemology*, ed. Ann Garry and Marilyn Pearsall. Boston: Unwin Hyman; and in *Gender/Body/Knowledge: Feminist Reconstructions of Being and Knowing*, ed. Alison Jaggar and Susan Bordo. New Brunswick, N.J.: Rutgers University Press.

Jones, Karen. 1998. Trust in Science and in Scientists: A Response to Kane. In *NOMOS 40: Integrity and Conscience*, ed. Ian Shapiro and Robert Adams. New York: New York University Press.

———. 2000. The Politics of Credibility. In *A Mind of One's Own*, 2nd edn., ed. Louise Antony and Charlotte Witt. Boulder, Colo.: Westview.

Jordan, Catherine. 2001. Getting the Lead Out: A Community-University Collaborative Approach. *Minnesota Physician* (September): 36–38.

———, S. Hughes, B. Roche, and E. Shapiro. 2004. The DREAMS Project: Risks and Developmental Outcomes in Inner-City Preschoolers. Symposium presented at the annual meeting of the International Neuropsychological Association, Baltimore, February 4–7.

———, ———, and E. Shapiro. 2003. Maternal Risk Factors Predict Child Lead Burden. Poster presented at the annual meeting of the International Neuropsychological Association, Honolulu, February 5–8.

———, P. Lee, R. Hampton, and P. Pirie. 2004. Recommendations from Lead Poisoning Prevention Program Participants: Best Practices. *Health Promotion Practice* 5(4): 429–37.

———, ———, and E. Shapiro. 2000. Measuring Developmental Outcomes of Lead in an Urban Neighborhood: The Challenges of Community-Based Research. *Journal of Exposure Analysis and Environmental Epidemiology* 10: 1–11.

———, B. Yust, L. Robison, P. Hannan, and A. Deinard. 2003. A Randomized Trial of Education to Prevent Lead Burden in High Risk Children: Efficacy as Measured by Blood Lead Monitoring. *Environmental Health Perspectives* 111: 1947–51.

Jordan, June. 1985. Nobody Mean More to Me Than You and the Future Life of Willie Jordan. In *On Call: Political Essays*. Boston: South End Press.

Kaminsky, Amy Katz. 1993. Issues for an International Literary Criticism. *Signs* 19(1): 213–27.

————. 1999. *After Exile*. Minneapolis: University of Minnesota Press.

Kant, Immanuel. [1771] 1960. *Observations on the Beautiful and Sublime*. Trans. John T. Goldthwait. Berkeley: University of California Press.

————. [1785] 1969. *Foundations of the Metaphysics of Morals*. Trans. Lewis White Beck. Ed. Robert Paul Wolff. Indianapolis: Bobbs-Merrill.

————. [1790, 1793] 2000. *Critique of the Power of Judgment*. Trans. Paul Guyer. New York: Cambridge University Press.

Kasher, Asa. 1993. Jewish collective identity. In Goldberg and Krausz (1993).

Keller, Evelyn Fox. 1985. *Reflections on Gender and Science*. New Haven, Conn.: Yale University Press.

————and Helen Longino, eds. 1996. *Feminism and Science*. Oxford: Oxford University Press.

Kellert, Stephen. 1999. Never Coming Home: Positivism, Ecology, and Rootless Cosmopolitanism. In *The Meaning of Being Human*, ed. Michelle Stoneburner and Billy Catchings. Indianapolis: University of Indianapolis Press.

Kershaw, Ian. 1999. Interview. *New York Times* (March 22).

Kessler, Suzanne J. 1990. The Medical Construction of Gender: Case Management of Intersexed Infants. *Signs* 16(1): 3–26.

————and Wendy McKenna. 1978. *Gender: An Ethnomethodological Approach*. Chicago: University of Chicago Press.

Kim, Jaegwon. 1984. Concepts of Supervenience. *Philosophy and Phenomenological Research* 45: 153–76. Reprinted in Kim 1993.

————. 1987. "Strong" and "Global" Supervenience Revisited. *Philosophy and Phenomenological Research* 48: 315–26. Reprinted in Kim 1993.

————. 1989. The Myth of Nonreductive Materialism. *Proceedings and Addresses of the American Philosophical Association* 63: 31–47. Reprinted in Kim 1993.

————. 1990. Supervenience as a Philosophical Concept. *Metaphilosophy* 21: 1–27. Reprinted in Kim 1993.

————. 1993. *Supervenience and Mind: Selected Philosophical Essays*. Cambridge: Cambridge University Press.

Kitcher, Philip. 1998. Truth or Consequences. *Proceedings and Addresses of the American Philosophical Association* 72: 49–63.

Klepfisz, Irena. 1990. *Dreams of an Insomniac: Jewish Feminist Essays, Speeches and Diatribes*. Portland, Ore.: Eighth Mountain Press.

Koertge, Noretta, ed. 1998. *A House Built on Sand*. New York: Oxford University Press.

Kukla, Rebecca. 2005. Conscientious Autonomy: Displacing Decisions in Healthcare. *Hastings Center Report* 35: 34–44.

Lafer, Gordon. 1993. Universalism and Particularism in Jewish Law: Making Sense of Political Loyalties. In Goldberg and Krausz 1993.

Langford, C. H. 1952. The Notion of Analysis in Moore's Philosophy. In *The Philosophy of G. E. Moore*, ed. Paul Arthur Schillp. New York: Tudor.

Latour, Bruno. 1979. *Laboratory Life: The Social Construction of Scientific Facts*. Beverly Hills: Sage.

Lear, Jonathan. 1982. Leaving the World Alone. *Journal of Philosophy* 79: 383–403.

————. 1984. The Disappearing "We". *Proceedings of the Aristotelian Society*. Supp. vol. 58: 219–42.

Lennon, Kathleen, and Margaret Whitford, eds. 1994. *Knowing the Difference: Feminist Perspectives in Epistemology*. New York: Routledge.

Liaschenko, Joan, and Debra DeBruin. 2003. The Role of Nurses in Ensuring the Responsible Conduct of Clinical Trials. *Minnesota Medicine* 86(10): 35–36.

Lindemann, Hilde. 2008. Verdi Requiem. In *Naturalized Bioethics: Toward Responsible Knowing and Practice*, ed. Hilde Lindemann, Marian Verkerk, and Margaret Urban Walker. Cambridge: Cambridge University Press.

Lloyd, Elisabeth A. 1996. Science and Antiscience: Objectivity and Its Real Enemies. In Nelson and Nelson 1996.

Longino, Helen. 1990. *Science as Social Knowledge: Values and Objectivity in Scientific Inquiry*. Princeton: Princeton University Press.

Lovibond, Sabina. 1983. *Realism and Imagination in Ethics*. Minneapolis: University of Minnesota Press.

———. 1994. The End of Morality? In Lennon and Whitford 1994.

Lugones, María. 1987. Playfulness, "World"-Travel and Loving Perception. *Hypatia* 2(2): 3–19. Reprinted in Lugones 2003a.

———. 1990a. Hispaneando y Lesbiando: On Sarah Hoagland's *Lesbian Ethics*. *Hypatia* 5(3): 138–46.

———. 1990b. Structure/Antistructure and Agency Under Oppression. *Journal of Philosophy* 87(10): 500–507. Reprinted in Lugones 2003a.

———. 1991. On the Logic of Pluralist Feminism. In Card 1991. Reprinted in Lugones 2003a.

———. 1994. Purity, Impurity, and Separation. *Signs* 19(2): 458–79. Reprinted in Lugones 2003a.

———. 2003a. *Pilgrimages/Peregrinajes*. Lanham, Md.: Rowman and Littlefield.

———. 2003b. Tactical Strategies of the Streetwalker/*Estrategias Tácticas de la Callejera*. In Lugones 2003a.

Mackenzie, Catriona, and Natalie Stoljar, eds. 2000. *Relational Autonomy: Feminist Perspectives on Autonomy, Agency, and the Social Self*. Oxford: Oxford University Press.

MacKinnon, Catharine A. 1987. *Feminism Unmodified: Discourses on Life and Law*. Cambridge, Mass.: Harvard University Press.

———. 1990. Sexuality, Pornography, and Method: Pleasure Under Patriarchy. In *Feminism and Political Theory*, ed. Cass R. Sunstein. Chicago: University of Chicago Press.

Miller, Alice. 1984. *For Your Own Good: Hidden Cruelty in Child-Rearing and the Roots of Violence*. Trans. Hildegarde Hannum and Hunter Hannum. New York: Farrar, Straus, and Giroux.

Mohanty, Chandra Talpede. 1991. Under Western Eyes: Feminist Scholarship and Colonial Discourses. In *Third World Women and the Politics of Feminism*, ed. Chandra Talpede Mohanty, Ann Russo, and Lourdes Torres. Bloomington: Indiana University Press.

Mohanty, Satya P., Paula M. L. Moya, Linda Martín Alcoff, and Michael Hames-García, eds. 2005. *Identity Politics Reconsidered*. New York: Palgrave Macmillan.

Monk, Ray. 1990. *Wittgenstein: The Duty of Genius*. New York: Free Press.

Morrison, Toni, and Claudia Brodsky Lacour, eds. 1997. *Birth of a Nation'hood: Gaze, Script, and Spectacle in the O. J. Simpson Case*. New York: Pantheon.

Moya, Paula M. L., and Michael Hames-García, eds. 2000. *Reclaiming Identity: Realist Theory and the Predicament of Postmodernism*. Berkeley: University of California Press.

Narayan, Uma. 1997. *Dislocating Cultures: Identities, Traditions, and Third World Feminism*. New York: Routledge.

Nelson, Hilde Lindemann. 2001. *Damaged Identities, Narrative Repair*. Ithaca, N.Y.: Cornell University Press.

———. 2002. Wittgenstein Meets "Woman" in the Language-Game of Theorizing Feminism. In Scheman and O'Connor 2002.

Nelson, Lynne Hankinson. 1990. *Who Knows: From Quine to a Feminist Empiricism*. Philadelphia: Temple University Press.

———and Jack Nelson, eds. 1996. *Feminism, Science, and the Philosophy of Science*. Dordrecht: Kluwer.

Nozick, Robert. 1998. Invariance and Objectivity. *Proceedings and Addresses of the American Philosophical Association* 72(2): 21–48.

Nussbaum, Martha. 1994. Feminists and Philosophy. *New York Review of Books* 41 (20 October): 59–63.

———. 1995. Reply to Scheman. *New York Review of Books* 42 (6 April): 48–49.

Nyiri, J. C. 1982. Wittgenstein's Later Work in Relation to Conservatism. In *Wittgenstein and His Times*, ed. Brian McGuinness. Oxford: Blackwell.

———. 1986. Wittgenstein 1929–31: The Turning Back. In *Ludwig Wittgenstein: Critical Assessments*, ed. S. G. Shanker. Vol. 4. *From Theology to Sociology: Wittgenstein's Impact on Contemporary Thought*. London: Croom Helm.

O'Connor, Peg. 2002. Moving to New Boroughs: Transforming the World by Inventing Language Games. In Scheman and O'Connor 2002.

O'Neill, Onora. 1986. The Power of Example. *Philosophy* 61: 5–29.

Outlaw, Lucius. 1992. Against the Grain of Modernity: The Politics of Difference and the Conservation of "Race." *Man and World* 25(4): 443–68.

Pears, David. 1988. *The False Prison: A Study in the Development of Wittgenstein's Philosophy*. Oxford: Oxford University Press.

Peskowitz, Miriam and Laura Levitt, eds. 1996. *Judaism Since Gender*. New York: Routledge.

Peterson, Susan Rae. 1977. Coercion and Rape: The State as a Male Protection Racket. In *Feminism and Philosophy*, ed. Mary Vetterling-Braggin, Frederick A. Elliston, and Jane English. Totowa, N.J.: Littlefield, Adams.

Phillips Neighborhood Health Housing Collaborative. 2000. PNHHC Supplement. *Alley Newspaper* 24 (November): 11.

Pickering, Andrew. 1995. *The Mangle of Practice: Time, Agency, and Science*. Chicago: University of Chicago Press.

Piper, Adrian. 1988. Cornered, a video piece produced by Bob Boilen. Posted on Google videos.

Porter, Bernard. 1999. Review of David Vincent, *The Culture of Secrecy in Britain 1832–1996*. *London Review of Books* 21(14): 13–15.

Post, J. F. 1995. "Global" Supervenient Determination: Too Permissive?. In *Supervenience: New Essays*, ed. E. E. Savellos and Ü. D. Yalçin. Cambridge: Cambridge University Press.

Potter, Nancy. 1994. Trustworthiness: An Aristotelian Analysis of a Virtue. Ph.D. dissertation, University of Minnesota.

———. 2002. *How Can I Be Trusted: A Virtue Theory of Trustworthiness*. Lanham, Md.: Rowman and Littlefield.

Prell, Riv-Ellen. 1992. Why Jewish Princesses Don't Sweat: Desire and Consumption in Postwar American Jewish Culture. In *People of the Body: Jews and*

Judaism from an Embodied Perspective, ed. Howard Eilberg-Schwartz. Albany: State University of New York Press.

———. 1999. *Fighting to Become Americans: Jews, Gender, and the Anxiety of Assimilation.* Boston: Beacon Press.

Putnam, Hilary. 1979. Reflections on Goodman's *Ways of Worldmaking. Journal of Philosophy* 76: 603–18.

Quine, W. V. O. 1960. *Word and Object.* Cambridge, Mass.: MIT Press.

———. 1969a. Epistemology Naturalized. In Quine 1969b.

———. 1969b. *Ontological Relativity and Other Essays.* New York: Columbia University Press.

Rawls, John. 1971. *A Theory of Justice.* Cambridge, Mass.: Harvard University Press.

Reagon, Bernice Johnson. 1983. Coalition Politics: Turning the Century. In *Home Girls: A Black Feminist Anthology*, ed. Barbara Smith. New York: Kitchen Table Women of Color Press.

Rey, Georges. 1997. *Contemporary Philosophy of Mind.* Oxford: Blackwell.

Rich, Adrienne. 1978. *The Dream of a Common Language: Poems 1974–1977.* New York: Norton.

———. 1979a. It Is the Lesbian in Us . . . . In Rich 1979b.

———. 1979b. *On Lies, Secrets, and Silence: Selected Prose 1966–1978.* New York: Norton.

———. 1979c. Women and Honor: Notes on Lying. In Rich 1979b.

———. 1986. Compulsory Heterosexuality and Lesbian Existence. In *Blood, Bread, and Poetry: Selected Prose 1979–1985.* New York: Norton.

Robison, S., C. Jordan, S. Hughes, D. Zelinsky-Goldman, and E. Shapiro. 2003. Can Sustained Attention Be Measured in Children Less Than Three Years. Poster presented at the annual meeting of the International Neurological Society, Honolulu, February 5–8.

Rooney, Phyllis. 1998. Putting Naturalized Epistemology to Work. In *Epistemology: The Big Questions*, ed. Linda Martín Alcoff. Oxford: Blackwell.

Root, Michael D. 1993. *Philosophy of Social Science: The Methods, Ideals, and Politics of Social Inquiry.* Oxford: Blackwell.

———. 1998. How to Teach a Wise Man. In *Pragmatism, Reason, and Norms*, ed. Kenneth R. Westphal. New York: Fordham University Press.

———. 2000. How We Divide the World. *Philosophy of Science* 67 (supp., pt. 2): S628–39.

Rosaldo, Renato. 1989. Grief and a Headhunter's Rage. In *Culture and Truth: The Remaking of Social Analysis.* Boston: Beacon Press.

Rouse, Joseph. 2002. *How Scientific Practices Matter: Reclaiming Philosophical Naturalism.* Chicago: University of Chicago Press.

Sager, Morten. 2006. *Pluripotent Circulations: Putting Actor-Network Theory to Work on Stem Cells in the USA, Prior to 2001.* Gothenburg: Acta Universitatis Gothoburgensis.

Scarry, Elaine. 1985. *The Body in Pain: The Making and Unmaking of the World.* Oxford: Oxford University Press.

Scheman, Naomi. 1980. Anger and the Politics of Naming. In *Women and Language in Literature and Society*, ed. Sally McConell-Ginet, Ruth Borker, and Nelly Furman. New York: Praeger. Reprinted in Scheman 1993b.

———. 1983. Individualism and the Objects of Psychology. In *Discovering Reality: Feminist Perspectives on Epistemology, Metaphysics, Methodology, and the*

Philosophy of Science, ed. Sandra Harding and Merrill B. Hintikka. Dordrecht: Reidel. Reprinted in Scheman 1993b.

————. 1991. Who Wants to Know? The Epistemological Value of Values. In *(En)gendering Knowledge: Feminists in Academe*, ed. Joan E. Hartman and Ellen Messer-Davidow. Knoxville: University of Tennessee Press. Reprinted in Scheman 1993b.

————. 1992a. "Though This Be Method, Yet There Is Madness in It": Paranoia and Liberal Epistemology. In Antony and Witt 1992. Reprinted in Scheman 1993b.

————. 1992b. Who Is That Masked Woman?: Reflections on Power, Privilege, and Home-ophobia. In *Revisioning Philosophy*, ed. James Ogilvy. Albany: State University of New York Press. Reprinted in Scheman 1993b.

————. 1993a. The Body Politic and the Impolitic Body. In Scheman 1993b.

————. 1993b. *Engenderings: Constructions of Knowledge, Authority, and Privilege*. New York: Routledge.

————and Peg O'Connor, eds. 2002. *Feminist Interpretations of Wittgenstein*. University Park: Pennsylvania State University Press.

Schulte, Joachim. 1986. Wittgenstein and Conservatism. In *Ludwig Wittgenstein: Critical Assessments*, vol. 4, ed. S. G. Shanker. Wolfeboro, N.H.: Croon Helm.

Sedgwick, Eve Kosofsky. 1990. *Epistemology of the Closet*. Berkeley: University of California Press.

Seigfried, Charlene Haddock. 1996. *Pragmatism and Feminism: Reweaving the Social Fabric*. Chicago: University of Chicago Press.

Shapin, Steven. 1994. *A Social History of Truth: Civility and Science in Seventeenth-Century England*. Chicago: University of Chicago Press.

Shapiro. Judith. 1991. Transsexualism: Reflections on the Persistence of Gender and the Mutability of Sex. In Epstein and Straub 1991.

Sherover-Marcuse, Erica. 1986. *Emancipation and Consciousness: Dogmatic and Dialectical Perspectives in the Early Marx*. Oxford: Blackwell.

Snitow, Ann. 1989. Pages from a Gender Diary: Basic Divisions in Feminism. *Dissent* 36: 205–24.

Sokal, Alan. 1996a. A Physicist Experiments with Cultural Studies. *Lingua Franca* (May/June): 62–64.

————. 1996b. Transgressing the Boundaries: Toward a Transformative Hermeneutics of Quantum Gravity. *Social Text* 46/47: 217–52.

Sokal, Alan, et al. 1996. Mystery Science Theater. *Lingua Franca*. (July/August): 54–64.

Specter, Michael. 1999. Decoding Iceland. *New Yorker* (18 January): 50–51.

Spelman, Elizabeth V. 1988. *Inessential Woman: Problems of Exclusion in Feminist Thought*. Boston: Beacon Press.

Steward, Helen. 1997. *The Ontology of Mind: Events, Processes, and States*. Oxford: Clarendon Press.

Stone, Sandy. 1991. The Empire Strikes Back: A Posttranssexual Manifesto. In Epstein and Straub 1991.

Stroud, Barry. 1983. Wittgenstein's "Treatment" of the Quest for "A Language Which Describes My Inner Experience and Which Only I Myself Can Understand." In *Epistemology and Philosophy of Science: Proceedings of the Seventh Annual Wittgenstein Symposium*, ed. Paul Weingartner and Johannes Czermak. Vienna: Hölder-Pichler-Tempsky.

————. 1984. The Allure of Idealism. *Proceedings of the Aristotelian Society*, supp. vol. 58: 243–58.

Stryker, Susan. 1994. My Words to Victor Frankenstein above the Village of Chamonix: Performing Transgender Rage. *GLQ: A Journal of Lesbian and Gay Studies* 1(3): 237–54.

Thomas, Laurence. 1993. *Vessels of Evil: American Slavery and the Holocaust*. Philadelphia: Temple University Press.

Traweek, Sharon. 1988. *Beam Times and Life Times: The World of High Energy Physicists*. Cambridge, Mass.: Harvard University Press.

Tuana, Nancy, ed. 1987. *Feminism and Science*. Bloomington: Indiana University Press.

———and Sandra Morgen, eds. 2001. *(En)Gendering Rationalities*. Albany: State University of New York Press.

Waldron, Jeremy. 1999. Review of John Rawls, *Collected Papers*, ed. Samuel Freeman. *London Review of Books* 21(14): 3–6.

Warner, Michael. 1993. *Fear of a Queer Planet: Queer Politics and Social Theory*. Minneapolis: University of Minnesota Press.

West, Cornel. 1989. *The American Evasion of Philosophy: A Genealogy of Pragmatism*. Madison: University of Wisconsin Press.

Williams, Patricia. 1991. *Alchemy of Race and Rights: Diary of a Law Professor*. Cambridge, Mass.: Harvard University Press.

Wilson, Robert A. 1995. *Cartesian Psychology and Physical Minds: Individualism and the Sciences of the Mind*. Cambridge: Cambridge University Press.

Wittgenstein, Ludwig. 1958. *Philosophical Investigations*. Trans. G. E. M. Anscombe. New York: Macmillan.

———. 1967a. *Remarks on the Foundations of Mathematics*, 2nd ed'n, ed. G.H. von Wright, Rush Rhees, and G.E.M. Anscombe. Trans. G.E.M. Anscombe. Oxford: Basil Blackwell.

———. 1967b. *Zettel*, ed. G. E. M. Anscombe and G. H. von Wright. Oxford: Blackwell.

———. 1969. *On Certainty*, ed. G. E. M. Anscombe and G. H. von Wright. Oxford: Blackwell.

Woese, Carl R. 2004. A New Biology for a New Century. *Microbiology and Molecular Biology Reviews* 68: 173–86.

Wylie, Alison. 2000. Rethinking Objectivity: Nozick's Neglected Third Option. *International Studies in the Philosophy of Science* 14(1): 5–10.

Zack, Naomi, ed. 1995. *American Mixed Race: The Culture of Microdiversity*. Lanham, Md.: Rowman and Littlefield.

Zita, Jacquelyn. 1981. Lesbian Continuum and Historical Amnesia. *Signs* 7(1): 172–81.

———. 1988. The Premenstrual Syndrome: "Dis-easing" the Female Cycle: Agency and Responsibility. *Hypatia* 3(1): 77–99.

———. 1992. The Male Lesbian and the Postmodernist Body. *Hypatia* 7(4): 106–27.

Index